Left: the spiky Esplanade – Theatres on the Bay makes a bold statement.

Pit Building and Paddock. The Grand Prix takes place in September.

SEE ALSO FESTIVALS AND EVENTS, P.58; SPORTS, P.119; WALKS AND VIEWS, P.131

Esplanade Park

If the weather is pleasant, it is worth making a detour to the left of the Esplanade Theatres, where a string of modest memorials stand, set in tree-lined open spaces. These include the **War Memorial**, in the park of the same name.

The **Esplanade Park,** stretching along Connaught Drive, is dotted with monuments like the Victorian-style **Tan Kim Seng Fountain**, built to mark the merchant's £13,000 contribution in 1857 to build the town's public water works. Further along, the **Cenotaph** pays homage to the soldiers who died in the two World Wars.

SEE ALSO MONUMENTS, P.79, 81

Marina Bay

Taking centre stage here is **Marina Bay Sands** ⑤, which was opened in phases from May 2010. At the heart of this development is the **Marina Bay Sands hotel**, made up of three towers, crowned by the **Sands SkyPark** on the 57th storey. Shaped like a boat perched at the top of the towers, the one-hectare sky oasis has restaurants, sculptured

Below: the Suntec City Mall's Fountain of Wealth.

gardens and an infinity pool.

The building also houses a casino, theatres, exhibition space and The Shoppes at Marina Bay Sands, with over 300 shops and restaurants.

The **ArtScience Museum** is a lotus-shaped museum that marries both art and science, resulting in unique, world-class exhibitions. A 280-m (918-ft) bridge, connects the two sides of the bay. Viewing platforms along the path allow superb bay vistas.

Opposite, **Gardens By The Bay** ⑥ is a sprawling horticultural attraction housing over 250,000 rare plants in huge, domed conservatories. The Supertrees are 25-50 metre-tall vertical gardens, with a suspended 128-metre-long walkway, giving you a bird's eye view of the Gardens and the Marina Bay area.

Discover more about the area's transformation at the **Marina Bay City Gallery**.

SEE ALSO ARCHITECTURE, P.29; HOTELS, P. 70; MUSEUMS & GALLERIES, P.82, 85; NIGHTLIFE, P.95; PARKS & GARDENS, P.100; RESTAURANTS, P.103; THEATRE, P.121

The **Marina Barrage**, built across the Marina Bay, is a clever addition to the island's reservoir stores. This unique three-in-one project encompasses a dam that acts as a tidal barrier to prevent flooding during high tides with a freshwater reservoir that sits behind the dam, while a 12-storey-high fountain has been built over a spot where undersea pipes continuously drain water from the reservoir for storage elsewhere. The reservoir's stable water level allows for a variety of water activities and events.

The Civic District

Roughly the area north of the Singapore River and between the City Hall and the Dhoby Ghaut MRT stations, the Civic District is where many colonial-era buildings stand. In his original town plan, Sir Stamford Raffles assigned the area north of the river to the British, ordering the building of offices, banks, hotels, churches and clubs there. He also built his house on the top of Fort Canning Hill. The city is today still governed from the colonial nucleus Raffles established, although many of the historical buildings have been restored and adapted for functions that are completely different from those in the past.

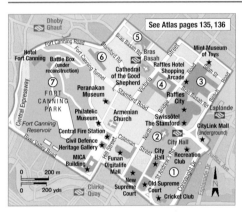

Above: the famous Singapore Sling was created at the Raffles.

City Hall

The expanse of green called the **Padang** ① ('field' in Malay), adjacent to the Esplanade Park, and the two leisure clubs flanking the field, the **Singapore Recreation Club** and the **Singapore Cricket Club**, used to be a focal point of the colonials for sport and social activities. The Padang, then known as the Esplanade, was earmarked in Raffles' town plan as a recreation area, and it remains so today as the site of cricket and rugby matches and public events.

Across St Andrew's Road from the Padang are a cluster of stately government build-ings that are also centre-pieces in Singapore's architectural landscape. Capped by a green dome and fronted by stout Corinthian columns is the **old Supreme Court**. It is now emptied of its law courts, which have moved to the glass-and-steel **new Supreme Court** behind it.

Next to the old Supreme Court is the stoic **City Hall**, once Singapore's most important government build-ing. Both the old Supreme Court and the City Hall are being converted into Singapore's **National Gallery**, which will open in 2015.

SEE ALSO ARCHITECTURE, P.26, 29, 30; PARKS AND GARDENS, P.101

Raffles City and Raffles Hotel

Standing above the City Hall MRT station amid verdant greenery is the gleaming white **St Andrew's Cathedral** ②, a gazetted monument that dates back to 1862.

The church spire rises tall, but not as high as the 72-storey **Swissôtel The Stam-ford**, formerly Southeast Asia's tallest hotel. It is linked to the **Raffles City**, another of the city's stylish malls, designed by I.M. Pei.

CityLink Mall extends from the City Hall MRT station to Suntec City (see p.8). This subterranean retail corridor, with over 50 stores, restau-rants and cafés, is a great rainy day route.

Left: the Raffles Hotel, grande dame of Singapore's hotel scene.

the **Peranakan Museum**, which offers a treasure trove of rare and typically intricate Peranakan (Straits Chinese) artefacts. Finding favour with stamp hobbyists is the **Singapore Philatelic Museum** at the top of Armenian Street.

Fort Canning Park ⑦ is uphill from the philatelic museum and well-marked paths weave through its lush greenery. **Battle Box** (currently closed for renovation), an underground war bunker used in World War II, adds interest for history buffs.
SEE ALSO MUSEUMS AND GALLERIES, P.86, 88; PARKS AND GARDENS, P.100

Hill Street

At the foot of the hill runs Hill Street, lined by a few architectural highlights. At the corner with Coleman Street are the atmospheric **Armenian Church** and the **Central Fire Station**, which also has the **Civil Defence Heritage Gallery** on site. With its 911 technicoloured window shutters, the **MICA Building** is hard to miss.
SEE ALSO ARCHITECTURE, P.26, 29; CHURCHES, MOSQUES AND TEMPLES, P.40; MUSEUMS AND GALLERIES, P.84

Making a stop at the **Raffles Hotel** ③ on Beach Road is de rigeur for many tourists, who come to admire its colonial-era architecture, sip a Singapore Sling, relax in its leafy courtyard or shop for luxury items at the **Raffles Hotel Shopping Arcade**.

Nostalgia continues across from the Raffles at the **Mint Museum of Toys**, a gem of a repository on Seah Street.
SEE ALSO CHURCHES, MOSQUES AND TEMPLES, P.43; HOTELS, P.72; MONUMENTS, P.80; MUSEUMS AND GALLERIES, P.85; SHOPPING, P.116

Churches Past and Present

At the corner of North Bridge and Bras Basah roads are two churches, both significant in history but now offering contrasting facets. **Chijmes** ④, a former convent school with a chapel, has been converted into a collection of restaurants and shops. The **Cathedral of the Good**

Enjoy a Singapore Sling at the Long Bar of the Raffles Hotel, where it was first concocted in 1910. The fruity gin-based drink packs a punch.

Shepherd is a tranquil place of worship offering Roman Catholic service, built in 1846 in the design of a crucifix.
SEE ALSO CHURCHES, MOSQUES AND TEMPLES, P.41; MONUMENTS, P.78

Museum District

The Civic District is the city's museum district. The **Singapore Art Museum** ⑤ on Bras Basah Road has regular exhibitions of works from its permanent collection of 4,000 Southeast Asian paintings. A stone's throw away on Stamford Road is the recently rejuvenated **National Museum of Singapore** ⑥, displaying a collection of Singapore treasures in a handsome neoclassical building.

On Armenian Street is

Below: St Andrew's Cathedral.

11

Chinatown and the Central Business District

The area south of the Singapore River comprises two distinct districts – Chinatown and the CBD. It may seem odd that this city, with a predominantly Chinese population, has a Chinatown. But this can be traced to Raffles' original town plan, which assigned the different races to various districts. Immigrants from China huddled in Chinatown then, living in dark and cramped quarters in the shophouses. Closer to the river, within the CBD's glass-and-steel maze, are historical and cultural gems worth visiting.

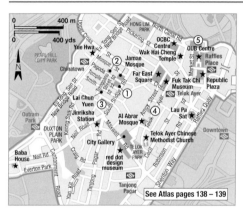

See Atlas pages 138 – 139

Chinatown

Today's Chinatown is hemmed in by soaring high-rises, but vestiges of the traditional can still be seen. Conservation shophouses house decades-old businesses, which stand shoulder to shoulder with even older places of worship. Medical halls dispense traditional herbal cures, and families flock to restaurants for dim sum at the weekends.

Exotic sights and smells still dominate. There are rare Asian ingredients and frogs to be skinned in the fresh-produce market. At certain times of the year, the streets are filled with the pungent aroma of durians (a thorny Southeast Asian fruit).

SOUTH BRIDGE ROAD

Chinatown has its fair share of Chinese temples, but it also has some of the most well-known places of worship of other faiths, such as the **Sri Mariamman Temple** ① and **Jamae Mosque** along South Bridge Road.
SEE ALSO CHURCHES, MOSQUES AND TEMPLES, P.41, 43

CHINATOWN STREETS

The heart of Chinatown embraces **Pagoda, Temple, Trengganu, Smith** and **Sago streets**. In the evenings, vendors of the **Chinatown Night Market** set up stalls along these streets, selling tourist souvenirs and Chinese trinkets. After browsing at the night market, have supper at the hawker stalls which line the open-air **Chinatown Food Street** on Smith Street.

The former Chinese opera house of **Lai Chun Yuen** stands at the corner of Trengganu and Smith streets. The hardships of early residents are showcased in the excellent **Chinatown Heritage Centre** ②, which occupies three shophouses on Pagoda Street.

The ostentatious **Buddha Tooth Relic Temple and Museum** ③, which claims to hold a sacred Buddha's tooth, stands between Sago Street and Sago Lane.

The pedestrian bridge extending from Pagoda Street across New Bridge

Below: Chinatown's shops are fascinating to browse.

MEI HEONG YUEN DESSERT

CBD is another conservation zone. **Ann Siang Road and Club Street** used to hum with the activities of Chinese clan associations but are now taken over by restaurants and bars.

The area boasts the **Singapore City Gallery**, which charts the city's urban development, and the **Fuk Tak Chi Museum**, which displays articles donated by early Chinatown residents.

Telok Ayer Street is a street for the faithful, lined by the **Thian Hock Keng Temple** ④, **Al Abrar Mosque** and **Telok Ayer Chinese Methodist Church**. At the street's southern end, the **red dot design museum** in the red dot Traffic building stages industrial-design exhibitions.
SEE ALSO CHURCHES, MOSQUES AND TEMPLES, P.40, 45; MUSEUMS AND GALLERIES, P.84, 86, 88

Sago Street is lined with age-old shops. **Fong Moon Kee** (No.16) sells traditional healing oils. **Leung Sang Hong** (No.18) has delicious Chinese pastries.

Road and Eu Tong Sen Street leads to **Yue Hwa**, a one-stop emporium for all things Chinese.
SEE ARCHITECTURE, P.28; CHURCHES, MOSQUES AND TEMPLES, P.40; MUSEUMS AND GALLERIES, P.83; SHOPPING, P.114, 116

Tanjong Pagar

To best appreciate the architectural flourishes of Chinatown's Chinese Baroque-style shophouses, walk around the **Tanjong Pagar Conservation District**, along Tanjong Pagar, Duxton, Craig and Neil roads. The European-style **Jinriksha Station** at the corner of Tanjong Pagar and Neil roads,

where rickshaw pullers used to congregate, offers a contrast in architectural style.

Nearby in the former red-light district of **Keong Saik Road**, splendid shophouses have been converted into hip boutique hotels and bars.

The **Baba House** is further along on Neil Road. It boasts most of its original mouldings and intricate tile work. Restored and redecorated, it offers a fascinating glimpse into old Peranakan life.
SEE ALSO ARCHITECTURE, P.28, 30; MUSEUMS AND GALLERIES, P.83

Ann Siang Road and Club Street

Between Chinatown and the

Central Business District

Singapore's financial boom-town centres on **Raffles Place** ⑤, an open-air plaza surrounded by skyscrapers, including OUB Centre, **UOB Plaza** and **Republic Plaza**.

In the shadow of the I.M. Pei-designed **OCBC Centre** is the incense-filled **Wak Hai Cheng Temple**, built by Chinese Teochew immigrants to give thanks to the gods for their safe passage between China and Singapore.
SEE ALSO ARCHITECTURE, P.29, 30, 31

13

Orchard Road and Surroundings

Orchard Road is to Singapore what Fifth Avenue is to New York – one seemingly interminable line of smart boutiques, shopping malls and hotels stretching from one end of a very long road to the other. But there is more to this former plantation area than just retail glamour and enchantment. The fashion strip also has a few leafy parks, a presidential palace, sidewalk cafés and a charming enclave filled with some of Singapore's finest examples of Chinese Baroque-style shop- and terrace houses.

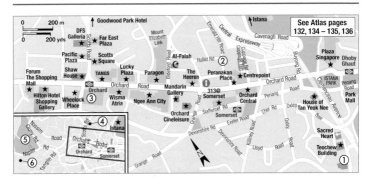

Dhoby Ghaut

The Dhoby Ghaut MRT station marks the top end of Orchard Road, around where shopping centres like **Plaza Singapura** and **Park Mall** stand. Park Mall, on Penang Road and named after Fort Canning Park behind it, is a favourite hunting ground for furniture shoppers.

A detour from Penang Road up Clemenceau Avenue leads to Tank Road, where three institutions stand in testimony of Singapore's polyglot character: the Roman Catholic **Church of the Sacred Heart**, the Chinese-style **Teochew Building** and the Hindu **Sri Thendayuthapani Temple** ①.

At the corner of Clemenceau Avenue and Penang Road is the former **House of Tan Yeok Nee**, one of the only two southern Chinese-style courtyard houses left in Singapore, now home to a business school.

Just beyond Plaza Singapura on Orchard Road is the **Istana**, the official residence of Singapore's president, set amid manicured lawns. **Istana Park** opposite is a pleasant patch of landscaped greenery with a café.
SEE ALSO ARCHITECTURE, P.28; CHURCHES, MOSQUES AND TEMPLES, P.44; MONUMENTS, P.80

The Main Stretch

Orchard Road gets its name from the nutmeg and pepper orchards that once blanketed the area in the 1840s. The only glimpses of this rural past are the roads named after plantation owners, such as Scotts, Cairnhill and Cuppage.

Cuppage Terrace, a strip of restored shophouses housing pubs and eateries, sits behind **Centrepoint**, a mall well loved by Singaporeans. Its anchor tenant is **Robinsons**, a large department store that offers some of the best service in the city. Next door is **Peranakan Place**, a complex of ornate shophouses. At its shaded terrace café, relax with an ice-cold drink, before exploring the lovely Chinese Baroque-style terrace houses further up the slope on **Emerald Hill** ②.

Across the road are two malls: **313@Somerset**, found above Somerset MRT, and **Orchard Central**, whre the rooftop offers several dining options with views of Orchard Road. It also houses New York's Dean & Deluca gour-

Left: ION Orchard brims with high-end stores.

Many alfresco cafés along Orchard Road are located on the street level, fantastic spots from which to people-watch.

the main stretch, is home to upscale hotels and eclectic malls. On one side is **Shaw House**, with plenty of eateries and cineplexes, the youngster hangout **Pacific Plaza**, and the striking red duty-free store **DFS Galleria**. On the other side of the street are **Scotts Square** and **Far East Plaza**, popular with teens looking for affordable streetwear. Perched at the top of a gentle rise is the castle-like **Goodwood Park Hotel** ④.

SEE ALSO HOTELS, P.73; MONUMENTS, P.80; SHOPPING, P.114, 115

met store on the fourth level.

At the junction of Orchard and Cairnhill Roads are the **Singapore Visitors Center** and **The Heeren** (currently undergoing renovations). It enjoys a younger clientele, as does **Orchard Cineleisure**, a complex of cineplexes and games arcades at the corner of Orchard and Grange roads. The malls that follow cater to a decidedly more upmarket crowd. Beside Orchard Cineleisure is the Mandarin

Gallery, full of posh boutiques, eateries and designer labels. **The Paragon** is another haven of designer goods, while the massive **Ngee Ann City** houses Takashimaya departmental store and an impressive food hall in its basement. **Wisma Atria**, further down, is also a popular fashion destination. The darling of Singapore shopping, however, is the sprawling **ION Orchard** ③ on the corner of Orchard and Paterson roads.

Across Mount Elizabeth Road from The Paragon is the comparitively dowdy **Lucky Plaza**, nevertheless a favourite with tourists for its electronics goods. Adjacent to it is the home-grown retail darling of **TANGS** department store.

SEE ALSO ARCHITECTURE, P.27; SHOPPING, P.114, 115, 116

Scotts Road

Scotts Road, extending from

Left: Chinese Baroque-style houses on Emerald Hill.

Lower End of Orchard

Back on Orchard Road, **Wheelock Place**, a complex designed by architect Kisho Kurokawa, houses Marks & Spencer and casual eateries. More elegant designer boutiques are found in the **Hilton Hotel Shopping Gallery**, **Palais Renaissance** and **Forum The Shopping Mall**.

Tanglin Road

Tanglin Road, often regarded as an extension of Orchard Road, offers a change of pace from frenetic shopping action. You can wind down in the lush **Singapore Botanic Gardens** ⑤ or relax in **Tanglin Village** ⑥ further west. Also known as the Dempsey Road area, Tanglin Village is now flourishing with stylish cafés and restaurants. Antiques and home décor shops here specialise in Asian furnishings.

SEE ALSO PARKS AND GARDENS, P.101

15

Little India and Kampong Glam

Perhaps the most colour- and scent-saturated areas in Singapore, Little India and Kampong Glam still bustle with traditional businesses and religious centres. Beginning first as a camp for Indian convict workers, Little India's abundant grass and water later made it an ideal cattle-breeding ground. Kampong Glam had a more idyllic beginning as the location of the palace of Sultan Hussein, the Malay ruler who ceded the island to the British. A walk through these areas is a trek through Singapore's past.

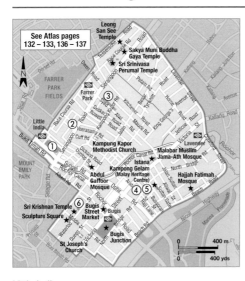

Little India comes alive in October or November for the annual Deepavali light-up. Twinkling fairy lights and colourful decorations adorn the streets, and the Deepavali bazaar, selling snacks, religious paraphernalia and home décor items, is always worth a browse.

On Syed Alwi Road is the sprawling **Mustafa Centre** ③, a 24-hour shopping complex that is hugely popular with bargain hunters.
SEE ALSO CHURCHES, MOSQUES AND TEMPLES, P.40, 42, 43, 44; FOOD AND DRINK, P.65; SHOPPING, P.114

Little India

Serangoon Road is the main thoroughfare that runs through Little India. Its sidestreets, such as Campbell Lane, Dunlop Street and Buffalo Road, are lined with brightly-lit shops spilling over with spices, fabrics, floral garlands and glittering jewellery. A landmark at the junction of Serangoon and Bukit Timah roads is **Tekka Centre** ①, a bustling fresh-produce market worth a look.

Although Little India is the hub of the Hindu community,

religious centres of various faiths call the area home. Also marvellous examples of various architectural styles, these places of worship include the **Abdul Gaffoor Mosque** on Dunlop Street, and **Sri Veeramakaliamman Temple** ② and **Sri Srinivasa Perumal Temple** along Serangoon Road. The stunning **Sakya Muni Buddha Gaya Temple** and the ornately decorated **Leong San See Temple** also attract the Chinese faithful to the area.

Kampong Glam

To the east of Little India is **Kampong Glam**, which means 'village of the *gelam* tree' in Malay. Malays used to use the bark of the *gelam* tree to caulk boats, although it would be difficult to find this tree here today.

The first Arab settlers, along with the Bugis, Javanese, Boyanese and people from the Riau Islands, turned Kampong Glam into a commercial hub. Today the area still draws those in search of bargains, but beyond that, Kampong Glam is also a lovely enclave that offers plenty to see on a

Left: a henna tattooist in Little India.

now converted into the **Malay Heritage Centre**. The **Malabar Muslim Jama-Ath Mosque**, at the corner of Jalan Sultan and Victoria Street, and the **Hajjah Fatimah Mosque**, off Beach Road, are two of the prettiest mosques in the city.

SEE ALSO CHURCHES, MOSQUES AND TEMPLES, P.41, 43, 44; MUSEUMS AND GALLERIES, P.85; WALKS AND VIEWS, P.128

Bugis

Above the Bugis MRT station is another shopping hub with the overcrowded Bugis Street Market and the Bugis Junction mall, featuring a glass-covered retail 'street' with boutiques and cafés.

Nearby **Waterloo Street** is a hive of activity with Buddhist worshippers, medicine sellers and fortune tellers crowding the entrance to the **Kwan Im Thong Hood Cho Temple** ⑥. Hindu devotees congregate at **Sri Krishnan Temple** on its right.

At the junction of Waterloo Street and Middle Road is the **Sculpture Square**, dedicated to three-dimensional art.

SEE ALSO CHURCHES, MOSQUES AND TEMPLES, P.42; MUSEUMS AND GALLERIES, P.87; SHOPPING, P.115

leisurely stroll. Lately it has even earned a reputation as Singapore's coolest neighbourhood, where boutiques and antiques shops sit side by side with Middle Eastern restaurants and cosy bistros, all set in restored two-storey shophouses. Many of these houses were built in the Early Shophouse style in the 1840s, resembling unadorned dollhouses with their squat upper levels and simple lines.

Batiks, linens and baskets of every shape, size and colour are sold on **Arab Street** ④. **Bussorah Street** holds a treasure trove of shops selling Asian and Muslim-inspired crafts. At the end of the street is the golden-domed **Sultan Mosque** ⑤.

Dotting the Kampong Glam area are several other cultural sights. At the centre is **Istana Kampong Gelam**, the former royal palace built in the 1840s,

Below: religious posters in Little India *(left)*; shopping in Kampong Glam *(right)*.

Sentosa and the Southern Islands

G et away from the urban sprawl and head offshore for a spot of island hopping. The most popular of Singapore's offshore islands is Sentosa, the site of the country's other major Integrated Resort. Younger adults love it for its beautiful beaches and laid-back bars, while families visit for its child-centric attractions. Several other islands lie within easy access of the mainland, ranging from tiny specks like Sisters' Islands to larger gems like St John's Island.

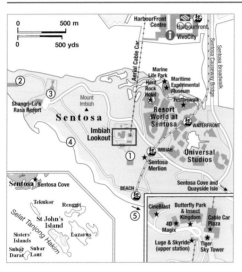

Admission fees to Sentosa (depending on mode of transport) apply and include access to all park areas and beaches, unlimited rides on the light rail, buses and beach trams on Sentosa.

world's largest oceanarium, and other attractions.

GETTING THERE
From the HarbourFront Centre, take a taxi or bus, or walk across the 710-m (2,329-ft) causeway that links Sentosa to Singapore island.

However, for a more exciting start to your trip, hop on the recently upgraded cable car ride that floats 60m above the harbour into the

Below: a Sentosa Express train passes the Sentosa Merlion.

Sentosa

Sentosa, located to the south of the main Singapore island, was once known as Pulau Blakang Mati ('island at the back of death' in Malay), in reference to the frequent fatal disease outbreaks on the island. It was also a refuge for pirates in the 19th century before the British used it as a military fortress. When the British pulled out their troops in 1968, the island was turned into a leisure playground and renamed Sentosa ('isle of peace and tranquillity').

In the past two years, Sentosa has re-emerged as the latest lifestyle enclave away from the city. Sentosa Cove, an upmarket residential project, now boasts swish multi-million-dollar homes by the water. In the area is Quayside Isle which has a bevy of restaurants. **Resorts World Sentosa**, the first Integrated Resort to open in Singapore, is headlined by a glitzy casino, a variety of hotels and dining options, the Universal Studios theme park, Marine Life Park, the

ones will love is the **Underwater World** ③, a small but excellent oceanarium with a submerged acrylic tunnel.
SEE ALSO CHILDREN, P.37

BEACHES

The best beaches are on Sentosa. Sun worshippers gravitate to the soft, clean sands of **Palawan Beach** and **Siloso Beach** ④, both of which have cool bars and watersport equipment for hire. Siloso Beach is also the site of *Songs of the Sea* ⑤, a multimedia spectacle combining shooting jets of water, fire and laser lights. **Tanjong Beach** is a more peaceful spot.
SEE ALSO BEACHES AND ISLANDS, P.34

island. Cable cars depart from HarbourFront Tower 2 and The Jewel Box on Mount Faber. The lofty ride offers a bird's-eye view of the city and the port.

The quickest way into the island is to take the light rail **Sentosa Express** from VivoCity shopping mall on the main island. Once on the island, you can walk or take the shuttle bus or tram services to the various attractions.

IMBIAH LOOKOUT

A whole day should be set aside for Sentosa. There are plenty of attractions, and choosing the right ones can make all the difference.

Many of Sentosa's attractions are grouped in a cluster named the **Imbiah Lookout**, near the Imbiah Station. A number of sights here provide wonderful vistas of Singapore's skyline and the nearby islands. These include the **Tiger Sky Tower** and the

Sentosa Merlion statue. The Imbiah Lookout's best attraction is **Images of Singapore** ①, a waxwork museum. Sentosa's other major historical display is **Fort Siloso** ②, located on the western tip, which was originally built in the 1880s for Singapore's defence.
SEE ALSO MUSEUMS AND GALLERIES, P.84

SENTOSA FOR CHILDREN

Sentosa has plenty of sights to keep children entertained. The **Butterfly Park** and **Insect Kingdom**, with some 1,500 fluttering butterflies and over 3,000 mounted bugs, also includes some of the world's rarest creepy crawlies.

Near the Butterfly Park is the **Skyline Luge Sentosa**, where you ascend on a gondola and slide downhill in a luge. The **Sentosa 4D Magix** theatre thrills with four-dimensional visual entertainment. Another attraction the little

Southern Islands

Beyond Sentosa is an archipelago of tiny islands. These include **Kusu Island**, a place of both rest and worship, **St John's Island**, a holiday haven with an easygoing air, and **Sisters' Islands** and **Pulau Hantu**, both popular for diving.
SEE ALSO BEACHES AND ISLANDS, P.34

Southern and Western Singapore

Southern Singapore is the gateway to the leisure resort of Sentosa and also harbours the world's busiest port, the Port of Singapore. It has also gained cachet of late as a bona fide entertainment destination with the opening of several nightlife venues and the city's largest shopping mall, VivoCity. Western Singapore, although designated as the country's industrial zone with factories and petroleum refineries, is also the location of a major recreation zone with sprawling green spaces and theme parks.

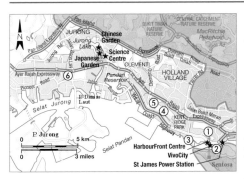

Mount Faber

Begin exploring the west coast from the south at **Mount Faber** ①, off Kampong Bahru Road. This bluff is covered by one of the oldest rainforests in Singapore, with various vantage points looking out to the harbour. The name Mount Faber is in fact a misnomer, as the hill is only 110m (361ft) high. Formerly called Telok Blangah Hill, it was renamed in 1845 after Captain C.E. Faber of the Madras Engineers, who constructed the serpentine road up to the summit. The **Jewel Box** on the hilltop is a dining and drinking venue with the best views, especially at night. From here, you can also board a cable car to Sentosa.

SEE ALSO WALKS AND VIEWS, P.131

HarbourFront Precinct

At the base of Mount Faber is the **HarbourFront Centre**, where cable cars en route from Mount Faber pick up passengers to Sentosa. The nearby **Singapore Cruise Centre** receives passenger ships. Next to the HarbourFront Centre is one of Singapore's largest malls **VivoCity** ②, a shopping experience with covetable retail and dining options. The **Sentosa Express** light rail to Sentosa stops at the third level. An overhead bridge joins the mall to the red-brick **St James Power Station**, a

Below: the twinkling Jewel Box, which offers fantastic views.

> For a taste of the high life, dine 70m above sea level in a cable car. 'Sky Dining' is available nightly, during which guests are served a three-course Western dinner accompanied by views of the twinkling skyline. For bookings, call 6337 9688 or check www.mountfaber.com.sg.

SEE ALSO MUSEUMS AND GALLERIES, P.86

Left: kitschy Haw Par Villa is a unique theme park.

Holland Village

Holland Village is a villagey enclave with two-storey shophouses. It is well loved by both expatriates and locals for its good cafés, watering holes, fashion boutiques and art galleries. **Chip Bee Gardens** here is the locale of a variety of restaurants.

Jurong

Further west, in the industrial zone of Jurong, lie a few gardens that are good for a tranquil stroll, and some theme attractions. The **Singapore Science Centre** and adjacent **Omni Theatre** on Science Centre Road provide educational entertainment that is welcomed by families. Close by on Yuan Ching Road are the **Chinese and Japanese gardens** with serene Asian-style landscaped gardens.

Just off the Ayer Rajah Expressway is the **Jurong BirdPark** ⑥, where many of its 9,000 birds fly free.

SEE ALSO CHILDREN, P.36, 39; PARKS AND GARDENS, P.100

massive nine-venue nightclub housed in a former coal-fired power station.

SEE ALSO NIGHTLIFE, P.96; SHOPPING, P.116, TRANSPORT, P.123

Pasir Panjang Road

At the western end of the harbour, off Pasir Panjang Road, is **Labrador Park** ③, a World War II site offering tours of its hidden war tunnels.

Also in the vicinity is another World War II site, **Reflections at Bukit Chandu**. It pays tribute to the Malay Regiment who fought Japanese troops at the Battle of Pasir Panjang in 1942.

Haw Par Villa ④, on Pasir Panjang Road, is a collection of macabre statues illustrating stories and the various stages of Hell in Chinese mythology.

SEE ALSO CHILDREN, P.36; MUSEUMS AND GALLERIES, P.84, 87

NUS Museums

Along Kent Ridge Crescent is the National University of Singapore (NUS), which houses the first-rate **NUS Museums** ⑤, with three galleries offering insights into Chinese, Asian and local art. The **Raffles Museum of Biodiversity Research** here displays specimens of rare plants and animals.

Right: at the NUS Museum.

The East Coast

The East Coast offers a melange of different lifestyles. Friendly Geylang Serai is the heart of Malay history and culture, while in Katong, there are glimpses into the Peranakan and Eurasian ways of life. The East Coast Park lures watersport enthusiasts, romancing couples and family picnickers from all over the island with its sun, sand and sea, and day trippers set off to rural Ubin island on an idyllic boat ride from the Changi Coast. Perhaps due to its restful and breezy atmosphere, the east also has a host of alfresco cafés and restaurants in its various neighbourhoods, from Siglap and Joo Chiat to Changi Village and the East Coast Park.

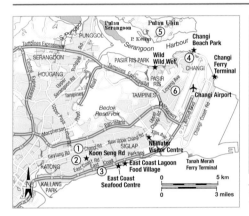

Above: the Katong area is famous for its *laksa*.

Geylang

Geylang is Singapore's red-light district, but is worth a visit for its more salubrious facets. Food-mad Singaporeans swarm to this gourmet heaven with a high density of well-known eateries.

Its ethnic flavour is the strongest in **Geylang Serai** ①, roughly the section of Geylang Road between Jalan Eunos and Aljunied Road. The area was named after the *serai* (lemon grass) fields that once covered it. By the early 20th century, flamboyantly decorated shop- and terrace houses, similar to those found in Chinatown and Kampong Glam, had taken over. Many of these, con-

served and refurbished, are found in the lanes between Geylang Road and Sims Avenue.

The best time to visit Geylang Serai is the Ramadan fasting month that leads up to Hari Raya Puasa every year. The streets are ablaze with blinking lights, and a boisterous open-air, night-time bazaar offers Malay snacks, colourful apparel, home furnishings and fascinating fodder for photographers.

At other times, a more subdued cultural experience awaits in the Malay shops and restaurants, found opposite the Paya Lebar MRT station.

Katong

Opposite the Malay Village is the **Joo Chiat** area, which like **Katong** ② further south, is a stronghold of the Eurasian and Peranakan communities. Katong, which used to be by the coast, gets its name from a now-extinct species of sea

Katong's favourite stalwart is **Chin Mee Chin Confectionery** (204 East Coast Road; tel: 6345 0419), where two generations of Katongites have snacked on their toasted buns with *kaya* (coconut and egg jam) and old-fashioned cakes. The staff and menu of the confectionery have not changed since it opened in the 1960s.

SEE ALSO ARCHITECTURE, P.28; WALKS AND VIEWS, P.129

turtle. Many wealthy English, Portuguese and Chinese settlers were once owners of plantations beside the sea.

The Peranakan and Eurasian influence is discernible today in the antiques shops and restaurants. But perhaps the finest clues to the area's Peranakan heritage are the florid Chinese Baroque-style terrace houses along **Joo Chiat Road** and **Koon Seng Road**.

Siglap and East Coast Park

Continuing east along Upper East Coast Road brings you to **Siglap**, a residential enclave peppered with alfresco cafés and wine bars.

South of Siglap, the **East Coast Park** ③ stretches more than 10km (6 miles), where people jog, rollerblade

Left: sailing is a popular sport on the East Coast.

and indulge in watersport.

Dining options are plentiful here, from Singapore-style seafood at the **East Coast Seafood Centre** to hawker fare at the **East Coast Lagoon Food Village**.

SEE ALSO BEACHES AND ISLANDS, P.32; FOOD AND DRINK, P. 64; RESTAURANTS, P.113

Changi

Before the Changi Airport opened in the early 1980s, laid-back **Changi Village** ④ was the only reason to venture to the far-eastern coast. The shops in this slice of old Singapore, such as George Photo and the Salvation Army Thrift Shop, are tinged with nostalgia.

The **Changi Village Food Centre**, serving local fare, is often a refuelling stop for day trippers to **Pulau Ubin** ⑤, who take boats from the nearby Changi Point Ferry Terminal.

A footbridge leads to **Changi Beach Park**, a small, quiet beach popular with picnickers and anglers. The stretch of sea is dotted with dinghies and keelboats from the nearby sailing clubs.

Near the Changi Airport on Upper Changi Road North is the historic **Changi Chapel and Museum** ⑥, dedicated to the memories of World War II POWs.

SEE ALSO BEACHES AND ISLANDS, P.32, 33; FOOD AND DRINK, P.64; MUSEUMS AND GALLERIES, P.83

Pasir Ris

Pasir Ris Park, on the northeastern coast, offers another pleasant stretch of beach. The **Wild Wild Wet** water theme park is ideal for families and energetic children.

SEE ALSO BEACHES AND ISLANDS, P.33; CHILDREN, P.36

Below: boats from the Changi Point jetty depart for Ubin island.

Central and Northern Singapore

Central and Northern Singapore are a paradox. The two areas have some of the country's most heavily populated housing districts, yet at the same time hold most of its pockets of nature, including three of the four gazetted reserves and two open-concept zoos set in lush greenery. In fact, these parts of the island offer such large tracts of tropical forest and mangrove swamp that getting close to nature here is as much a part of the Singaporean lifestyle as eating and shopping.

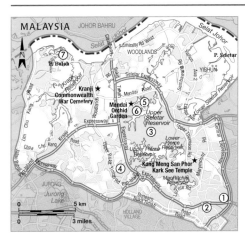

The four gazetted nature reserves in Singapore are the **Central Catchment Nature Reserve**, **Bukit Timah Nature Reserve**, **Sungei Buloh Wetland Reserve** and **Labrador Nature Reserve**. Together they comprise more than 3,340 hectares (8,235 acres) of untouched greenery – which is by no means a small number in land-scarce Singapore.

Temples and Memorials

With Central Singapore home to a large proportion of the population, it is no surprise it is also the locale of a few of the country's most important Chinese temples. **Lian Shan Shuang Lin Monastery** ①, better known as Siong Lim Temple to locals, is located in Toa Payoh, one of Singapore's oldest housing estates, about 5km (3 miles) north of Orchard Road. A number of its buildings are noted for carvings and sculptures crafted by artisans from China.

A few kilometres north of Shuang Lin Monastery is the **Kong Meng San Phor Kark**

See Temple, located on Bright Hill Drive. Built in 1980, it is the largest Buddhist temple in Singapore.

The national monument of **Sun Yat Sen Nanyang Memorial Hall** ② lies further south. This two-storey Victorian-style bungalow, built in 1900, was gifted to Dr Sun, the leader of China's nationalist movement. The museum chronicles his revolutionary activities.

SEE ALSO CHURCHES, MOSQUES AND TEMPLES, P.42; MUSEUMS AND GALLERIES, P.88

Central Catchment Nature Reserve

West of the Kong Meng San

Temple is a lush expanse known as **MacRitchie Reservoir Park**, which forms the **Central Catchment Nature Reserve** ③, one of the four gazetted nature reserves in Singapore, together with the Pierce Reservoir Park and the Upper Seletar Reservoir Park further north.

A highlight worth exploring in the reserve is the **Treetop Walk**, an excursion on a suspension bridge that allows memorable views of the rainforest canopy.
SEE ALSO WALKS AND VIEWS, P.130

Bukit Timah Nature Reserve

To the west of MacRitchie is the **Bukit Timah Nature Reserve** ④, located in the geographic centre of Singapore, 12km (7.5 miles) from the city. Most of Singapore's

Left: the Kranji War Memorial
is dedicated to the fallen of
World War II.

SEE ALSO CHILDREN, P.37, 39;
PARKS AND GARDENS, P101

Kranji

The peaceful, solemn **Kranji
Commonwealth War Ceme-
tery**, further west on Woodlands Road, is the final
resting place of two presidents and Allied soldiers who
were killed in World War II. In
its middle is the War Memorial, engraved with names of
over 24,000 men who died in
the Asia Pacific battles.

The **Sungei Buloh
Wetland Reserve** ⑦, on the
extreme northwestern tip, is a
favourite with birders and
trekkers. Mangroves thrive
here, as do freshwater flora
like water lilies and lotuses.
The abundant birdlife, such as
plovers, egrets and sand-
pipers, can be observed along
its boardwalk and trails.

Over the last few years,
Kranji has been developed as
a rustic getaway from Singapore's urban sprawl. Called
Kranji Countryside, a slice
of this rural area now boasts
various organic, goat, egg
and frog farms and an aquarium that are worth a day trip.
SEE ALSO PARKS AND GARDENS,
P.101; WALKS AND VIEWS, P.131

forest was heavily logged
until the mid-19th century. In
1883, in response to research
by the Straits Settlement government on climatic changes
arising from deforestation, the
Bukit Timah Nature Reserve
was established.

With its moist, dark greenery overlaid by the buzzing of
cicadas, this isolated patch of
land seems almost surreal in
this concrete jungle of a city.
SEE ALSO WALKS AND VIEWS, P.128

Mandai

About 15km (9 miles) north-
east of the Bukit Timah
reserve is the much-lauded
Singapore Zoo ⑤ on Mandai
Lake Road. The world's first
night wildlife park, the **Night
Safari** ⑥, is next door with
nocturnal animals in
recreated habitats.

West of the zoo is the
Mandai Orchid Garden on a
hillside, covered with orchids
in all shapes and shades.

Below: admiring nature from the Treetop Walk at the Central Catchment Nature Reserve *(left)* and
the boardwalk at the Sungei Buloh Wetland Reserve *(right)*.

Architecture

Singapore has seen numerous buildings come and go. A common lament is the lack of sentimentality shown towards old buildings, which get razed in favour of modernisation. However, in such a land-scarce city, redevelopment is par for the course. But look closer and you'll find a good number of old buildings that have stood their ground over generations. In 2001, the Preservation of Monuments Board has listed up to 64 buildings as national monuments. Singapore's architecture is much like its population – a melting pot of ethnicities, styles and sensibilities that invariably find their own harmony.

Central Fire Station

62 Hill Street; tel: 6332 2996; www.scdf.gov.sg; gallery Tue–Sun 10am–5pm; free; MRT: City Hall or Clarke Quay; map p.136 A1

The oldest fire station in Singapore is housed in this distinctive red-and-white 'blood and bandage' building completed in 1901. Its architecture is Edwardian England, a departure from the usual Palladian and classical styles prevailing in Singapore at the time. The 'blood' is the exposed brick, while the 'bandage' refers to the brick covered in white-washed plaster. The building

also holds the **Civil Defence Heritage Gallery**.

SEE ALSO MUSEUMS AND GALLERIES, P.84

City Hall

St Andrew's Road; MRT: City Hall; map p.136 A1

Completed in 1929, this was once Singapore's most important government building, featuring Grecian architecture, dignified columns and a grand staircase. It has seen numerous ceremonies in history, including the World War II surrender of the Japanese on its steps in 1945, the declaration of Singapore's city status by

King George VI and governor Sir Franklin Gimson in 1951, and the proclamation of self-government by Lee Kuan Yew in 1959. Lee later declared the nation's independence on the very same steps in 1963.

Together with the old Supreme Court (*see p.30*), the City Hall will be home to the National Art Gallery from 2015.

Clarke Quay

River Valley Road; MRT: Clarke Quay; map p.135 E1

Clarke Quay was named after the second governor of the Straits Settlement, Lieutenant-General Sir Andrew Clarke. Until the 1970s, it hummed with activity as bumboats carried cargo from ships to the warehouses on its banks. Today it has a hum of a different kind, with trendy bars, clubs and restaurants nestled in the restored warehouses lining its lanes. But look a little closer and discover some of its history. For instance, at its

Left: restored warehouses at Clarke Quay.

Left: colourful and ornate terrace houses.

1903, is particularly outstanding – it features a grand Chinese entrance that was carefully restored by craftsmen from China.

Esplanade – Theatres on the Bay

1 Esplanade Drive; tel: 6828 8222; www.esplanade.com; free; MRT: City Hall or Esplanade; map p.136 B1

The design of this landmark – which people either love or hate – with its distinctive facade of sharp-edged metal sunshades, has been mired in controversy since the model was first unveiled in 1992. Michael Wilford, the British architect who designed the edifice, quit the project in 1995 over unexplained differences, leaving home-grown company DP Architects to complete the job. The result is a glazed building that is protected from the tropical sun and heat by triangular aluminium sun shields. The shields are set to open or close at varying angles, depending on the angle of the

southern end, on the wall of the last shophouse is a sign proclaiming that it was once Whampoa's Ice House. A wealthy Chinese landowner, Whampoa gifted the land where the Singapore Botanic Gardens sits today to the British, who gave him the land at Clarke Quay in return.

Emerald Hill and Peranakan Place

Orchard Road, between Midpoint Orchard and Centrepoint; MRT: Somerset; map p.135 D3–4
This area was once settled by the Peranakan people, or Straits-born Chinese, whose unique culture evolved through intermarriage between Chinese immigrants and local Malay women in the 17th century. Peranakan Place is a complex of ornate Peranakan-style shophouses that have been transformed into a commercial hub. Its shady terrace café is popular with tourists for its drinks and a great place to watch Orchard Road go by.

Up the slope on Emerald Hill is a collection of lovely old restored terrace houses

Once dilapidated and shunned, many shop- and terrace-houses are much sought-after properties today because of their unique facades and historical value. Strict guidelines govern the restoration of these houses, many of which have been turned into chic restaurants, bars and boutique hotels, as well as offices for advertising and publishing firms.

that once belonged to wealthy Peranakan families. The 30 or so homes along the slightly curved road were built between 1901 and 1925 in the Chinese Baroque style, typified by ornamental mouldings, shuttered wooden windows, pastel colours and colourful ceramic tiles. These houses were also the first to be given conservation status in 1981, which means the owners cannot alter their facades. Look out for the four terrace houses numbered 39 to 45, with forecourts and gates and topped with ornate Chinese roofs. No.45, designed by M.T. Moh in

Below: the spiky facade of the Esplanade Theatres.

27

sun's rays. And so arose the building's myriad nicknames, everything from 'fish scales' and 'bug eyes' to what most people seem to have settled on, the 'Durian'.
SEE ALSO DANCE, P.47; MUSIC, P.90; THEATRE, P.121

The Fullerton Hotel

1 Fullerton Square; tel: 6733 8388; www.fullertonhotel.com; MRT: Raffles Place; map p.139 D4

This grand building was built in 1924. Named after Sir Robert Fullerton, the first governor of the Straits Settlements, it was Singapore's largest and is now a wonderful example of the Edwardian Baroque neoclassical style that once dominated the Civic District. Before it was artfully renovated for an astounding S$400 million and reopened as a hotel in 2001, it was the heart of social, official and commercial life, having housed the Singapore Club, the Chamber of Commerce and the General Post Office. The hotel, whose central atrium was created by punching out several floors and the old ceiling, is deceptively contemporary within its stately walls.
SEE ALSO HOTELS, P.70

House of Tan Yeok Nee/Chicago Graduate School of Business

101 Penang Road; MRT: Dhoby Ghaut; map p.135 E3

The eponymous Teochew, cloth peddler turned wealthy gambier and pepper merchant, built this elegant house in 1885. Over the years, the mansion has variously served as the residence of a station master and a bishop, a boarding school for girls, accommodation for Japanese army officers in World War II and the Salva-

Above: the Fullerton's stately walls belie its contemporary interior.

tion Army headquarters. It is a rare example of a southern Chinese-style courtyard house, with a grand entrance and sloping roofs with spiral ornamentation. A business school since 2000, it is not open to visitors but there's nothing against a potential student wandering in.

Jinriksha Station

Corner of Tanjong Pagar and Neil roads; MRT: Chinatown or Tanjong Pagar; map p.138 B2

An eye-catching triangular edifice built in 1903 in the classical style, Jinriksha Station is crowned by a square tower with an octagonal cupola. It served as the main station for *jinriks* (two-wheeled rickshaws

In land-scarce Singapore, providing housing for the masses means building upwards. More than 80 percent of Singaporeans own and live in high-rise flats built by the Housing and Development Board. In many other parts of the world, public housing is associated with poverty and social unrest, but not in Singapore. In fact, its public housing programme is one of its finest achievements, with other fast-growing countries seeking to emulate its success.

pulled by men), which first arrived in Singapore in the 1880s from Shanghai. They were the main means of transport in Singapore in the early 1900s. The rickshaw coolies found it convenient to live around the station, renting bed space in tiny Chinatown cubicles.

Joo Chiat Road and Koon Seng Road

MRT: Paya Lebar; bus: 40, 43, 76 or 135

The Joo Chiat area was once home to Peranakan families. The area still retains traces of its Peranakan heritage, such as the beautifully restored Chinese Baroque shop- and terrace houses along **Joo Chiat Road** and **Koon Seng Road**. Built in the 1930s, in what has come to be known as the Late Shophouse Style (the most florid of all shophouse styles), they feature richly decorated facades and ornate details that testify to the wealth of the original homeowners.

Lai Chun Yuen

36 Smith Street; MRT: Chinatown; map p.138 B3

Built in 1887, this restored three-storey building, with gleaming wooden floors and carved banisters, was formerly called Lai Chun Yuen, a Cantonese opera house that packed in the fans in its heyday. Famous opera stars performed here in the 1920s. If there is a faint similarity between the facade of the theatre and that of the Raffles Hotel, it is because both were designed by R.A.J. Bidwell. The building has unfortunately been renovated into a budget hotel.

Marina Bay Sands

10 Bayfront Avenue, Marina Bay Sands; MRT: Bayfront, Promenade or Marina Bay; map p.139 E3

When this Integrated Resort was built, it changed Singapore's skyline completely. Designed by Moshe Safdie Architects, the three soaring hotel towers are crowned by the Sands SkyPark on the 57th floor, offering an amazing 360 degree view. Another iconic structure in the vicinity by the same architect is the **ArtScience Museum**. Perched at the Marina Bay waterfront, the round shaped building features 10 'fingers' designated as gallery spaces. These fingers feature skylights that allow natural light to flood in. The dish-like roof allows rainwater to flow through the building's central atrium.
SEE ALSO HOTELS, P.71; MUSEUMS & GALLERIES, P.82; NIGHTLIFE, P.94;

RESTAURANTS, P.103; THEATRE, P.121

MICA Building

140 Hill Street; MRT: Clarke Quay or City Hall; map p.136 A1
The MICA Building, built in 1934, is also commonly known as the Old Hill Street Police Station, which once occupied the premises. The more delicate features of this classical Renaissance-style building with horseshoe arches are now rather overwhelmed by its startling multicoloured shutters – there are 911 altogether – but experts agree that it is one of the city's premier examples of British colonial architecture.

After undergoing extensive restoration, the building reopened in 2000 and today houses the offices of the Ministry of Information, Communication and the Arts, the National Arts Council and the National Heritage Board. The **ARTrium** courtyard on the ground level is occupied by a number of art galleries.
SEE ALSO MUSEUMS AND GALLERIES, P.89

New Supreme Court

1 Supreme Court Lane; tel: 6336 0644; MRT: City Hall or Clarke Quay; map p.136 A1

Designed by the renowned architect Lord Norman Foster, the new Supreme Court building houses Singapore's main law courts. The civil courts are located on the lower floors and the criminal courts are above. Singapore's highest court, the Court of Appeal, is symbolically raised above the other courtrooms, occupying the dramatic aluminium steel-and glass-clad disc on top. The architect intended the disc, on par with the dome of the old Supreme Court (see p.30), as the latter's modern interpretation. With its palette of materials, including glass and stone, the building allows light to filter through it by day and emits a warm lantern-like glow by night.

There is a public **observation deck** (free) on the 8th floor with excellent views of the Singapore River. On the ground level is the **Supreme Court Gallery**, which traces Singapore's legal history (Mon–Fri 8.30am–6pm, Sat 8.30am–1pm; free).

OCBC Centre

65 Chulia Street; MRT: Raffles Place; map p.139 C3
This 52-storey monolith had the honour of being the first foreigner-designed skyscraper after independence. The city's tallest building when it was completed in 1976, it is a fine example of architect I.M Pei's vision of the modern brutalist style, which is often defined by the use of concrete and repetitive angular configuration. Designed to symbolise permanence and strength, this stoic building bears three distinctive tiers separating striking windows that resemble button pads. Because of these windows and its slim profile, it has earned the nickname of 'the Calculator'.

Below: the old (left) and new (right) Supreme Courts.

Architecture

29

the forest of skyscrapers around the building, the top floors enjoy unobstructed sea views, made possible by the unconventional strategy of turning the building's axis on the upper floors 45 degrees from that of the ground floor.

Robertson Quay

MRT: Clarke Quay, then taxi; bus: 32, 54, 64, 123, 139, 143 or 195; map p.135 D1

Robertson Quay lies upriver of Clarke Quay. In the old days, European and Chinese merchants used this part of the river mostly for storing goods. Although a few warehouses still exist along Rodyk Street, Robertson Quay has been taken over by some of Singapore's most exclusive riverside apartments. A number of restored 19th-century warehouses are now occupied by restaurants, bars and the **Singapore Tyler Print Institute**.

SEE ALSO MUSEUMS AND GALLERIES, P.88

Tanjong Pagar Conservation District

Tanjong Pagar, Craig, Neil and Duxton roads; MRT: Chinatown or Tanjong Pagar; map p.138 B2

Once a Malay fishing village, the land around Tanjong Pagar was turned into a nutmeg plantation in the 1830s. The area then became a thriving commercial hub, but by the 1960s, it fell into disrepair, and would have met the wrecker's ball if the authorities had not started its massive conservation drive. Tanjong Pagar soon became an archetype for how the remainder of historic Singapore would be restored.

The 190 shophouses were

Old Supreme Court

St Andrew's Road; MRT: City Hall or Clarke Quay; map p.136 A1

Completed in 1939, the old Supreme Court was the swansong of Frank Dorrington, then chief architect of the Public Works Department. The imposing edifice is most notable for its Corinthian and Ionic columns and green copper dome, as well as its pediment, which is ornamented by a tympanum sculpture crafted by the Milanese sculptor Cavalieri Rudolfo Nolli. The centre figure of the sculpture is Justice, distinguished by the scale she is holding. Flanking her are figures representing a lost soul, the law, gratitude, prosperity and abundance.

The law courts have all moved to the glass-and-steel new Supreme Court located just behind (see p.29). Together with the City

Hall (see p.26) next door, the old Supreme Court is awaiting its new lease of life in 2015 as the National Art Gallery, which will be the largest visual arts gallery in Singapore.

Republic Plaza

9 Raffles Place; MRT: Raffles Place; map p.139 D3

Architect Kisho Kurokawa's clever ways around the design constraints for the Republic Plaza won him a top architectural award, the World Best Architecture 1997 Award from FIABCI. Built at a height of 280m (918ft), the maximum allowed by Singapore's aviation regulations, the Republic Plaza is one of the three tallest skyscrapers in Singapore – the other two are OUB Centre and UOB Plaza One (see opposite). The tower tapers upwards, a design that ensures stability against gales. And despite

From the 1960s to the 1970s, anything that stood in the way of economic progress, including colonial-era buildings, was razed. By the 1970s Singapore had achieved prosperity, but was criticised for its lack of character and culture. In the 1980s the government began to restore older buildings, focusing on four conservation areas, namely Boat Quay, Little India, Kampong Glam and Chinatown/Tanjong Pagar. More areas have been added since, but many still feel that the preservation efforts have come too late.

Above: 'five-foot-ways' front many conservation houses.

American company.

UOB Plaza
80 Raffles Place; MRT: Raffles Place; map p.139 D4
Completed in 1992, the twin towers of UOB Plaza are the most well known icons of Singapore's CBD skyline, designed by Japanese architectural maestro Kenzo Tange. His concept was built on that of the original octagonal 38-storey UOB Building designed by Lim Chong Keat. Taking the sculptural concept a step further, Tange added more storeys that are turned at 45 degrees relative to one another, rendering the building's chiselled look.

The ground floor is hollowed out as an atrium, which connects the Singapore River and Raffles Place. Salvador Dali's large bronze statue *Homage to Newton* stands in the middle of the atrium, overlooking the constant stream of smartly dressed executives.

renovated for 'adaptive reuse' as restaurants, shops and offices. The first units were put up for tender in 1987 and almost overnight Tanjong Pagar became hot property for creative people, who were drawn by its traditional architectural elements.

The two- and three-storey narrow yet deep structures typically feature ornate plaster facades, wooden window shutters and stairways, high ceilings and 'five-foot-way' footpaths, which are so named because they always measure 5ft (1.5m) wide.

The area takes on a magical glow at night when the lights come on and people unwind in the pubs and restaurants. The art deco Tanjong Pagar Railway station which ceased operations on 30 June 2011 was gazetted as a national monument that same year.

Thong Chai Medical Institute
50 Eu Tong Sen Street; MRT: Clarke Quay; map p.138 C4
The former Thong Chai Medical Institute was built in 1892 as a free hospital. Modelled after a southern Chinese palace with two inner courtyards, it is distinctive for its ornately decorated ridges and green-tiled gabled roofs shaped like clouds. The building is now a national monument, although it also serves as the headquarters of an

Right: Salvador Dali's *Homage to Newton* at the UOB Plaza.

31

Beaches and Islands

With its urban sprawl, it is often easy to forget that Singapore is a tropical island. There are beaches aplenty, good for walks, picnics and watersport, while the outlying islands are lovely respites from the shopping malls, office buildings, museums and restaurants. You can spend the night on most of the islands, although accommodation is the bare basics on the smaller ones, while the larger ones like Sentosa boast plush retreats that are a mere bus or boat ride away from the main island.

Changi Beach Park

Along Changi Coast Road; free; bus: 2, 29, 59 or 109

A short walk from Changi Village Food Centre (see p.64) is the Changi Point Ferry Terminal, which offers a boat service to Pulau Ubin (see opposite). This ferry terminal is also the start of the **Changi Point Coastal Walk**, a 2.2-km (1.4-mile) boardwalk, heading west, which offers pleasant views of the sea, Pulau Ubin and Malaysia. A footbridge in the opposite direction leads to Changi Beach Park, a short but pleasant stretch of sand

Look out for the **Changi Beach Massacre Site** along Changi Beach, marked by a storyboard. This was where 66 male civilians were killed by a Japanese firing squad in World War II.

with views across the water to Malaysia and Pulau Tekong. Changi Beach is not as popular as the East Coast Park and therefore far less crowded.

East Coast Park

Along East Coast Park Service Road; free; MRT: Bedok, then bus: 401

The visitor's first encounter with Singapore starts with the lush east coast as one travels into town from the Changi Airport. The area could be described as Singapore's 'riviera', with coconut groves and sandy beaches on one side of the coastal highway, and expensive condos on the other.

East Coast Park stretches for more than 10km (6 miles) along the coast between the Changi Airport and Marina Bay. Fringed with casuarinas and coconut palms, the park affords superb views of ships anchored in the Straits of Singapore. The sea breeze blows gently and it's often peaceful enough for birds to flock to special tall-grass sanctuaries found along the coastline.

The park is the playground for residents living in the eastern part of the island. Tai chi practitioners can be seen exercising in the park as early as 6am, together with joggers and cyclists. Picnic tables and barbecue pits are set up under the trees, and happy campers pitch their

Below: rollerblading at the East Coast Park.

Left: locals enjoying the beach.

detail Ubin's flora and fauna and things to do. It's best to see the island on a bicycle, which can be rented from shacks in the main village, where there are also rustic seafood restaurants.

Ubin has vast tracts of secondary jungle and mangrove swamp that sustain a wide variety of animals, such as long-tailed macaques and monitor lizards and birds like sunbirds, kingfishers and brahminy kites.

A walk in the swamp or forest may reveal unexpected surprises, such as sightings of oriental whip snakes curled up on trees and fruit bats rustling in the evenings. There are also wild orchids and flowers to be found and, if one is lucky, carnivorous pitcher plants with trapped insects.

Accommodation is available at the **Celestial Ubin Beach Resort**, which offers air-conditioned rooms with basic facilities, outdoor activities and a fish spa (tel: 6542 9749; ubinbeach.celestial

Below: cycling on Pulau Ubin.

colourful tents. The park is especially packed at weekends as Singaporeans escape to the beach, but on weekdays the beach and picnic areas are blissfully quiet. Although the water and beach are clean, don't expect crystal-clear waters and powdery white sand.

Watersport and other recreational facilities are available along the beach. And like everywhere else in Singapore, there are plenty of food options, from hawker favourites to local seafood at the **East Coast Seafood Centre**.
SEE ALSO RESTAURANTS, P.113 AND SPORT, P.119

Pasir Ris Park

Along Pasir Ris Drive 3; free; MRT: Pasir Ris
The idyllic Pasir Ris Park is another pleasant stretch of beach, overlooking Pulau Ubin just across the water. Part of the park, near car park C (entry via Pasir Ris Green), encloses a reserve that protects a 6-hectare (14.8-acre) mangrove

swamp, where many migrating birds feed and build their nests.

A wooden boardwalk leads across the mudflats and brackish ponds, with signboards that provide details about the flora and fauna. Nature lovers will also enjoy Sungei Api Api nearby. This river is one of the few remaining natural rivers in Singapore and about 26 species of mangrove have been identified in this swamp.

If flora and fauna does not interest you, then spend a lazy afternoon relaxing on or swimming by this undulating sand stretch. A string of casual eateries are also located here.

Pulau Ubin

Off Singapore's northeastern tip; free; boat from Changi Point Ferry Terminal
Ubin island measures just 8km (5 miles) across and 1.5km (1 mile) wide. An information kiosk run by the National Parks Board (tel: 6542 4108; daily 8.30am–5pm) has maps and leaflets that

resort.com). You can also pitch tents on **Jelutong, Noordin** and **Mamam beaches**.

CHEK JAWA WETLANDS

Call it nature's outdoor classroom if you will. Thanks to passionate nature lovers, the Chek Jawa wetlands, located on Pulau Ubin's southeastern coast and discovered only in 2000, has been saved from reclamation. The vast expanse of sand and mudflats is so fertile it has created an astonishingly diverse ecosystem found nowhere else in Singapore. The wetlands with several habitats – seagrass bed, rocky shore, sand bar, mudflats and mangrove forest – teems with endangered flora and fauna.

Visitors can now enjoy the wildlife of Chek Jawa along a boardwalk and from a floating pontoon and viewing tower.

Guided tours of Chek Jawa are conducted at low tides by the National Parks Board and must be booked in advance. Schedules are posted on www.nparks.gov.sg; for more information, tel: 6542 4108.

Sentosa's Beaches

Southern Sentosa; tel: 1800-736 8672; www.sentosa.com.sg; entrance charge to Sentosa; MRT: HarbourFront, then Sentosa Express from VivoCity or cable car from HarbourFront Centre; cable car from Mount Faber

If you disregard the views of ships in the distance, Sentosa's beaches are probably Singapore's finest stretches of sand, running some 3km (1.8 miles) along the southern shore of the resort island, interspersed with scenic saltwater lagoons and coconut groves.

Watersport enthusiasts should head for **Palawan Beach** or **Siloso Beach**, where windsurfers, canoes and pedal boats can be hired. Beach volleyball has attracted a lively crowd of bikini-clad girls and bare-chested young men, especially at weekends. Throughout the year, events like sand-sculpting competitions, jazz evenings and bazaars keep the beaches a hotbed of activity. Hotspots like Coastes and Wave House Sentosa are great spots to have a bite and beer by the beach.

The *Songs of the Sea* multimedia show comes on nightly at Siloso Beach. At

Above: imbibing the good life on Siloso Beach.

Palawan Beach, you can also climb on its **suspension bridge** to get to the southernmost point of Continental Asia.

If you prefer something laid-back, head to **Tanjong Beach** at the eastern end of the island. Tanjong Beach Club, a stylish restaurant-bar by the beach, lures in the trendy set.

A beach tram plies all three beaches daily from 9am to 7pm.

SEE ALSO CHILDREN, P.37; NIGHTLIFE, P.95

Southern Islands

South of Sentosa; www.sen-

Below: Sentosa has the best beaches in Singapore; Siloso Beach is perfect for a game of volleyball.

tosa.com.sg; ferry from Marina
South pier

The archipelago of tiny
islands that lie beyond
Sentosa range from
uninhabited coral outcrops to
popular weekend retreats.

GETTING THERE

The ferry to Kusu and
St John's islands departs at
10am and 2pm Mon–Fri, at
9am, 12pm and 3pm Sat and
at 9am, 11am, 1pm, 3pm and
5pm on Sun and public holidays, from the **Marina South
Pier** (tel: 6534 9339; www.island-
cruise.com.sg). To get to the
pier, take bus 402 from the
Marina Bay MRT station. The
last ferry departs
St John's at 2.45pm Mon–Fri,
3.45pm Sat and 5.50pm on
Sun and public holidays, and
leaves Kusu at 4pm Mon–Fri,
4.30pm Sat and 6.15pm on
Sun and public holidays.

Sisters' and Hantu islands
are not served by regular
ferries, so you will have to
hire a boat at the Marina
South Pier. An alternative
way to see the harbour and
islands is on the *Cheng Ho*,
a replica Chinese junk that
cruises around the southern
islands with a half-hour
stopover at Kusu (tel: 6533
9811; www.watertours.com.sg).

If you are visiting Sisters'
and Hantu islands, be sure to
pack a picnic as the islands
do not offer food or drinks or
facilities of any sort. Camping
is allowed on Sisters' and
Hantu islands, but a permit
from Sentosa is required.
Bungalows on St John's
Island can be booked with
Sentosa as well.

KUSU ISLAND

Kusu Island, also called Turtle
Island, is a place of both
relaxation and worship.
Legend has it that two shipwrecked sailors – one Malay,

Above: a Chinese pavilion on Kusu Island.

one Chinese – were saved
when a giant turtle transformed itself into an island.
Each man gave thanks
according to his own belief,
and so today the Taoist **Tua
Pek Kong Temple** with its
turtle pool and the Muslim
keramat (shrine) on the hill
are popular pilgrimage sites,
especially during the ninth
month of the lunar calendar,
usually straddling October
and November.
SEE FESTIVALS AND EVENTS,
P.59

PULAU HANTU

Many of the southern islands
are enveloped by coral reefs,
including Pulau Hantu, or
Ghost Island, to the north-
west of Sentosa. Named so
because it is said to be
haunted by the spirits of two
ancient warriors who fought
to their deaths here, Hantu is
regarded as one of Singa-
pore's best diving spots.
Contact The Hantu Blog, a
non-profit environmental
group that raises funds by
organising monthly dive trips
to Hantu (www.pulauhantu.org).

ST JOHN'S ISLAND

Also called Pulau Sakijang
Bendera, this was where
Raffles anchored before
meeting the Temenggong,

or Malay chief, on the
Singapore River in 1819.
The island served as a quar-
antine centre for immigrants
until the 1950s when it was
used as a holding centre for
political detainees. In 1975
St John's was turned into a
holiday resort with lagoons,
shady paths and picnic
spots, making it a popular
weekend getaway.

SISTERS' ISLANDS

Pulau Subar Darat and Pulau
Subar Laut are the two small
islands collectively known as
Sisters' Islands. With one of
Singapore's richest coral
reefs, they are an ideal venue
for diving. The currents can
get pretty strong, so take
care when swimming.

Below: terrapins are released
at the tortoise sanctuary on
Kusu Island for good luck.

35

Children

If nothing else, Singapore is one of the world's most family-friendly places. Movies are censored and rated, shopping malls offer road shows with popular television and cartoon characters almost all year round, and incentives like the Baby Bonus are dished out to willing parents. In the same vein, the city's attractions offer all things educational and entertaining for children of all ages. The island resort of Sentosa is an obvious choice, but there are also a number of quirky tours and amusement parks as well as exceptional zoos. Some of them are so good that adults will find them hard to resist.

Haw Par Villa

262 Pasir Panjang Road; tel: 6872 2003; daily 9am–7pm; free; MRT: Buona Vista, then bus: 10, 20, 188 or 200

Also known as Tiger Balm Gardens, this theme park houses a collection of 1,000 statues and 150 tableaux that illustrate Chinese mythological stories and notorious crimes from Singapore's history. These gaudy exhibits are the only remaining collection of this genre in Asia.

Haw Par Villa ('villa of the tiger and the leopard') was built by Aw Boon Haw ('Gentle Tiger') for his brother Aw Boon Par ('Gentle Leopard') in 1937. The Aw brothers were philanthro-pists who made their fortune with Tiger Balm, the cure-all that is now world-famous. When Boon Par died in 1945, Boon Haw turned Haw Par Villa into public property as a way of preserving Chinese culture.

The **Wild Wild Wet** theme park (1 Pasir Ris close; tel: 6581 9128; www.wildwild wet.com; Mon, Wed–Fri 1–7pm, Sat–Sun and public and school holidays 10am–7pm; entrance charge), features eight different water-based rides and slides, and massive wave pools. Younger children can muck about in a shallow splash area.

Jacob Ballas Children's Garden

Singapore Botanic Gardens, 1 Cluny Road; tel: 6471 7361; www.sbg.org.sg; Tues–Sun 8am–7pm; free; MRT: Orchard, then taxi; bus: 7, 105, 123 or 174

If your kid needs to get in touch with the great out-doors, this children's park at the Botanic Garden's Bukit Timah Core might just do the trick. Children up to the age of 12 will be treated to adventures in the **A-Maze-ing maze garden**, learn about photosynthesis at the **Magic of Photosynthesis** interactive exhibit, and hang out at the tree house and suspension bridge in the **Fantastic Forest**, among other themed attractions.

SEE ALSO PARKS AND GARDENS, P.101

Jurong BirdPark

2 Jurong Hill; tel: 6265 0022; www.birdpark.com.sg; daily 8.30am–6pm (last admission 5.30pm); MRT: Boon Lay, then bus: 194 or 251

Left: Universal Studios Singapore is great for families.

Left: the little ones will have a splashing good time in Singapore.

Children

3411; www.nightsafari.com.sg; daily 7.30pm–midnight (last admission 11pm); MRT: Ang Mo Kio, then bus: 138 or MRT: Choa Chu Kang, then bus: 927
Next door to the Singapore Zoo, the Night Safari is the world's first night wildlife park, with over 2,500 nocturnal animals awake and active in seven geographical zones of the world. These re-created habitats feature clever unobtrusive lighting resembling moonlight.

From 7.30pm, a series of trams (separate charge) with guides aboard takes about 45 minutes to encircle the themed zones on a 3.2-km (2-mile) track.

Deer and other small animals wander freely by the tram. You can disembark to take a closer look at the animals in their open enclosures by following one of the four walking trails. One of the newest is the Wallaby Trail – inspired by the wildlife of the Australian Outback. Visitors are separated from the larger animals by natural barriers such as moats, vegetation and near-invisible wires. Flash photography is not allowed.

Don't miss the interactive **Creatures of the Night** show (daily 7.30pm, 8.30pm and 9.30pm) featuring nocturnal animals such as the puma, leopard cat and spotted hyena.

Home to 5,000 birds and 380 species from all over the world, this 20-hectare (49-acre) park attracts well over a million visitors each year. A relaxing way to explore the park is by the **Panorail** (daily 8.30am–5.45pm; separate charge), which affords panoramic vistas.

The park is split into various themed areas. These include the **Penguin Coast**, which is a re-created Antarctic habitat for penguins and puffins; the **Flamingo Lake** with delicate pink flamingos; and the walk-in **African**

Waterfall Aviary housing over 600 species of African birds and a 30-metre high waterfall. The **Lory Loft** is another walk-in free-flight aviary resembling Australia's rural landscape.

Also unique is the **World of Darkness**, a nocturnal bird house with a reversed lighting system such that when it is day outside, it is night inside. Residents here include the snowy owl, tundra and buffy fish owl.

Night Safari

80 Mandai Lake Road; tel: 6269

Sentosa

South of Singapore island; tel: 1800-736 8672 or 6736 8672; entrance charge to Sentosa; opening times and entrance charges for attractions vary; MRT: HarbourFront, then Sentosa Express from VivoCity

Below: the Night Safari's open concept allows gentle animals to wander freely.

or cable car from HarbourFront Centre; cable car from Mount Faber

Sentosa has a plethora of sights to keep children entertained throughout the day. Here is a selection of some favourites.

4D MAGIX

Imbiah Lookout; tel: 6274 5355; www.sentosa4dmagix.com.sg; daily half-hourly shows 10am–9pm

At Southeast Asia's largest four-dimensional theatre, enjoy an engaging multi-sensory experience complete with images leaping out at you and precisely timed environmental effects like water sprays and blowing wind.

DOLPHIN LAGOON

Palawan Beach; tel: 6275 0030; www.underwaterworld.com.sg; daily 10am–7pm; entrance charge includes admission to Underwater World

The endangered Indo-Pacific humpbacked pink dolphins here endear themselves to the crowd with their antics. Meet-the-Dolphin and Fur Seals live shows take place daily (11am, 3pm and 5.45pm).

SKYLINE LUGE SENTOSA

Near Sentosa Express Beach Station; daily 10am–9.30pm

Riders ascend a slope by chairlift and hurtle down in a luge, a part go-kart, part-toboggan, at a speed that suits their fancy.

UNDERWATER WORLD

Northwestern Sentosa; tel: 6275 0030; www.underwaterworld.com.sg; daily 10am–7pm

The oceanarium's highlight is the 83-m- (272-ft-) long acrylic tunnel with a travellator, which leads under a huge tank containing over 2,500 sea creatures – think bright, luminous reef dwellers, sinister stingrays and sharks. Stone fish, sea urchins and moray eels lurk behind the rocks and amid colourful corals.

There are also 'touch pools' and aquariums of jelly fish, sea dragons and other colourful marine life.

Throughout the day, you can watch these denizens of the deep being hand-fed by divers. The more adventurous can 'Dive with the Sharks' while intrepid scuba-certified divers can sign up for the 'Extreme Bull Shark Encounter'.

UNIVERSAL STUDIOS SINGAPORE

8 Sentosa Gateway, Sentosa Island; tel: 6577 8888; www.rwsentosa.com; daily 10am–7pm, Sat 10am–8pm; MRT: HarbourFront then take the Sentosa Express at VivoCity and alight at Waterfront Station

The biggest attraction for families in Singapore, this theme park draws kids of all ages to experience its thrilling rides, shows and attractions based on your favourite blockbuster films and TV shows. There are seven zones: Hollywood, New York, Sci-fi City, Ancient Egypt, Lost World, Far Far Away and Madagascar. Besides the highly publicised Transformers The Ride: The Ultimate 3D Battle, the world's first Sesame Street ride *(Sesame Street Spaghetti Space Chase)* is the park's newest attraction.

MARINE LIFE PARK

8 Sentosa Gateway, Sentosa Island; tel: 6577 8888; www.rwsentosa; S.E.A. Aquarium, daily 10am–7pm, Adventure Cove Waterpark daily 10am–6pm; MRT: HarbourFront, then take the Sentosa Express at VivoCity and alight at Waterfront Station

Resorts World Sentosa is home to the world's largest oceanarium. Explore its S.E.A. Aquarium which has more than 800 species of marine animals and over 200 sharks.

At the Adventure Cove Waterpark, snorkel with 20,000 tropical fish and other sea creatures, grab a tube and float down Adventure River which passes through 14 themed zones, or enjoy thrilling waterslides.

The Maritime Experiential Museum

8 Sentosa Gateway, Sentosa Island; tel: 6577 8888; daily 10am–7pm; MRT: HarbourFront, then take the Sentosa Express at VivoCity and alight at Waterfront Station

Left: lugers at the Skyline Luge Sentosa.

Don't miss the Living Fossils exhibit at Underwater World, where about 20 fish have been tagged with microchips. When a tagged fish passes by a sensor, visitors can read facts about it, such as its name, species and origins, on a touchscreen.

This multi-sensory museum showcases an interactive voyage along the ancient Maritime Silk Route. Explore artefacts, interact with exhibits and experience a shipwreck in the exciting 360-degree Typhoon Theatre.
SEE MUSEUMS AND GALLERIES, P.85

Above: catch animals in lively action at feeding time at the zoo.

Singapore Science Centre

15 Science Centre Road; tel: 6425 2500; www.science.edu.sg; daily 10am–6pm; MRT: Jurong East, then bus: 66 or 335
Inquisitive minds will find the 1,000 interactive exhibits in the Science Centre's 14 galleries a thorough joy.

Highlights include the **Genome Exhibit**, where DNA structures and their functions are explored through three-dimensional exhibits. There are optical illusions in the **Mind's Eye** gallery, and kids will find the **Kinetic Garden**, with sculptures and water features, especially engaging.

The adjacent **Omni-Theatre** presents several wide-screen Omnimax movies each day (10am–8pm; separate charge) on a five-storey-high hemispheric screen.

Singapore Zoo

80 Mandai Lake Road; tel: 6269 3411; www.zoo.com.sg; daily 8.30am–6pm (last admission 5.30pm); MRT: Ang Mo Kio, then bus: 138 or MRT: Choa Kang, then bus: 927
Spread over 28 hectares (69 acres), the zoo stands out in nearly every category by which animal collections are judged: variety of wildlife (more than 2,800 animals from 300 species); open-air, naturalistic enclosures; captive breeding of endangered species; and attractive landscaping.

Popular attractions include the **Elephants of Asia** exhibit, reminiscent of the hills of Burma; and the **Fragile Forest**, showcasing various rainforest ecosystems. The zoo also has the world's largest captive **orangutan colony**. The little ones will be enthralled with **Children's World**, where they can pet animals, watch a sheep dog at work, and take a ride on a miniature train.

If your child fancies having a **Jungle Breakfast with Wildlife** among orangutans and other forest animals, book a place at Ah Meng Restaurant in advance (daily 9–10.30am; separate charge). Animal shows take place several times a day at the open-air amphitheatre.

Note: The zoo's parent company, Wildlife Reserves Singapore, will be introducing **River Safari**, Asia's first and only river-themed wildlife park in 2013. Check the website for details.

The park's biggest attraction is the Giant Panda Forest (pandas.riversafari.com.sg) which will house two pandas from China. Visitors can have a special preview of the panda's new home, which is accessible through the zoo for a limited time.

Tours

Ducktours

Tickets at Ducktours Counter, Suntec City Mall Galleria, 3 Temasek Boulevard; tel: 6338 6877; www.ducktours.com.sg; daily 10am–6pm; MRT: City Hall, then shuttle bus to Suntec City or Promenade; map p.136 C2
If you can't decide between a bus tour and a river cruise for the family, simply go with a Ducktour. Kids will love the one-hour ride on the Duck, a converted amphibious vehicle that first splashes into the Kallang Basin for a scenic cruise up to the Merlion at Marina Bay, and then goes ashore, waddling through the historical Civic District.

The same company also offers **Hippotours**, which are city sightseeing trips on open-top double-decker buses. You can hop on and off at designated stops along the way.

39

Churches, Mosques and Temples

Singapore has an enviable record of religious and ethnic harmony, although it was not one that was won lightly. The country was wrecked by two communal riots in the 1950s and 1960s, but for the most part today, its people are accepting of one another's faiths. Naturally then, there are plenty of places of worship, many of which have been declared national monuments for their architectural and historical value.

Abdul Gaffoor Mosque
41 Dunlop Street; tel: 6295 4209; Sat–Thur 9am–8pm, Fri 9am–12.30pm, 2.30pm–8pm; free; MRT: Little India; map p.133 C1
Built in 1859 and named after a lawyer's clerk, this Renaissance- and Arabian-style mosque is an oasis of calm in exuberant Little India. The prayer hall, decorated with Moorish arches, has a tableau tracing the origins of Islam.

Al Abrar Mosque
192 Telok Ayer Street; tel: 6220 6306; daily 11am–9pm; free; MRT: Tanjong Pagar; map p.139 C2
This mosque was built between 1850 and 1855 by the Muslim Chulia community from South India. Declared a national monument in 1974, it is a mansion compared to the earlier structure that sat here in the 1830s, which was a mere thatched building known as Kuchu Palli ('hut mosque').

Armenian Church
60 Hill Street; tel: 6334 0141; www.armeniansinasia.org; daily 9am–6pm; free; MRT: City Hall; map p.136 A2
Also called St Gregory the Illuminator, this exquisite church was built in 1835 and designed by colonial archItect George Coleman. The oldest in Singapore, it houses a cemetery in its grounds, where the tombstones of some eminent names in Singapore's history lie. Among them are the Sarkies brothers who founded Raffles Hotel and Agnes Joaquim, after whom Singapore's national flower is named.

Agnes discovered a purple bloom, later named Vanda Miss Joaquim, behind her home in Tanjong Pagar in 1893.

Buddha Tooth Relic Temple and Museum
288 South Bridge Road; tel: 6220 0220; www.btrts.org.sg; daily 7am–7pm; free; MRT: Chinatown; map p.138 B3
Right in the heart of Chinatown lies this five-storey-high Buddhist shrine housing

Below: the graceful Armenian Church is a quiet sanctum in the bustling Civic District.

Left: worshippers at Sri Veeramakaliamman Temple *(see p.44)*.

Archbishop of Singapore. It was gazetted as a national monument in 1973. Two colonial architects, Denis Loolcy Sweeney and J. Turnbull Thomson, submitted designs for the cathedral in a competition. The former was eventually the victor, for his design, inspired by St Paul's in Covent Garden and St Martin-in-the-Fields in London, was less expensive than Thomson's.

Hajjah Fatimah Mosque

4001 Beach Road; tel: 6297 2774; daily 9am–9pm; free; MRT: Lavender; map p.137 D4

Built by a British architect in 1846, this mosque was named after a faithful Muslim woman who, after her husband's death, ran his shipping business so well that the proceeds enabled her to build the mosque on the site of their home. Its Gothic-style spire, which tilts at six degrees, has earned the mosque the nickname 'Leaning Tower of Singapore'.

Jamae Mosque

218 South Bridge Road; tel: 6221 4165; daily 10am–7pm; free; MRT: Chinatown; map p.138 C3

Sporting an eclectic mix of architectural styles, this mosque features pagoda-like minarets that are rare in mosque architecture, perhaps as a gesture of deference to the predominantly Chinese neighbourhood. It has a South Indian-style entrance gate and neoclassical-style prayer halls and shrine. The mosque was constructed in 1826 by Muslim Chulia immigrants who came from South India's Coromandel Coast.

Over 85 percent of Singapore residents say they have a faith: 43 percent are Buddhist, 15 percent are Muslim, 15 percent are Christian, 8 percent are Taoist and 4 percent are Hindu. Others profess to minority beliefs.

---

sacred objects dedicated to the Maitreya Buddha (Future Buddha). Its architecture, interiors and statuary are inspired by the styles of the Tang dynasty – a golden age for Buddhism in China.

Entering the 80-m- (262-ft-) high main hall, you will see an intricately carved 5-m (16-ft) wooden Maitreya Buddha image. A hundred other Buddha statues line both sides of the hall. The next floor is designated as an exhibition hall for religious artworks and a library of Buddhist texts. A permanent collection of cultural artefacts, some of which were purchased from Sotheby's and Christie's auctions, is kept in a climate-controlled hall on the third floor.

The temple's centrepiece is one of the Buddha's sacred teeth, an object dogged by much controversy; its authenticity has been doubted by Buddhism scholars and some members of the public. It is held on the fourth floor in a golden stupa and only taken out for viewing on Vesak Day and Chinese New Year. About 220kg (485lb) of the 420kg (925lb) of gold needed to construct the 3.5-tonne stupa was donated by devotees. Curtains obscuring the stupa from view are unveiled two times a day (9am and 3pm). On the roof, you can admire the blooms of the Dendrobium Buddha Tooth, an orchid hybrid specially named after the temple.

Cathedral of the Good Shepherd

Queen Street; tel: 6337 2036; Mon–Fri 7am–5.30pm, Sat 7am–7.30pm, Sun 7.30am–7pm; free; MRT: City Hall or Bras Basah; map p.136 A2

Built in 1846 in the design of a crucifix, the cathedral is the oldest Roman Catholic church in Singapore and home to the present

Above: Kwan Im Thong Hood Cho Temple.

Kong Meng San Phor Kark See Temple

88 Bright Hill Road; tel: 6849 5300; daily 8.30am–4pm; free; MRT: Bishan, then taxi or bus: 410

Built in 1980, Singapore's largest Buddhist temple is spread over 12 hectares (30 acres). Its **Hall of Great Compassion** houses a 9-m- (29.5-ft-) high marble Goddess of Mercy (Guan Yin), crafted in the Indian tradition with 1,000 arms and eyes. Also look out for the huge image of the Medicine Buddha, which sits beneath a golden stupa in the **Pagoda of 10,000 Buddhas**. **Vesak Day** celebrations are held here on a grand scale, sometimes stretching over three weeks.
SEE ALSO FESTIVALS AND EVENTS, P.57

Kwan Im Thong Hood Cho Temple

178 Waterloo Street; tel: 6337 3965; daily 6.15am–6.15pm; free; MRT: Bugis; map p.136 B3

Built in 1895 and refurbished in 1982, the temple is a highlight not for its architecture but rather for the glimpses of colourful local life it offers. Pensive supplicants inside the temple kneel before the Goddess of Mercy in prayer. Some shake canisters with numbered bamboo fortune sticks until one falls out, then consult with the fortune tellers who wait outside along with traditional medicine and flower sellers. From lottery numbers to prospects for offspring, the goddess tries to unravel everything about the future.

> Some Chinese worshippers can also be seen offering incense sticks to Lord Krishna and other Hindu deities at the highly ornamented **Sri Krishnan Temple** next door to the Kwan Im Thong Hood Cho Temple – perhaps for double assurance.

Leong San See Temple

371 Race Course Road; tel: 6298 9371; daily 6am–6pm; free; MRT: Farrer Park; map p.133 D3

The ornately decorated Leong San See Temple (Dragon Mountain Temple) is dedicated to the Goddess of Mercy. Dating back to 1913, it also bears an image of Confucius at its altar and is hence popular with many parents who bring their children here to pray for success at examinations and filial piety. Note especially the dragon sculptures on top of its roofs. At the back is a courtyard with old ancestral tablets.

Lian Shan Shuang Lin Monastery

184E Jalan Toa Payoh; tel: 6259 6924; daily 8.30am–5pm; free; MRT: Potong Pasir

Its name means 'Twin Grove of the Lotus Mountain Temple'. Completed in 1912, the temple was modelled after Xi Chan Si, a well-known *cong lin* temple in Fuzhou. *Cong lin* means 'layers of forest' and Xi Chan Si is a monastery that was built according to an established layout that allows monks to move around in a set pattern to perform rituals. This enables them to find their way about in any *cong lin* temple they might be in, whatever its size.

Shuang Lin Monastery was the fulfilment of Low Kim Pong's (1838–1908) dream. Low was a successful trader and a leader of the local Hokkien community. The story goes that one day in 1898, he had a dream in which he saw a golden light shining from the west. He found out the next day that his son had the same dream. Taking it as an omen, father and son went to the harbour and waited. At sunset a boat sailed in from the west, carrying 12 Buddhist monks and nuns who were on their way back to China after six years of pilgrimage in India, Sri Lanka and Burma. Inspired, Low persuaded the group to stay and donated substantial funds to build Shuang Lin Monastery, which took over a decade to finish.

The **Main Hall** is noted for its decorative panels, wood-carvings and sculptures of deities. The temple under-went major restorations from 1991, with new structures built in traditional style. In 2002 the new seven-storey granite **Dragon Light Pagoda** – topped with a golden spire – was com-pleted by craftsmen from China as a spectacular finale to the 11-year restoration programme that cost over S$40 million.

Malabar Muslim Jama-Ath Mosque

471 Victoria Street; tel: 6294 3862; daily 10am–noon and 2–4pm; free; MRT: Lavender; map p.133 E1
This beautiful mosque is covered in pretty blue

Above: a giant Buddha at the Sakya Muni Buddha Gaya Temple.

mosaics and topped by a golden dome. It harks back to the era Kampong Glam was founded. The mosaic tiles were only added after the mosque opened in 1963. This is the only mosque in Singapore built by Indian Muslims from the Malabar coastal region of Kerala.

St Andrew's Cathedral

11 St Andrew's Road; tel: 6337 6104; Mon–Sat 9am–5pm, guided tours Mon–Sat 10.30am–noon (except Wed) and 2.30pm–4pm (except Sat); free; MRT: City Hall; map p.136 B1
The grandest church in Sin-gapore, St Andrew's Cathe-dral is, befittingly, a gazetted monument. It owes its smooth white surface to the curious plaster used by the Indian convict labourers who built it. Called Madras *chunam*, the plaster was made of egg white, eggshell, lime, sugar, coconut husk and water, and gave the building a smooth polished finish.

The original cathedral, designed in Palladian style by George Coleman, was twice struck by lightning and demolished in 1852. The present cathedral, in the style of an early Gothic abbey and designed by Ronald

MacPherson, was conse-crated in 1862. The gleaming white exterior contrasts with the dark pews inside, as sunlight gently filters through the stained-glass windows in the morning.

Sakya Muni Buddha Gaya Temple

366 Race Course Road; tel: 6294 0714; daily 8am–4.30pm; free; MRT: Farrer Park; map p.133 D3
Also known as the Temple of 1,000 Lights, this stunning temple has a 15-m- (49-ft-) high Buddha image that sits under a halo of lightbulbs, on a base depicting scenes from the life of the Buddha. Wor-shippers may illuminate the lights around the statue for a small donation or have their fortune told by spinning a wheel on the left of the prayer hall. Visitors are advised to dress conservatively.

Sri Mariamman Temple

244 South Bridge Road; tel: 6223 4064; daily 7am–noon and 6–9pm; free; MRT: China-town; map p.138 C3
This temple is synonymous with its tall *gopuram* (tower), adorned with colourful renditions of Hindu deities, at the entrance. Dedicated to

43

Below: at the Lian Shan Shuang Lin Monastery.

the goddess Mariamman – who is known for curing serious illnesses – it is the oldest and most important Hindu shrine in Singapore. Here, devotees perform prayers amid gaudy statues and vivid ceiling frescoes. Built in 1827 by Naraina Pillai, the first recorded Indian immigrant to enter Singapore, it was a simple shed that eventually became the annual site of **Thimithi**, the Hindu fire-walking festival in October. In an elaborate ceremony that honours the goddess Draupathi, the faithful work themselves into a trance and walk over burning embers to fulfil their vows. Curiously, it is a ritual that also draws participation from a small number of Chinese devotees. The right to take photographs in the temple will cost a donation of S$3.
SEE ALSO FESTIVALS AND EVENTS, P.59

Sri Srinivasa Perumal Temple

397 Serangoon Road; tel: 6298 5771; daily 6.30am–noon and 6–9pm; free; MRT: Farrer Park; map p.133 D3

This temple's five-tier tower was a donation from P. Govindasamy Pillai, one of the earliest Indian immigrants who made good. He set up a chain of popular general-goods stores in Little India and was known for his philanthropic work, a legacy continued by his sons today. The temple is at the centre of the Hindu trinity made up of Brahma the Creator, Vishnu the Preserver and Shiva the Destroyer. It is dedicated to Krishna, one of the incarnations of Vishnu. Perumal is another name for Krishna and statues of him – coloured blue to signify blue blood – are everywhere in the temple. The temple ceiling is dominated by a colourful circular pattern depicting the nine planets of the universe.

The annual **Thaipusam** procession sets off from here and makes its way to the Sri Thendayuthapani Temple on Tank Road (see below).
SEE ALSO FESTIVALS AND EVENTS, P.56

Sri Thendayuthapani Temple

15 Tank Road; tel: 6737 9393; daily 8am–noon and 5.30–8.30pm; free; MRT: Dhoby Ghaut; map p.135 E2

Better known to most Singaporean Hindus as the Chettiar Temple, this was built in 1859, by the Chettiars, an Indian caste of moneylenders. Take a good look at the 48 glass panels on the roof, designed to catch the sun's rays. It is also here, during the annual **Thaipusam** festival, that hundreds of pilgrims end their walk from the Sri Srinivasa Perumal Temple (see left) on Serangoon Road.
SEE ALSO FESTIVALS AND EVENTS, P.56

Sri Veeramakaliamman Temple

141 Serangoon Road; tel: 6295 4538; daily 5.30am–noon and 4–9pm; free; MRT: Little India; map p.133 C1

Dating to 1855 and built by indentured Bengali labourers, this temple is dedicated to the multi-armed goddess Kali, the manifestation of anger in the face of evil, who is both loved and feared. In one of her images at the temple, she is shown ripping a hapless victim apart. As consort to Shiva, the goddess is also known as Parvati in her benign form. The main shrine has a striking Kali statue, flanked by those of her sons Ganesh, the Elephant God, and Murugan, the Child God.

Tuesdays and Fridays are considered sacred days and are especially busy with devotees streaming in to pray and ask for blessings.

Sultan Mosque

3 Muscat Street; tel: 6293 4405; Sat–Thur 9am–noon, 2–4pm, Fri 2.30–4pm; free; MRT: Bugis; map p.136 C4

The largest mosque in Singapore, this dates back to 1924. Swan and Maclaren, the architectural firm responsible for the mosque, adopted the design of the Taj Mahal and combined it with Persian, Moorish, Turkish and classical themes. The muezzin calls the faithful to prayer five times a day; the women to their enclave upstairs, and the men to the

Below: a temple musician at the Sri Srinivasa Perumal Temple.

Above: the Sultan Mosque is one of the most important places of worship for Muslims in Singapore.

During renovations of Thian Hock Keng in 1999, a rare silk scroll bearing the calligraphy of Qing-dynasty emperor Guang Xu (1871–1908) was found. The emperor inscribed four large characters, *bo jing nan ming* ('the wave is calm in the South Seas'), on the scroll and gifted it to the temple to mark the completion of its first major restoration in 1906. He also gave Yueh Hai Ching Temple a similar piece of calligraphy.

main prayer hall. With its striking golden domes and soaring minarets, this is one of the loveliest places of Muslim worship in Singapore.

Telok Ayer Chinese Methodist Church

235 Telok Ayer Street; tel: 6324 4001; Mon–Fri 9am–5pm, Sat 9am–1pm; MRT: Tanjong Pagar; map p.139 C2

The building that houses the church today was built 1924–25 and gazetted as a national monument in 1989. Its unusual architecture is a blend of East and West – with a flat-roofed Chinese pavilion and a ground floor graced by European-style columns.

Thian Hock Keng Temple

158 Telok Ayer Street; tel: 6423 4616; daily 7.30am– 5.30pm; MRT: Tanjong Pagar; map p.139 C2

Telok Ayer Street, which means 'Water Bay' in Malay, once stood on Singapore's shoreline. Today the reclaimed land is blocked from the sea by a wall of skyscrapers. It was here that seafarers and immigrants from the Fujian province in China set up a joss house in the 1820s in gratitude for their safe arrival in Singapore.

The joss house eventually became the Thian Hock Keng Temple, the Temple of Heavenly Happiness, dedicated to Ma Chu Po, by 1842. The Goddess of the Sea could reputedly calm rough waters and rescue those in danger of drowning.

Visually extravagant and built without the use of a single nail with imported materials from China and Europe, Thian Hock Keng is a must-see among Singapore's many Chinese temples. Dragons, venerated for protection on sea voyages, leap along the roof and curl around granite pillars. Incense wafts from giant brass urns in front of altars laden with offerings.

Yueh Hai Ching Temple

30B Phillip Street; tel: 6533 8537; daily 6am–6pm; free; MRT: Raffles Place; map p.139 D3

Built in the 1830s by the local Teochew community for the protection of traders travelling between Singapore and China, this temple combines the practices of Buddhism and Taoism. Its ornate roof depicts scenes from Chinese village life, including an opera stage and houses. Huge, distinctive incense coils are hung and burnt in the courtyard. There's also a large terracotta furnace in the courtyard, where paper money is burnt to assist the deceased in their journey to the netherworld.

Below: an image of Kali at the Sri Veeramakaliamman Temple.

Dance

Singapore's dance offerings are often based on cross-cultural exchanges of interpretations from the East and West, and dancers and choreographers tend to move between projects and ensembles. Increasingly, as the corp of local dancers mature, there is also a burgeoning of professional ensembles. One pivotal company is the Singapore Dance Theatre, hailed as an 'Asian Jewel'. Its repertoire ranges from *Sleeping Beauty* and *The Nutcracker* to contemporary ballet set to pop music. The venues for performances are also diverse, from the superb Esplanade Theatre to the lawn at the Fort Canning Park.

Companies

Arts Fission

01-07/09 and 03-03/04 ONE-TWO-SIX Cairnhill Arts Centre, 126 Cairnhill Road; tel: 6238 6469; www.artsfission.org

One of the most cutting-edge dance laboratories in Singapore, Arts Fission adopts a multidisciplinary approach and draws inspiration from cultural roots and heritage to create a new genre of contemporary Asian dance. Besides productions on stage, it has an affinity for site-specific performances.

Odyssey Dance Theatre

28 Aliwal Street, Aliwal Arts Centre; tel: 6221 5229/6221 5516; www.odysseydance theatre.com; MRT: Bugis

This contemporary-dance company busies itself with

three main performances a year and with showcases at international festivals. It also organises a biennial dance festival, Xposition 'O'.

Singapore Dance Theatre

201 Victoria Street, Bugis +#07-02/03; tel: 6338 0611; www.singaporedancetheatre. com; MRT: Bugis

The grande dame of the Singapore dance scene, the Singapore Dance Theatre (SDT) is a melting pot of dancers and choreographers from all over the world, who deliver modern dance interpretations and classical dance pieces such as *The Nutcracker* and *Giselle* with equal aplomb. It performs at the Esplanade Theatre and the Victoria Theatre, and features its outdoor dance showcase *Ballet Under the Stars* outside its studios on the lawn of the Fort Canning Park. SDT is also a regular at the Singapore Arts Festival.

Venues

Esplanade Theatres

Esplanade – Theatres on the Bay, 1 Esplanade Drive; tel:

Above: *Swan Lake* is one of the classic ballets performed by the Singapore Dance Theatre.

6828 8222; www.esplanade.com; MRT: City Hall or Esplanade; map p.136 B1

The Esplanade is the city's premier performing arts centre, and its 2,000-seat Theatre has played host to numerous dance performances, including those of the Singapore Dance Theatre. Full-scale ballets have also been held here by internationally renowned groups, in addition to contemporary and avant-garde performances by companies like the

Tickets to performing arts and sport events can be purchased in person or booked by phone or online (and paid for in the latter two cases by credit card) with **SISTIC** (tel: 6348 5555; www.sistic.com.sg). Check the website for Sistic's ticketing outlets.

Left: fluid movements in the Singapore Dance Theatre's performance of the contemporary work *Negro Y Blanco*.

and a 450-seat theatre.

Victoria Theatre
11 Empress Place; tel: 6330 8283; www.vch.gov.sg; MRT: Raffles Place; map p.139 D4
In 1905 this former town hall was converted into a 900-seat theatre, used by amateur English-drama troupes. Until the Esplanade was opened in 2002, Victoria Theatre was the most prestigious performance venue in Singapore for almost a century. It is closed for renovations and due to reopen in 2013.

Ballet Under The Stars is possibly the most popular of Singapore's outdoor arts events. Held several times a year at Fort Canning Park, the event sees ballet buffs bringing out their picnic baskets and rugs for an evening of performances by the Singapore Dance Theatre under the stars. For schedules, see www.singaporedancetheatre.com.

Bill T. Jones/Arnie Zane Dance Company and Italy's

Company Il Posto. Experimental dance presentations are also staged in the smaller, 220-seat **Theatre Studio**.
SEE ALSO ARCHITECTURE, P.27; MUSIC, P.90; THEATRE, P.121

University Cultural Centre
National University of Singapore, 50 Kent Ridge Crescent; tel: 6516 2492; www.nus.edu.sg; MRT: Clementi, then bus: 96
Used mostly by students, this has also hosted acclaimed international performers. It has a 1,700-seat concert hall

Festivals

Da:ns Festival
www.dansfestival.com
Organised by the Esplanade – Theatres on the Bay in October, this is probably the best dance-genre festival in Singapore. Past festivals featured performances by the Compañia de Danza Española Aida Gómez from Spain, the Eifman Ballet of St Petersburg as well as screenings of movies centred on dance.

Below: the Victoria Theatre is a sought-after dance venue, set in a beautiful building.

Environment

The smallest country in Southeast Asia, Singapore has an area of just 699sq km (270 sq miles). Yet this geographical blip has one of the highest road densities. With more than 957,000 vehicles on the roads, the island has a road density that is more than double the UK's. One would expect such a large car population and Singapore's urban sprawl to result in a polluted city, but dedicated measures have made this island one of the least polluted places in the world. These include keeping a tight rein on vehicular growth and efforts to promote recycling and green the cityscape.

Air Pollution

A tiny island filled with too many people with high disposable incomes faces a potential problem: too many cars choking the roads and causing air pollution. But while traffic in the rest of Asia crawls at a snail's pace during rush hour, in Singapore it cruises at a reasonable 60–70km/h (37–44 miles/h) on the expressways at peak times. Air quality is maintained at a good level. Despite having one of the highest car densities in the world, Singapore has found a solution to a problem that has stumped traffic authorities elsewhere, using a combination of regulation and technology.

VEHICULAR POPULATION CONTROL

To control the number of vehicles and minimise pollution, Singapore uses various measures. For starters, cars in Singapore are probably among the most expensive in the world. After a hefty 45 percent tax on car imports, a registration fee of 150 percent and an annual road tax pegged to the engine capacity of the car, a 1,600cc saloon can be incredibly exorbitant. In addition, a potential vehicle owner needs to bid for a Certificate of Entitlement (COE) in order to be 'entitled' to a new vehicle. If successful, the vehicle entitlement is valid for only 10 years from the vehicle's date of registration. In 2013, the COE for small cars up to 1,600cc increased to over $10,000, and the premium hit a record high of about $92,000. The premium for cars above 1,601cc increased to $96,210.

ELECTRONIC ROAD PRICING

In 1999 the government struck another brainwave in the form of the Electronic Road Pricing (ERP) system. Overhead ERP gantries are strategically located in the Central Business District and along expressways. These deduct a fixed toll during peak hours from cash cards inserted in the special in-vehicle units (IU) installed in cars. Sensors on the gantries

Above: an ERP gantry.

are linked to a central system that logs all vehicles passing under them. Motorists without IUs or with insufficient cash on their cards will have their licence plates photographed. A few days later, summonses to pay fines arrive in the mail.

The ERP system has drawn a mixed response. Government coffers have swelled, but the scheme has also succeeded in reducing traffic during peak hours. Traffic during ERP operating hours has dropped by 15 percent.

OTHER MEASURES

While discouraging car own-

plans for recycling efforts in Singapore, setting a recycling rate and monitoring it closely. Since 2001 recycling efforts have gone door-to-door. Residents living in flats are given specific bins and bags for the disposal of cans, paper, glass bottles and plastic containers. Another of NEA's efforts is a green pact supported by numerous companies that aims to systemically reduce packaging waste. Singapore produces about 1,200 tonnes of packaging waste a day; NEA hopes this voluntary agreement will lower the stress on the country's landfills.

Water

For years Singapore has depended on Malaysia for its water supply, but as its contracts are reaching an end and the threat of non-renewal looms, the island has looked into producing its own supply. NEWater – the brand name given to reclaimed water produced by the Public Utilities Board – is essentially treated sewage water. It is supplied to industries requiring high-purity water and is also blended with reservoir water before undergoing further treatment for human consumption.

ership, the authorities have also poured in millions of dollars to facilitate a more efficient public transport system as an alternative to driving. In addition, car-sharing schemes also maximise vehicle use, while the Park-and-Ride Scheme, which allows drivers to park their cars near MRT stations and bus interchanges, encourages drivers to continue their journeys by MRT or bus.

Those who can't live without a car are persuaded to use smaller-capacity cars with lower road tax. Owners of hybrid vehicles and compressed natural gas (CNG) vehicles enjoy green-vehicle tax rebates.

Climate

To combat the urban heat, the city has a legion of green belts, such as parks nestled between skyscrapers. The National Parks Board spends millions every year to keep the city verdant, and a large part of its budget goes towards maintaining nature reserves in the suburbs as well.

Temperatures range between 24–33°C (75–91°F), with humidity around 75 percent. Residents escape the heat by retreating into air-conditioned homes, shopping malls and offices. With indoor temperatures often set at 22°C (72°F) or lower, and cardigans and jackets permanent fixtures of office wardrobes, it has been said Singapore indulges in air-conditioning overkill. The demand for air conditioning in this tropical land is unlikely to diminish, and has thus led to a pressing need for more energy-efficient buildings.

Recycling

The National Environment Agency (NEA) has grand

Below: heed the sign.

No Littering

> The **NEWater Visitor Centre** offers tours of the NEWater treatment process, plus interactive games and multimedia shows (20 Koh Sek Lim Road; tel: 6546 7874 or 6593 1533; www.pub.gov.sg; Tue–Sun 9am–5.30pm; free; MRT: Tanah Merah, then bus 12, 24, 31, 38 or free shuttle service at specified times).

Essentials

Travelling in Singapore is a cinch. English is widely spoken, public transport is generally efficient, and streets and addresses are clearly marked. When you first arrive in Singapore, head to one of the Singapore Visitors Centres run by the tourism board to get maps, brochures and advice on things to do and see. In addition, this section offers the practical information you need to know to enjoy this city, from currency and entry regulations to telecommunications and advice on taxes and tipping. Also included are details on where to get medical help and assistance in emergencies.

Embassies

Australia
25 Napier Road; tel: 6836 4100
Canada
11-01 One George Street;
tel: 6854 5900
New Zealand
15-10 Ngee Ann City Tower A,
391A Orchard Road;
tel: 6738 6700
UK
100 Tanglin Road;
tel: 6424 4200
USA
27 Napier Road; tel: 6476 9100

Emergencies

Fire and ambulance: **995**
Police: **999**

Entry Requirements

Visa requirements vary from time to time, so check with a Singapore embassy or consulate. Most visitors are given a 30-day social visit pass on arrival. Renewals can be made at the **Immigration and**

Metric to Imperial Conversions
1 metre = 3.28 feet
1 kilometre = 0.62 mile
1 hectare = 2.47 acres
1 kilogram = 2.2 pounds

Checkpoints Authority
(10 Kallang Road; tel: 6391 6100;
www.ica.gov.sg).

Health

Singapore has no free medical care and medical evacuation is very expensive, so be sure you are covered by insurance. Most hotels have doctors on call.

HOSPITALS
Raffles Hospital
585 North Bridge Road;
tel: 6311 1111;
www.rafflesmedical.com
Singapore General Hospital
1 Hospital Drive; tel: 6222 3322;
www.sgh.com.sg

PHARMACIES
Pharmacies, many with qualified pharmacists, are open 9am–9pm, but it is wise to travel with your own prescriptions and medication.

Internet

Wireless@SG is a scheme that provides free wireless connection at selected hot spots. You will need a mobile device with WiFi facility, and

will need to register online with a service provider: **Wireless@SG by M1** (tel: 6655 5833; www.m1net.com.sg),
iCELL (tel: 6309 4520;
www.icellnetwork.com), or
Singtel (tel: 1688;
www.singtel.com). Check the Infocomm Development Authority website
(www.ida.gov.sg) for locations of hot spots.

Money

The Singapore dollar (S$ or SGD) is divided into 100 cents, with coins of 5, 10, 20, 50 cents and S$1. Bills in common circulation are S$2, S$5, S$10, S$20, S$50, S$100, S$500 and S$1,000.

ATMS
ATMs are found in banks, shopping malls and MRT stations; many feature the Cirrus and PLUS systems.

CREDIT CARDS
Major credit cards are widely accepted. Report lost or stolen cards immediately to the police (tel: 1800-353 0000 for locations) and to your card company.

Left: don't be deterred by the many do's and don'ts in Singapore; it's still a great city.

S$100. Show your passport to the retailer and fill out a voucher. Before departure, validate the voucher at the airport customs, then present it together with your items at the Global Refund Counter (tel: 6225 6238) or Premier Tax Free Scheme Counter (tel: 1800-829 3733).

Telephones

The country code for Singapore is 65; there are no area codes. To call overseas from Singapore, dial the access code 001, 013 or 019, followed by the relevant country code.

Only GSM mobile phones with roaming facility can hook up automatically to the local networks. All local mobile numbers begin with '8' or '9'.

Some public phones can be used for international calls. Phone cards are available from post offices and convenience stores.

Tipping

Most hotel and restaurant bills come with a 10 percent service charge on top of the 7 percent GST. Tipping is optional, although appreciated.

Tourist Information

The Singapore Tourism Board (24-hour infoline: 1800-736 2000; www.yoursingapore. com) has visitors centres at the following locations: junction of Orchard Road and Cairnhill Road (opposite Somerset MRT); ION Orchard Level 1 Concierge, Chinatown Visitor Centre at Kreta Ayer Square; and the arrival halls and transit lounges of Changi Airport terminals 1, 2 and 3.

American Express
Tel: 1800-396 6000
Diners Club
Tel: 6416 0800/0900
MasterCard
Tel: 800-110 0113
Visa
Tel: 800-448 1250

CURRENCY EXCHANGE
Money-changing services are available at the airport and in banks, hotels and shopping malls. Moneychangers give slightly better rates than banks; hotels give the worst.

TRAVELLERS' CHEQUES
These can be cashed at banks and are accepted at many establishments.

Postal Services

Postal services are provided by **Singapore Post** (tel: 1605). Branches include: **1 Killiney Road** (Mon–Sat 9am–9pm, Sun and public holidays 9am–4.30pm); **Changi Airport Terminal 2** (daily 8am–9.30pm).

You can also buy stamps and weigh letters and small packages at self-service automated machines found in MRT stations.

> Singapore is 8 hours ahead of GMT.

Taxes

A Goods and Services Tax (GST) of 7 percent is charged on most purchases. This is refundable for purchases from shops participating in the **Global Refund Scheme** and the **Premier Tax Free Scheme**. The refund applies to purchases exceeding

Below: the Singapore Post is highly reliable.

Fashion

When it comes to fashion, Singaporeans are not an adventurous lot, tending to opt for comfort over style. Traipse the heartlands and you will see their denizens in their 'uniform' of T-shirt and shorts – or if they are feeling dressy that day, T-shirt and jeans. In the CBD, corporate types stride purposefully in plain pastel business shirts and trousers or skirts. But thankfully, changes are afoot: in the hipper districts of the city, trendy boutiques chalk up fashion credits for the rest of the island with threads designed by local style mavens and those inspired by the latest international fashion trends.

Local Designer Boutiques

With its small domestic market, Singapore's local fashion industry is miniscule compared to cities like Paris and Milan. The few local fashion designers who have found success have had to venture abroad. Singaporean names that have made it on the world fashion map include **Andrew Gn**, whose dazzling coats are much sought after in Europe and New York, and **Ashley Isham**, who first won attention at London Fashion Week in 2003. That said, there are also smaller labels that have found a following of fans at home and in the Asian region.

Some local labels have chain stores, much like Topshop in London. These include **GG>5** and **M)phosis**, which are firm favourites of young women in search of funky wear for the office, and can be found in just about every mall. Their shoe equivalent, **Charles & Keith**, also available in most malls, offers myriad affordable styles.

Fru Fru & Tigerlily
19 Jalan Pisang (off Victoria Street); tel: 6296 8512; MRT: Bugis; map p. 136 C4
Ginette Chittick, Jasmine Tuan and Cheryl Tan form the design collective called FruFru & Tigerlily. Their clothes and accessories are

> The **Asia Fashion Exchange** - also known as AFX - (www.asiafashionexchange.com.sg) which takes place in May replaces the annual Singapore Fashion Festival. The AFX consists of four key events: the Audi Fashion Festival (AFF) (showcases collections from top and emerging designers from around the world); the Star Creation Designer Competition (a regional fashion design competition to spot budding talents); Asia Fashion Summit (AFS) (a business conference featuring key speakers from the fashion industry); and the Blueprint trade show (offering business opportunities between international buyers and designers). During this period, there will also be fashion concerts, catwalk shows and after-parties to look forward to.

Below: ritzy Orchard Road is the style capital of Singapore.

love their multi-brand boutiques, which stock hard-to-find, cult labels from around the world. Here are some of their favourites.

Antipodean
27A Lorong Mambong, Holland Village; tel: 6463 7336; www.antipodeanshop.com; MRT: Buona Vista and Holland Village

Carries top designer names from Australia and New Zealand, including Akira Isogawa, Morrison, and the cult jewellery designer Elke Kramer.

Front Row
02-08-09 Raffles Hotel Shopping Arcade, 328 North Bridge Road; tel: 6224 5501; www.frontrowsingapore.com; MRT: City Hall; map p.136 B2

This fashion-art multi-label concept store stocks contemporary men's and women's apparel and accessories from various labels. It showcases collections by young designers from Singapore and Southeast Asia and also collaborates with progressive and cult international brands. It is the exclusive stockist in Singapore for brands such as A.P.C., Cosmic Wonder, United Bamboo, Woods & Woods and others.

Drifters
141 Jalan Besar; tel: 6297 1280; www.atwhiteroom.com; MRT: Farrer Park; map p.133 D1

Designer Arthur Chua formed a partnership with White Room to design local ready-to-wear menswear brand Drifters, The label's aesthetics incorporate the characteristics of military, utility, rock and roll, and Japanese street style, and feature design details such as colour

---

Many local labels go by the sizes 'small', 'medium' and 'large'. As a rough guideline, 'small' is equal to a US0–2/UK6–8; 'medium' is US4/UK10, and 'large' is equivalent to US8/UK12. The largest size is often 'extra large' (US10/UK14).

---

creatively reconstructed with a punk sensibility.

Hansel
02-14 Mandarin Gallery, 333A Orchard Road; tel: 6337 0992; www.ilovehansel.com; MRT: Orchard Road; map p.135 C4

'Quirky, intelligent and vibrant – with understated minimalism' best describes this kooky label by Central St Martin's alumnus Jo Soh. The label which offers wearable pieces for confident women is a hit in Singapore and Australia.

Nicholas
02-323 Marina Square, 6 Raffles Boulevard; tel: 6337 3726; www.nicholasnic.com; MRT: City Hall; map p.136 A2

Designer Nic Wong has won myriad fashion awards in Singapore, including the Mercedes Benz Fashion

Award in 2004. His eponymous label was created for the stylish, contemporary, professional lady. He aims for geometrically quirky details and understated designs, featuring a juxtaposition of monochromatic palette with bold vibrant colours for his apparels and accessories.

Boutiques

Beyond cookie cutter mall boutiques, Singapore's fashionistas have come to

Asian sizing is small, to say the least. Many Westerners lament the fact that it is hard to find clothes that fit them in Singapore. For larger sizes, or simply clothes that fall longer, check out international chain stores like Country Road, Mango, Zara and Topshop.

blocking and fabric mixing.

Know It Nothing

51 Haji Lane; tel: 6392 5475; www.knowitnothing.com; MRT: Bugis; map p.136 C3

A collection of international and local labels for menswear including shirts, trousers, shoes, caps and accessories.

Custom Classics

CYC Shanghai Shirt Co

02-21 Raffles Hotel Shopping Arcade, 328 North Bridge Road; tel: 6336 3556; www.cyc customshop.com; MRT: City Hall; map p.136 B2

This stalwart bespoke tailor offers great value for money, with its finely crafted shirts designed for both men and women. You can customise yours according to fabric, colour and shape, all the details down to the buttons and monograms.

PIMABS

32B Boat Quay; tel: 6538 6466; www.pimabs.com; MRT: Raffles Place or Clarke Quay; map p.139 D4

Helmed by local fashion designer Leslie Chia, PIMABS' specialises in bespoke tailoring services for men at reasonable prices.

Cheap Chic

77th Street

B3-35 ION Orchard, Orchard Turn; tel: 6509 9354; www.77thstreet.com; MRT: Orchard; map p.134 B1

This streetwear pioneer is a favourite with younger people for its affordable togs. You'll find t-shirts, low-slung jeans, sexy

Above: vintage remains very popular in Singapore.

tops, backpacks and just about every accessory you can think of. Other locations in malls such as Bugis Junction and Bishan Junction 8.

Flesh Imp

03-27/28 Wisma Atria, 435 Orchard Road; tel: 6238 6738; www.fleshimp.com; MRT: Orchard; map p.134 C4

Hot both in the club and fashion scenes, this mid-priced streetwear label has

seen collaborations with American graffiti artists. It is particularly popular with DJs.

Fourskin
03-349/354 Marina Square, 6 Raffles Boulevard; tel: 6333 1878, MRT. City Hall; map p.136 C1
Hip limited edition t-shirts with fantastic graffiti prints are this local label's signature. You'll also find plenty of Japanese-inspired street fashion, trendy flip-flops, sling bags, skull caps and other accessories.

Odette
02-29 Change Alley, 30 Raffles Place, Chevron House; tel: 6438 8380; www.odette.com.sg; MRT: Raffles Place; map p.139 D3
A collection of pretty dresses designed in-house. There are incredibly feminine pieces for any occasion for the girly girl here, many of which are made with vintage fabrics and in very small quantities.

Above: stylish shoppers perusing Singapore's boutiques.

Shoes and Accessories

Charles & Keith
B1-18/19 Wisma Atria, 435 Orchard Road, tel: 6238 3312; www.charleskeith.com; MRT: Orchard; map p.134 C4
The dizzying variety of shoes, bags and accessories is enough to send any footwear-addicted woman into a frenzy. Shoe addicts are known to cart home shoes by the boxes, aided, of course, by prices that go easy on the pocket.

LeftFoot
02-07A Orchard Cineleisure, 8 Grange Road; tel: 6736 3227; www.leftfoot.com.sg; MRT: Somerset; map p.135 C3
Open till late at weekends, this stocks streetwear trainers and limited editions from brands like A Bathing Ape, Vans and Visvim.

On Pedder
02-12P/Q Tower B, Ngee Ann City, 391 Orchard Road; tel: 6835 1307; MRT: Orchard; map p.134 C4
This boutique stocks the hottest looks of the season from both the world's most coveted names and more obscure designers. There's a range of lovely jewellery, handbags and of course, shoes that keep the chi-chi crowd coming back for more. For cheaper options, its sister label Pedder Red is found one level down.

TANG + Co
02-12 Paragon, 290 Orchard Road; tel: 6737 8281; www.tangs.com; MRT: Orchard; map p.134 C4
The shoe department at **TANGS** department store has proved so popular over the years that it has evolved into a boutique of its own. Career women come here for affordable, stylish and mid-range designer shoes and handbags.

Vintage

The Attic Lifestyle Store
04-146A Far East Plaza, 14 Scotts Road; tel: 6732 3459; MRT: Orchard; map p.134 B1
Packed to the rafters with vintage clothes, costume jewellery, 1970s lamps and all sorts of old-school knick-knacks, it truly is a treasure hunt in this crammed space.

Left: a model on the catwalk during an Asia Fashion Exchange (AFX) event at Paragon Shopping Centre.

55

Festivals and Events

W ith its multi-racial character, it's no surprise Singapore is a constant hive of activity, celebrating one cultural festival after another. Almost every month of the year, its streets, temples and ethnic enclaves come alive with a motley assortment of religious and cultural celebrations. A boom in world-class venues and a growing population of fun-seeking city-dwellers have led to a significant increase in contemporary events, from the Singapore Biennale to the New Year Countdown Party.

Public Holidays

New Year's Day	1 Jan
Labour Day	1 May
National Day	9 Aug
Christmas Day	25 Dec
Variable dates	
Chinese New Year	Jan/Feb
Good Friday	Mar/Apr
Vesak Day	May
Deepavali	Oct/Nov
Hari Raya Puasa	
Hari Raya Haji	

Festivals and Events

JANUARY TO MARCH
Chinese New Year

Chinese New Year falls on the first day of the lunar calendar, usually between mid January and mid February. Chinese custom decrees that the previous year's debts be paid, the home cleaned and new clothing purchased. It is also a time for reaffirming ties at the family reunion dinner which takes place on the eve. The 15-day festival, beginning with a two-day holiday, is commemorated by feasting and the giving of *hong bao*, red packets of 'lucky money'.

On the days leading up to Chinese New Year, Chinatown streets are lit and packed with people jostling for festive goods. Dragon and lion dancers throng the streets, making plenty of noise to keep the mythical monsters associated with the New Year at bay. The area then mostly empties out for the first few days of the New Year.

A riverside carnival called River Hongbao usually takes place at the Marina Bay Promenade with all sorts of entertainment and food stalls.

The celebrations end with the **Chingay** parade, an exuberant procession held on the Sunday following the New Year. There are lavish floats, stilt walkers, martial arts performances and more.

Thaipusam

This Hindu festival is observed between January and February, in the Tamil month of Thai. Devotees honour Lord Muruga, god of bravery, power and virtue, by performing feats of mind over spirit. The festival begins at dawn at the Sri

Srinivasa Perumal Temple in Serangoon Road. Here, devotees who have entered a trance have their bodies pierced with metal hooks or spikes attached to a *kavadi*, a cage-like steel contraption that is carried on their shoulders. The procession makes its way to the Sri Thendayuthapani Temple on Tank Road.

Right: the Chinese New Year bazaar in Chinatown.

Left: a Hindu devotee carries a *kavadi* as an act of penance during Thaipusam.

Asian and Western performing arts. Past performers have included the Washington Ballet and the London Philharmonic Orchestra, and also more cutting-edge ventures like a Lithuanian adaptation of Shakespeare's *Othello*. The festival also features an eclectic fringe segment and workshops by visiting companies.

Dragon Boat Festival

Every fifth Chinese lunar month (usually May or June) colourful boats with prows carved to represent dragons and birds crest the waves of Marina Bay, propelled by dozens of men. The Dragon Boat Race is an international-class event that draws teams from Australia, Europe and the US, among others. The festival honours a Chinese patriot, Qu Yuan, who drowned himself in 278 BC to protest against the corruption in the imperial court. Fishermen tried to rescue him but failed. Small packages of rice were then thrown into the water to distract fishes from his body. Drums and gongs

For the most current list of events and celebrations, check the Singapore Tourism Board website at www.your singapore.com or go to any of its Visitors Centres. *The Straits Times* and tourist magazines like *I-S*, *Changi Express* and *Time Out Singapore* also provide details.

APRIL TO JUNE

Singapore International Film Festival

SEE ALSO FILM, P.60

World Gourmet Summit

A two-week-long event with workshops on fine food and wines. Singapore's best chefs and restaurants are feted with awards while guest chefs from around the world play host at selected restaurants with special menus.

Vesak Day

Usually celebrated in May, this is the most important event in the Buddhist calendar, honouring Buddha's birth, death and enlightenment. Temple celebrations begin at dawn with a candlelight procession.

As part of the celebrations, caged birds are released and free meals are distributed to the poor. On the eve of Vesak, monks at the Kong Meng San Phor Kark See Monastery lead devotees through a 'three-step-one-bow' ritual around the temple grounds. This is believed to purify negative actions of the past and is an act of homage to Buddha.

Singapore Arts Festival

This annual event in June showcases a bonanza of

Below: fireworks explode in New Years' celebration, watched by Singapore's icon, the Merlion.

57

were sounded to frighten away predators and villagers decorated their boats with dragon heads and tails with the same purpose in mind. Today several varieties of these rice dumplings are available throughout the year.

The Great Singapore Sale

Held islandwide from end May–early July, the Great Singapore Sale indulges those with a passion for shopping – with goods at shopping malls slashed to bargain prices.

JULY TO SEPTEMBER
Singapore Food Festival

The island celebrates another favourite pastime – eating – with a month-long food fiesta in July. Various food-tasting events and unique dining experiences that cover a gamut of cuisines are held.

National Day

The parade, which marks the anniversary of the island's independence in 1965, is being held at the newly built Marina Bay Floating Stadium until the new Sports Hub at Kallang is built. The pomp and pageantry culminates in a stunning firework display.

Festival of Hungry Ghosts

Traditional Chinese believe

> The **Formula 1 Singapore Grand Prix** made its debut in September 2008. The annual night race promises dramatic twists and turns on 5.05km (3.15 miles) of public roads in the Marina Bay area. See www.singaporegp.sg for details.

the gates of hell are opened throughout the seventh lunar month, usually August/September, to allow ghosts to wander the earth. To appease the spirits, joss sticks and paper money are burnt and feasts whipped up as offerings. After the ghosts have had their fill, the food is eaten by the celebrants. Neighbourhood banquets, which include Chinese opera performances or *getai* (mini pop concerts), are held, climaxing in a lively auction.

Monkey God's Birthday

The Monkey God is a character from the Chinese classic *Journey to the West*, celebrated for protecting his master, a monk of the Tang dynasty dispatched to India to collect Buddhist sutras. During this festival in September, acrobats perform at various temples.

Singapore Grand Prix

In September 2008, the

Above: Chinese opera is often performed as entertainment to appease spirits during the Festival of Hungry Ghosts.

world's first F1 night race was held in Marina Bay and it has become a highly anticipated annual event since. The Singapore Grand Prix runs counter-clockwise, which makes it only one of three circuits in the world to do so. Held over one weekend in September, the organisers spare no expense in drawing the crowds with vibrant concerts featuring big names like Beyonce, Katy Perry and Maroon 5.
SEE ALSO SPORT, P.119

OCTOBER TO DECEMBER
Mid Autumn Festival

On the 15th day of the eighth lunar month, usually in October, the Chinese commemorate the 14th-century revolution that overthrew the Mongol dynasty in China. Mooncakes – rich pastries filled with lotus-seed or red-bean paste and salted egg yolks – are eaten. The cakes, as the legend goes, were used by rebel forces to smuggle messages about the revolution to the people, while lanterns were used to signal the start of the civilian

Below: Great Singapore Sale posters on Orchard Road.

THIS ITEM IS NOT ON SALE

But just about everything else is.

uprising. Today the festival is marked by an impressive display of lanterns at the Chinese Garden in Jurong.

Navaratri

Meaning 'nine nights' in Tamil, Navaratri pays homage to the three consorts of the Hindu gods with nine days of traditional Indian music and dance at Hindu temples. The festival concludes with a procession. It is also an opportunity to experience Indian arts; performances are held at the Sri Thendayuthapani and other Hindu temples.

Thimithi Festival

Thimithi is a breathtaking firewalking ceremony in October at the Sri Mariamman Temple on South Bridge Road. Male devotees sprint barefoot across glowing charcoals without any apparent injury to their feet, in honour of Draupathi, a legendary heroine deified by South Indian Tamils. On the eve of the festival, a magnificent silver chariot honouring Draupathi makes its way to the Sri Mariamman Temple from the Sri Srinivasa Temple in Little India.

Pilgrimage to Kusu Island

During this month-long festival falling between the first and 15th day of the ninth Chinese lunar month (usually October/November), Taoists and Muslims take the ferry to

Billed as an international event with an Asian flavour, the **Singapore Biennale**, (www.singaporeartmuseum.sg) held from October to February every two years, is the island's largest contemporary visual arts event. Exhibitions featuring some of the world's leading artists are held in various venues across the city.

Above: firewalkers prepare for their walk across hot charcoals at the Sri Mariamman Temple in Chinatown during Thimithi Festival.

Kusu Island to make offerings and pray at the Tua Pek Kong Temple and at the Malay shrine. The legend behind the pilgrimage tells of a turtle (*kusu*) that turned itself into an island in order to save two shipwrecked sailors.
SEE ALSO BEACHES & ISLANDS, P.35

Deepavali

Also known as the Festival of Lights, to symbolise the conquest of good over evil, this is the most important festival in the Hindu calendar. Usually occurring in October or November, it is celebrated by the traditional lighting of oil lamps at home and in Little India, which is turned into a fairyland of twinkling lights. Prayers are recited in temples and statues of deities carried around the grounds.

Christmas

A sizeable percentage of the population is Christian but almost everyone, regardless of religion, gets into the spirit and exchanges gifts come Christmas time. A yuletide light-up transforms Orchard Road into a riot of lights and glitzy displays. As with all things Singaporean, Christmas here is celebrated with a difference – just tuck into a tandoori turkey and you'll see!

VARIABLE DATES
Hari Raya Puasa

This Muslim celebration falls on the first day of the 10th Muslim month; the date varies from year to year. During Ramadan, the month preceding Hari Raya Puasa, all able Muslims observe a strict fast from sunrise to sunset so that they are better able to commiserate with the less fortunate. On Hari Raya Puasa, Muslims ask for forgiveness from family members, make new resolutions and feast on traditional food. The other Muslim festival celebrated with a holiday is **Hari Raya Haji**, which marks the sacrifices made by Muslims who undertake the pilgrimage to Mecca.

Below: malls dress up in dazzling lights for Christmas.

F

Film

Singaporeans love going to the movies – which explains the glut of cineplexes across the island. They love a good Hollywood blockbuster, so much so that some movies open here even before they do in the US. When it comes to Singapore-produced movies, the output has been slim, with about half a dozen Singaporean feature films made each year. Admittedly, there are some duds that feature wooden acting and overused clichés, but for the most part, Singaporean films are slowly but steadily winning critical and commercial success, both at home and abroad.

Singapore's Film Industry

Singapore had its golden age of cinema in the 1950s and 1960s when it was home to two powerhouse movie studios, Cathay and Shaw Brothers. Movies then were mainly made in Bahasa Melayu and exported to the region.

Following Singapore's separation from Malaysia in 1965, the film industry moved to Kuala Lumpur. Over the next few decades, Singapore served more as an exotic location for foreign films, including Noel Coward's *Pretty Polly* (1967) and Paul Theroux's *Saint Jack* (1979).

The 1990s saw a revival for the film industry. Director Eric Khoo's *12 Storeys* (1997) was the first Singaporean film shown at the Cannes Film Festival. In 1998 Glen Goei's *Forever Fever*, a *Saturday Night Fever*-inspired tale, was picked up by Miramax and released in the US as *That's the Way I Like It*. But it was local TV comic-turned-filmmaker Jack Neo's *Money No Enough* (1998) that really warmed Singaporeans to local filmmaking efforts. Produced

The **Singapore International Film Festival** in April presents a varied diet of arthouse films from various countries. Local films are also screened. Fringe events include retrospectives, tributes, seminars and film-appreciation workshops.

for less than S$1 million, the film raked in S$5.8 million.

Milestone Films
12 Storeys (1997), directed by Eric Khoo
Its indulgently lengthy frames capture the lives of lonely residents in a block of flats. The only Singaporean film to date to be selected for the *Un Certain Regard* section at Cannes.
15 (2002), directed by Royston Tan
This film about restless Chinese teenagers who turn to gangs was heavily censored on release (references to gangs are considered risky in Singapore). It's available uncut on DVD only in the UK and US.
881 (2007), directed by Royston Tan
Tan achieved commercial success with this film about the

trials and tribulations of two friends who pursue their dream of becoming *getai* (concerts held during the Festival of Hungry Ghosts) singers.
Ah Boys To Men (2012-3), directed by Jack Neo
This two-part film revolves around the lives of a group of recruits serving their National Service in Singapore. It is to date the highest-grossing Singaporean movie of all time.
Be With Me (2005), directed by Eric Khoo
Inspired by the life story of Theresa Chan, an elderly woman who has been deaf and blind since she was a teenager, this film is made up of three poignant stories interwoven around the desire for love and companionship. It was the opening film for the Directors' Fortnight programme at Cannes in 2005.
Money No Enough (1998), directed by TL Tay
This film is very telling of Singaporean heartlanders' taste for local movies. They loved this wacky story of working-class Chinese Singaporeans striving to make a quick buck in a ruthless society.

Left: Royston Tan's *881* was a commercial hit.

My Magic (2008), directed by Eric Khoo

After the screening of My Magic at the 61st Cannes Film Festival, a 15-minute plus standing ovation ensued. The film – a mostly Tamil drama about an alcoholic magician struggling to repair his relationship with his young son – was Singapore's first contender for the Palme d'Or. Its lead, first-time actor Bosco Francis, won Best Male Actor at the Asian First Film Festival.

Perth (2004), directed by Djinn

Lim Kay Tong plays a taxi driver who aspires to save enough money to retire in Perth, Australia. He takes on a job ferrying prostitutes to their clients, becomes obsessed with one, and finds himself in a bloody mess.

Singapore Dreaming, (2006), directed by Colin Goh and Woo Yen Yen

A cogent portrayal of the local obsession with what are known locally as the 5Cs: cash, credit card, car, condo and country club. The story revolves around family members who try to win over their parents' favour and hard-earned cash.

Singapore GaGa (2005), directed by Tan Pin Pin

In this acclaimed documentary, the director explores what it means to be Singaporean through the aural landscape created by ordinary people.

Cinemas

Cineplexes mostly screen commercial movies and are found in most malls. Listed below are screens that are more likely to show arthouse films that have toured the festival circuit. Screening times are available in daily papers.

Alliance Française de Singapour

1 Sarkies Road; tel: 6737 8422; www.alliancefrancaise.org.sg; MRT: Newton

The Alliance Française's Cine Club screens French films regularly at the AF Theatre for members and non-members.

The Arts House

1 Old Parliament Lane; tel: 6332 6900; www.theartshouse.com.sg; MRT: City Hall; map p.139 D4

Its theatre screens foreign-language and local films.

Cinema Europa

2–3F VivoCity, 1 HarbourFront Walk; tel: 1900-912 1234; www.gv.com.sg; MRT: HarbourFront

Part of the Golden Village VivoCity cineplex, this screens foreign-language arthouse flicks throughout the year.

Cinematheque

National Museum of Singapore, 93 Stamford Road; tel: 6332 3659; www.nationalmuseum.sg; MRT: City Hall or Dhoby Ghaut; map p.136 A2

Home of the museum's film programme, which is inclined towards historical and significant Singapore-produced films, and foreign classics.

The Picturehouse

5–6/F, Cathay Cineplex, 2 Handy Road; tel: 6235 1155; www.thepicturehouse.com.sg; MRT: Dhoby Ghaut; map p.136 A3

The first dedicated arthouse cinema in Singapore, a venue for international film festivals.

Below: Eric Khoo's *Be With Me* is inspired by Theresa Chan's life story.

Spread over five floors of an old shophouse, the **Screening Room** (12 Ann Siang Road; tel: 6221 1694; www.screeningroom.com.sg; map p.138 C3) is an entertainment hub boasting a film theatre which regularly screens arthouse films that would otherwise be bypassed in Singapore.

Food and Drink

There are few places in the world where life revolves around food like it does in Singapore. Singaporeans talk about food all the time, displaying remarkable critical abilities in all matters gastronomic. They can debate on where to get the freshest seafood, the spiciest chilli sauce, the best chicken rice or finest satay for hours on end – and preferably over a meal. Whether served on polystyrene plates in a rough-and-ready food centre or on bone china in a chi-chi restaurant, food is a major focus in Singapore. There are few cuisines that are not represented here – the choice is wonderfully daunting.

Cultural and Culinary Diversity

Singapore's extraordinary cultural diversity has given it an explosion of flavours – Chinese, Malay, Indian – and the hybrid Peranakan cuisine that is entirely its own.

PERANAKAN CUISINE

Peranakans are descendants of early immigrants from China who settled in Penang, Melaka and Singapore and married local Malay women. The product of this union is the unique Peranakan culture and a cuisine that imaginatively blends Chinese ingredients with Malay spices and herbs.

Central to the cuisine is *rempah*, a mixture of spices and herbs such as chillies, shallots, lemon grass, candlenuts, turmeric and *belacan* (shrimp paste), ground by hand in a pestle and mortar. It is this nose-tickling mixture that imparts a distinctive flavour and aroma to Peranakan cuisine.

Although best eaten in a Peranakan home, the food can be enjoyed in a small number of restaurants. Look out for dishes like *otak otak*, a blend of fish, coconut milk, chilli paste, galangal and herbs wrapped in banana leaf. Another is *ayam buah keluak*, which combines chicken with Indonesian black nuts to produce a rich gravy. Be sure to leave room for the desserts, which are colourful cakes and sticky sweet delicacies usually with coconut milk as the main ingredient.

CHINESE CUISINE

While there are unique Singapore-inspired Chinese dishes like chilli or pepper crabs, the large Chinese population here generally ensures the authenticity of the cuisine. The meal is usually eaten in the traditional style – by helping oneself with chopsticks to a selection of dishes shared by all diners.

The adaptation to regional and climatic demands, as well as foreign influence, has led to a great variety of cuisines from all over China. In Singapore you don't just say you'll eat Chinese; it will be Sichuan, Cantonese, Teochew or any of a dozen distinct types of food from China's various regions.

Below: a favourite get-together for Chinese families is a dim sum brunch at a Chinese restaurant or teahouse.

Left: South Indian fare features fiery-hot dishes.

generally mild, although anything prefixed by the word *masala* is likely to be spicy. The so-called 'banana leaf' restaurants in Little India are well known for their spicy fare served on banana leaves.

Indian Muslim food is very popular in Singapore. One speciality is *murtabak*, which is a fluffy pan-fried bread stuffed with minced lamb or chicken. When the bread is served plain, it is called *prata*. Another is *nasi briyani*, a fragrant rice dish redolent of saffron and cooked with seasoned mutton or chicken.

MALAY CUISINE
Malay food in Singapore is an amalgam of traditional dishes from Peninsular Malaysia with strong influences from the Indonesian islands of Sumatra and Java. Rice is the staple that counterbalances the spiciness of the food. Malay dishes are flavoured with a wide array of spices and herbs such as lemon grass, kaffir lime leaves, galangal, tamarind, turmeric, cumin and garlic. Coconut milk is used in gravies, cakes, desserts and drinks. Another vital ingredient is *belacan*, a pungent dried

Below: satay is a signature of Malay cuisine.

shrimp paste often combined with pounded fresh chillies to make *sambal belacan*.

Nasi padang, originally from the Padang area in West Sumatra, with a variety of spicy meat, chicken and vegetable dishes served with rice, is a perennial favourite. Another well-loved snack is satay, small bamboo skewers of marinated beef, mutton or chicken that are grilled over charcoals and served with sliced onion, cucumber, rice cakes and peanut sauce.

INDIAN CUISINE
Indian food, characterised by the complex use of spices, is not always spicy. Northern Indian cuisine is more aromatic than spicy, its rich flavour resulting from the use of spices tempered by yoghurt. The tandoor or clay oven is used for baking leavened *roti* (bread) or naan, and to produce delicious marinated fish or chicken dishes.

Fiery curries are a speciality of southern Indian cuisine, and coconut milk is often used in the gravy instead of yoghurt. *Korma* dishes are

SEAFOOD
Next to Peranakan food, seafood-based cuisine is perhaps the closest there is to a home-grown culinary art. Asian spices combined with Chinese cooking methods create dishes like chilli or pepper crabs, steamed prawns and crispy fried baby squid. Singaporeans adore seafood and will happily make the pilgrimage to the East Coast to find the best seafood restaurants.

Singapore Signatures
A visit to Singapore would not be complete if you did not try these signature dishes. The best versions are usually found in hawker centres.

If you don't fancy local fare, take your pick from the large number of French, Italian, Mediterranean, Greek, Thai, Japanese, Korean or Vietnamese restaurants. Some of the best chefs in the world have been drawn to these shores and set up restaurants here.
(See Restaurants, p.102–13)

Chilli Crabs

Singaporeans will tell you this dish is best made with meaty Sri Lankan crabs. The thick, tangy and spicy gravy is mopped up with fried or steamed buns.

Fish-head Curry

This speciality is unique to the Singaporean Indian community, although many Chinese restaurants are also drawing crowds for their versions. Massive heads of fish are stewed in a spicy gravy, which also holds vegetables like aubergines and okra.

Hainanese Chicken Rice

Chicken is poached in hot stock and then blanched in cold water, rendering it succulent and juicy. The chicken pieces are then served with rice that has been steamed with ginger, garlic and chicken stock, and a vinegary chilli sauce.

Laksa

Rice noodles are bathed in curried coconut gravy that is spiced with herbs and laced with fish cake, cockles, prawns and bean sprouts. The famous Katong laksa can now be found in franchises all across the island.

Sambal Stingray

Thin slabs of stingray (skate) are grilled and served on a banana leaf with a rich layer of chilli jam (sambal) made with chillies and garlic.

Drinks and Desserts

Teh halia, or ginger tea, a staple of Indian drink vendors, is a strong contender to the lattes of Starbucks. So are *kopi tarik* and *teh tarik*, 'pulled coffee' and 'pulled tea' that is poured from cup to pitcher and back again to ensure the ingredients are well mixed.

In hawker centres and food courts, try freshly squeezed fruit juice, cold soya bean milk or sugar-cane juice with a wedge of lemon. The local beer is Tiger, a refreshing pilsner-style beer.

Local desserts to try include *cendol*, which is shaved ice and green jelly strips in coconut milk, and *ice kacang* (or *ais kacang*), shaved ice with red beans, jelly cubes, evaporated milk and coloured syrups.

Hawker Centres

The hawker centre offers multi-ethnic Singapore food at its best. Whether it is a simple dish of noodles for S$3 or a S$20 three-course meal of barbecued fish, chilli prawns and stir-fried vegetables with rice, the cost is a fraction of what you would pay for a similar meal in a restaurant. Low prices aside, the experience is unique, and an enjoyable thing to remember from your stay in this food-crazy city.

Changi Village Food Centre

Block 2 Changi Village Road; daily 7.30am–late; bus: 2, 29, 59 or 109

It's most famous for *nasi lemak*, a coconut-milk-based rice dish with fried chicken, *ikan bilis* (whitebait) and egg; the longest queues are at stall 57. The food centre was recently renovated – it is cleaner and brighter now.

Chinatown Complex Food Centre

335 Smith Street, Chinatown Complex; daily early morning–late; MRT: Chinatown; map p.138 B3

The stalls here offer a mind-boggling array of Chinese favourites, from *wonton* noodles to roast meats. The basement fresh-produce market is also worth exploring. There's live fish, poultry, flowers and all manner of Asian vegetables.

East Coast Lagoon Food Village

1220 East Coast Parkway, next to car park E2; daily 11am–late; MRT: Bedok, then bus: 401; bus: 31, 36, 43 or 196

Where else can you have some of the best local food in a lovely Indonesian-style structure and just a stone's throw from the sea? Try the curry puffs (stall 28), barbecued-pork noodles (stall 45) and vermicelli with satay

Below: freshly baked buns.

Here's how you order a meal at a hawker centre. If there's a group of you, have one person sit at a table to reserve the seats. The others, having noted the table number, should order their food and tell the hawkers where they are seated at, unless the hawker stall is a self-service operation. If you are on your own, you may have to share a table with strangers if the hawker centre is crowded.

Above: hotels serve local hawker food too.

Above: numerous hawker stalls serving a wide variety of local fare are housed in the Lau Pa Sat Festival Market.

sauce (stall 17). Haron's (stall 55) has the best satay. Best visited at night when all the stalls are open.

Lau Pa Sat Festival Market
Corner of Boon Tat Street and Robinson Road; tel: 6220 2138; www.laupasat.biz; daily noon–10pm; MRT: Raffles Place; map p.139 D2
This Victorian octagonal-shaped structure, whose Hokkien name translates into 'old market', was built in Glasgow and shipped in 1894 to Singapore and reassembled on the waterfront. Formerly a fresh-produce market, it now has some 60 food stalls selling a variety of hawker fare. It underwent a S$4 million makeover in 1996. In the evenings, the adjacent **Boon Tat Street** is closed to traffic and transformed into an alfresco dining area with satay hawkers.

Makansutra Gluttons Bay
01-15 Esplanade Mall, 8 Raffles Avenue; tel: 6336 7025; www.makansutra.com; Mon–Thur 5pm–2am, Fri–Sat 5pm–3am, Sun 4pm–1am; MRT: City Hall; map p.136 B1
The people behind Singapore's hawker-food bible *Makansutra* have gathered up to 10 of the best

hawker stalls in Singapore together in this unbeatable waterfront location.

Newton Food Centre
Newton Circus, 500 Clemenceau Avenue; daily noon–1am; MRT: Newton; map p.132 A2
The prices at this noisy and packed hawker centre are higher than at other food centres, but it is still a great place to order barbecued seafood and Hokkien fried noodles.

Tekka Centre
665 Buffalo Road; daily 7am–10pm; MRT: Little India; map p.132 C1
Stalls selling Malay, Chinese and Indian food draw sizeable crowds here for breakfast. Tekka also has a fresh-produce market with an amazing array of fresh produce seldom found elsewhere in Singapore. Upstairs are clothing, brassware and antiques shops.

Cookery Schools

Coriander Leaf Cooking Studio
3A Merchant Court, 01-12 Clarke Quay, River Valley Road; tel: 6732 3354; MRT: Clarke Quay; map p.135 E1
This culinary school emphasises home cooking.

Its half-day courses are held in a studio and highlight the best of South Asian, Southeast Asian, Middle Eastern and fusion cooking. Coriander Leaf also runs an excellent fusion restaurant. SEE RESTAURANTS, P.102

Palate Sensations Cooking School
01-03 Chromos, 10 Biopolis Road; tel: 6478 9746; www.palatesensations.com; MRT: Buona Vista
A group of professional resident and guest chefs teach a variety of cuisines including Chinese, Italian, Mexican and French. Bread and French pastry making classes are available too. Chef instructors are friendly and informative.

Shermay's Cooking School
01-76 Chip Bee Gardens, Block 43 Jalan Merah Saga; tel: 6479 8442; www.shermay.com; MRT: Holland Village or Buona Vista
Cookbook author Shermay Lee teaches Peranakan cuisine based on her grandmother's traditional recipes. There are also other classes on French and Chinese cuisine and European and local pastries to suit both novice and advanced chefs.

65

Gay and Lesbian

Singapore has a thriving gay and lesbian community, despite the fact that homosexual sex is outlawed. The government has in recent years become more accepting of homosexuality, and has openly acknowledged that the civil service does not discriminate against the hiring of gay people. In general, though, Singapore society is still fairly conservative; public displays of gay affection are likely to draw stares. But that's as much response as you'll get, as Singaporeans do not usually react aggressively to homosexuality. There are a good number of gay and lesbian bars, mostly located in the Tanjong Pagar area.

Gay Bars and Clubs

BackStage Bar
13A Trengganu Street;
tel: 6227 1712; www.back-
stagebar.moon
fruit.com; Sun–Fri 6pm–1am,
Sat and the night before public
holidays 6pm–2am;
MRT: Chinatown; map p.138 B3
The posters of Broadway musicals set this venue's stall out. There are several floors in this place, so feel free to wander around. Watch an old movie on a sofa or pose at the bar. The booze here is very cheap, so guests are often very happy.

Play
21 Tanjong Pagar Road;
tel: 6227 7400;
www.playclub.com.sg;
Fri 9pm–3am, Sat 9pm–4am,
MRT: Chinatown;
map p.138 B2
A fun night out as the dance floor here is always packed, often with some shirtless eye candy to sweeten the deal too.
Hot local DJs play to a mixed crowd of gay men, lesbians and their straight friends.

Taboo
65/67 Neil Road; tel: 6225
6256; www.taboo.sg;
Wed–Thur 8pm–2am, Fri
10pm–3am, Sat 10pm–4am;
MRT: Outram Park or Tanjong
Pagar; map p.138 B2
One of the longest-surviving gay clubs in Singapore, Taboo is spread over three floors and boasts a happy hour that lasts till midnight.
On the first level, a DJ spins pop remixes and guests chill out at the long bar.
On the second floor, there are comfy sofas and a heaving dance crowd.
The attic is a decidedly cosier place, where groups of people sit around and chat over drinks.

In 2001 Singapore hosted its first national gay party on Sentosa that was such a hit, it evolved into a three-day annual event. Gay men from all over Asia flew into Singapore to partake of the revelry, so much so that the government soon put an end to it by withdrawing the organisers' permit.

There are special events aplenty here, such as Bodwatch (a swimsuit show) and Handbag Night every second Saturday of the month (expect handbag tunes and diva music).

Tantric
78 Neil Road; tel: 6423 9232;
www.backstagebar.moonfruit.
com; Sun–Fri 8pm–3am,
Sat 8pm–4am;
MRT: Outram Park or Tanjong
Pagar; map p.138 B2
It is hard to miss Tantric, thanks to the flashy rainbow flag at its front.
Like its sister bar BackStage, it has an alfresco area and a small interior. The vibe here tends to be a bit sleazy – the expat men draw plenty of local fans and the prices for drinks are often high. Most people come here for a few chasers before heading to Taboo.

Lesbian Bars and Clubs

Cows & Coolies
30 Mosque Street; tel: 6221
1239; Mon–Thur 5pm–1am,
Fri–Sat 5pm–2am;
MRT: Chinatown;

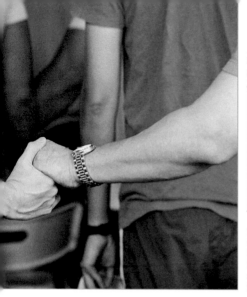

Left: homosexuality is still a sensitive issue in Singapore.

Girl parties are held regularly in Singapore. Check out **Two Queens Party** (tel: 6224 3188;www.twoqueens.me) for event listings. This community hub was established in 2000 for women in the region. It has since grown to become a weekly party, every Thursday at PLAY.

rules (at least in theory) against homosexual activity, it is no wonder that groups like **People Like Us** (www.plu.sg) are constantly campaigning for legislative changes.

For more information on gay events and issues, you can also head down to **Pelangi Pride Centre** (www.pelangipridecentre.org), which has a good library and archive.

map p.138 C3
This is where Mandarin-speaking ladies hang out and sing Chinese pop hits or play pool.

Crocodile Rock
05-29 Far East Plaza,
14 Scotts Road;
tel: 6738 0535; Tue–Wed
7.30pm–midnight, Thur
7.30pm–1am, Fri–Sat
7.30pm–3am;
MRT: Orchard; map p.134 B1
This lesbian pub has been in business for 15 years and counts a couple of men as part of their regular clientele. Like most lesbian crowds in Singapore, the guests here love a good karaoke session too. This pub will appeal to a more mature crowd.

Websites

Various websites offer excellent social networking for gay and lesbians in the Asian region. Check out www.fridae.com, www.utopia-asia.com and www.trevvy.com for the latest happenings and to see what's getting the community talking.

Given Singapore's strict

Right: despite the restrictions, Singapore still has a vibrant gay party scene.

History

1365
The Javanese *Nagarakretagama* records a settlement called Temasek – the old name that used to refer to Singapore.

1390S
Temasek is settled by a scion of the Srivijaya empire, Parameswara (also known as Iskandar Shah).

14–15TH CENTURIES
Siam (Thailand), followed by Java's Majapahit empire, seizes Temasek. Temasek exists as a vassal of the Malay kingdom of Melaka and is governed by a *temenggong* (chief) from Johor.

17TH CENTURY
Singapore is forgotten and left to the Orang Laut (sea nomads).

1819
Sir Thomas Stamford Raffles, representing the British East India Company, arrives in Singapore. The *temenggong* and Sultan Hussein allow Raffles to open a trading post in Singapore in exchange for money.

1824
The British agree to withdraw from Indonesia, in return for Dutch recognition of British rights over Singapore. Singapore is ceded to the British.

1826
The trading stations in Penang, Melaka and Singapore are named the Straits Settlements, under the administration of the East India Company.

1867
The Straits Settlements become a Crown Colony controlled by the Colonial Office in London.

1911
The population of Singapore grows to 250,000 and the census records 48 races, speaking 54 languages, on the island.

1920S
The Great Depression's effects are felt in Singapore as prices of commodities, such as rubber, collapse.

1942
The Japanese occupy Singapore for 3½ years. It is renamed Syonan, the 'Light of the South'.

1945
Japanese rule ends in August, with the landing of Allied troops.

1946
The British declare Singapore a Crown Colony.

1948
The British allow limited elections to the Legislative Council. A state of emergency is declared following the Malayan Communist Party's uprising against imperialism.

1951
Three Legislative Council elections. Singapore is formally proclaimed a city with a royal charter.

1955
Rendel Commission granted by the British leads to elections; David Marshall becomes the chief minister.

1956
PAP Central Executive Committee elections, in which the Communists decline to run, are held. Chinese students riot; PAP leaders are arrested.

1958
A constitutional agreement for partial independence for Singapore is signed in London.

1959
The People's Action Party (PAP) wins 43 out of 51 seats in the first elections. Lee Kuan Yew becomes the first prime minister.

1963
Singapore joins the Federation of Malaysia, made up of Malaya, Sabah (North Borneo) and Sarawak.

1964
PAP wins only one seat in the Malaysian general elections. Communal riots ensue.

1965
Singapore leaves the Malaysian federation, becoming an independent nation. The country joins the Commonwealth and the United Nations.

1907
Singapore, Malaysia, Thailand, Indonesia and the Philippines form the Association of Southeast Asian Nations (ASEAN).

1968
PAP sweeps the first parliamentary general elections, winning all 58 seats.

1978
The British Far East Command ceases.

1981
In a by-election, J.B. Jeyaretnam of the Workers' Party wins the first seat to be held by a member of an opposition party.

1987
The US$5 billion Mass Rapid Transit (MRT) system opens.

1990
Goh Chok Tong becomes prime minister. The amended constitution provides for an elected president.

1991
PAP's share of votes in the general elections falls to 59.7 percent, the lowest since it has been in power.

1996
Singapore is no longer regarded as a developing nation by the OECD.

1998
Singapore's economy is affected by the economic crisis in Southeast Asia.

1999
President Ong Teng Cheong steps down. S.R. Nathan is elected as the president.

2000
Economic growth hits 10.1 percent.

2001
Goh Chok Tong leads PAP to win 75.3 percent of votes in the general elections. Unemployment reaches 4.7 percent, a 15-year high.

2002
An Al-Qaeda-linked terrorist plot to bomb the US embassy is uncovered. The S$600 million Esplanade – Theatres on the Bay opens.

2003
Outbreak of Severe Acute Respiratory Syndrome (SARS) in April is quickly controlled. The North-East MRT line opens.

2004
Prime Minister Lee Hsien Loong takes office. The economy shows positive signs of recovery.

2005
Plans to build two 'Integrated Resorts', mega entertainment and leisure complexes, in Marina Bay and Sentosa are afoot.

2006
PAP wins 66.6 percent of votes in the general elections, sweeping all but two seats.

2007
Singapore acquires rights to host a leg of the Formula 1 World Championships.

2008
The 165-metre-high Singapore Flyer is launched, making it the world's tallest Giant Observation Wheel.

2009
Singapore hosts the Asia-Pacific Economic Cooperation (APEC) meetings for the first time.

2010
The two Integrated Resorts of Marina Bay Sands and Resorts World Sentosa and their casinos are launched.

2011
During the 2011 General Election, ruling party PAP faces its worst results since independence in 1965. It wins 60.1% compared to 66.6% in the 2006 election and 75.3% in 2001. S.R. Nathan steps down as president, and Tony Tan is elected.

2012
The sprawling Gardens by the Bay with its SuperTrees and Flower Domes were unveiled.

Hotels

There are myriad grades of hotels in Singapore to suit all budgets. Be it luxury accommodation from internationally renowned brand names, funky boutique outfits that appeal to the trendy jetsetter, or budget digs and backpacker hostels, visitors are – to put it mildly – spoiled for choice. Most visitors prefer to stay in the city, around the Civic District and Orchard Road, where the more expensive hotels are clustered. But if you want to avoid the crowds and stiff prices, head to Little India or Chinatown for cheaper-but-cheerful options. Here are our favourite places to lay your hat.

Singapore River

The Fullerton
1 Fullerton Square; tel: 6733 8388; www.fullertonhotel.com; $$$$; MRT: Raffles Place; map p.139 D4
Business travellers will appreciate its proximity to the financial district. Its contemporary art deco interior is filled with Philippe Starck fittings, and there are excellent restaurants and the trendy Post Bar on site. **One Fullerton** across the road entices with more waterfront wining and dining options. Within walking distance is its sister property **Fullerton by the Bay** which offers swanky interiors and excellent service.
SEE ALSO ARCHITECTURE, P.28

Gallery
1 Nanson Road; tel: 6849 8686; www.galleryhotel.com.sg; $$$;

MRT: Clarke Quay, then taxi; map p.135 D1
With its postmodernist architecture and compact rooms and suites artfully decorated by young artists, this is definitely a hotel for design-conscious visitors. Many rooms overlook the Singapore River. Complimentary internet access is provided in every room.

Grand Copthorne Waterfront
392 Havelock Road; tel: 6733 0880; www.millenniumhotels.com.sg; $$$; MRT: Clarke Quay, then taxi; map p.135 C1

This may be a modern business hotel but it is also ideal for partiers as it is situated right next door to one of Singapore's best dance clubs, Zouk. Rooms are all equipped with broadband internet access.

Marina Bay

Conrad Centennial
2 Temasek Boulevard; tel: 6334 8888; www.conradhotels.com; $$$$; MRT: Promenade; map p.136 C2
Stylish, modern business hotel adjacent to Suntec City and Marina Square, making it a

Below: the rooms at the Gallery are decorated by young artists.

Price categories are for a double room for one night without breakfast and taxes:
$$$$ = over S$300
$$$ = S$200–300
$$ = S$100–200
$ = under S$100

Left: funky furnishings in the New Majestic's lobby.

Cantonese and seafood cuisines. The bar with a riveting glass sculpture as its talking point is perfect for after-dinner drinks.
SEE ALSO RESTAURANTS, P.103

The Civic District

Carlton
76 Bras Basah Road; tel: 6338 8333; www.carlton.com.sg; $$$; MRT: City Hall; map p.136 B2
In the heart of the museum district and near the Chijmes entertainment hub. Premier rooms in the Annex Wing offer marble bathrooms and flat-screen TVs. It has an established Cantonese restaurant serving excellent dim sum.

Grand Park City Hall
10 Coleman Street; tel: 6336 3456; www.parkhotelgroup. com; $$$; MRT: City Hall; map p.136 A2
This business hotel is a combination of both traditional and modern architecture. It is located just across from sights like the Armenian Church and Fort Canning Park. Also well known for its Spa Park Asia.

Hangout@Mt Emily
10A Upper Wilkie Road; tel: 6438 5588; www.hangout hotels.com; $; MRT: Dhoby Ghaut; map p.136 A4
Funky budget-class hotel. Clean and comfortable but no frills. You sleep in Zonk Out rooms, meet fellow travellers in the Veg Out lounge, eat at the Pig Out café, and exercise at the Work Out room.

Hotel Fort Canning
11 Canning Walk; tel: 6559 6770; www.hfcsingapore.com; $$$$; MRT: Dhoby Ghaut; map p.135 C2
This grand colonial building was the British Far East Command Headquarters

www.yoursingapore.com is set up by the Singapore Tourism Board as a hotel directory and search facility. www.stayinsingapore.com is the Singapore Hotel Association's website.

great location for shopping. It has large rooms, marble-clad bathrooms and an outdoor swimming pool with a bar.

Mandarin Oriental
5 Raffles Avenue; tel: 6338 0066; www.mandarinoriental.com; $$$$; MRT: City Hall or Esplanade; map p.136 C1
Formerly known as the Oriental, this offers rooms with excellent views of the surrounding bay area on the higher floors. Located opposite Suntec City and next to Marina Square shopping mall. Several restaurants serving American, Chinese, Italian and Japanese cuisines.

Marina Bay Sands
10 Bayfront Avenue; tel: 6688 8888; www.marin-abaysands.com; $$$$; MRT: Marina Bay or Bayfront; map p.139 E2
Located in the massive Marina Bay Sands Integrated Resort, this hotel overlooks the city centre and bay area. Choose from 18 types of rooms. Among the many facilities in the complex are a stunning infinity pool, casino, shops and trendy bars and clubs.
SEE ALSO NIGHTLIFE, P.94; RESTAURANTS, P.103

Pan Pacific Singapore
7 Raffles Boulevard; tel: 6336 8111; www.singapore.pan pacific.com; $$$; MRT: Promenade; map p.136 C1
This John Portman-designed five-star hotel recently underwent a major revamp. It still boasts a lofty 35-storey atrium and comfortable, good-sized rooms, plus huge buffet restaurant, pool-side dining, Cantonese and Indian establishments and a lounge bar.
SEE ALSO RESTAURANTS, P.104

Ritz-Carlton Millenia
7 Raffles Avenue; tel: 6337 8888; www.ritzcarlton.com; $$$$; MRT: Promenade; map p.137 C1
With an impressive contemporary art collection and Singapore's largest guest rooms, plus stunning bathrooms with views to match. Restaurants serve Western,

71

Above: top-notch service at Raffles.

during World War II. Rooms are individually styled and there's also a gym, pool and a spa. Complimentary internet and Nespresso coffee and TWG tea in all rooms.

Hotel Rendezvous
9 Bras Basah Road; tel: 6336 0220; www.rendezvoushotels.com: $$$; MRT: Dhoby Ghaut; map p.136 A3
Modern-style hotel located close to the Singapore Art Museum. Its food and drink outlets include an Indonesian restaurant and the Palong Bar which is ideal for relaxing after a day of sightseeing.

Raffles
1 Beach Road; tel: 6337 1886; www.raffles.com; $$$$; MRT: City Hall; map p.136 B2
The city's most famous (and most expensive) luxury hotel, beautifully restored to its former grandeur. There is a

If yours is the child that gets nothing but the best, consider luxury hotel rooms specially created for children. The Four Seasons Singapore and Swissôtel The Stamford offer fully furnished children's rooms complete with plush toys, mini bathrobes, slippers and other child-friendly accessories.

host of restaurants and bars, offering everything from fine-dining French to exquisite sushi and local bites. Expect old-world atmosphere and charm.
SEE ALSO MONUMENTS, P.80; SHOPPING, P.116

Strand
25 Bencoolen Street; tel: 6338 1866; www.strandhotel.com.sg; $; MRT: Bugis or Dhoby Ghaut; map p.136 A3
Clean and comfortable and one of the better budget hotels around. Close to the museum district and Chijmes, and within walking distance of Orchard Road. Its café on the ground level is great for coffee and sandwiches.

Swissôtel The Stamford
2 Stamford Road; tel: 6338 8585; www.swissotel-the stamford.com; $$$; MRT: City Hall; map p.136 B2
Formerly the world's tallest hotel until it was supplanted in 1999, this hotel is practically part of the large shopping complex Raffles City and links to Fairmont Singapore. Business travellers are well catered to with its business and convention centres. Several restaurants and bars, including the excellent **Equinox** complex, plus a lux-

urious spa and well-equipped fitness centre.
SEE ALSO RESTAURANTS, P.105

Chinatown and the CBD

Amara
165 Tanjong Pagar Road; tel: 6879 2555; www.amara hotels.com; $$$; MRT: Tanjong Pagar; map p.138 B1
Chic hotel with a spa, fitness centre, swimming pool and tennis courts. Dining options include its award-winning Thai restaurant **Thanying**, as well as a Chinese restaurant and coffee shop.
SEE ALSO RESTAURANTS, P.107

Berjaya
83 Duxton Road; tel: 6227 7678; www.berjayaresorts.com; $$$; MRT: Tanjong Pagar; map p.138 B2
A boutique property occupying a row of restored shophouses. Rooms are smallish, but the Garden Suites have their own little courtyard.

Furama City Centre
60 Eu Tong Sen Street; tel: 6533 3888; www.furama.com/citycentre; $$$; MRT: Chinatown; map p.138 C4
After a major renovation to woo business travellers, the rooms are now comfortable and cosy. Good location for shopping and nightlife as it is near Boat Quay and Clarke Quay.

Hotel 1929
50 Keong Saik Road; tel: 6347 1929; www.hotel1929.com; $$; MRT: Outram Park; map p.138 B3
Ultra-hip boutique hotel in the heart of Chinatown that has made headlines in numerous design magazines. Highlights here include a rooftop jacuzzi, the well-known contemporary European restaurant **Ember**, and retro vintage furniture in the pretty, although small, rooms.
SEE ALSO RESTAURANTS, P.106

Above: Hotel 1929 has cosy, stylish rooms.

Link

50 Tiong Bahru Road; tel: 6622 8585; www.linkhotel.com.sg; $$; MRT: Tiong Bahru or Outram Park, then taxi

Luxury meets the heartlands in this boutique hotel converted from two blocks of apartments. Inside it is all plush and contemporary Asian design; outside is an experience all unto itself – at its doorstep are a popular hawker centre and an old-world bird arena where elderly folk make a sport of coaxing their birds to break into song.

M Hotel

81 Anson Road; tel: 6224 1133; www.mhotel.com.sg; $$$; MRT: Tanjong Pagar; map p.138 C1

Excellent location in the financial district for business travellers. It offers wireless internet access throughout the hotel and business facilities, including fully furnished and serviced offices. Rooms have harbour or city views.

New Majestic

31–37 Bukit Pasoh Road; tel: 6511 4700; www.newmajestichotel.com; $$$; MRT: Outram Park; map p.138 B2

So cool it almost hurts.

Price categories are for a double room for one night without breakfast and taxes:
$$$$ = over S$300
$$$ = S$200–300
$$ = S$100–200
$ = under S$100

Different themed rooms with unique murals are a draw, as is the small swimming pool with portholes at the bottom, which look down to the lauded modern Cantonese restaurant **Majestic**.

SEE ALSO RESTAURANTS, P.105

Scarlet

33 Erskine Road; tel: 6511 3333; www.thescarlethotel.com; $$; MRT: Tanjong Pagar or Chinatown; map p.138 C3

Sexy, gothic and like a deep, dark boudoir, this Baroque-inspired boutique hotel attracts media and design types who come here to drink at the rooftop bar and sup at the acclaimed restaurant. The rooms are small and there's a tiny jacuzzi and gym.

Orchard Road

Four Seasons

190 Orchard Boulevard; tel: 6734 1110; www.fourseasons.com/singapore; $$$$; MRT: Orchard; map p.134 B4

A statement in understated elegance, this hotel is located just behind Orchard Road. Luxurious interiors, large plush rooms and expensive artworks belie its rather plain façade. Restaurants serve grills and local fare and refined Cantonese cuisine, plus a cosy alfresco bar with views of Orchard Road. Its air-conditioned tennis courts are a dream in humid Singapore.

SEE ALSO RESTAURANTS, P.108

Goodwood Park Hotel

22 Scotts Road; tel: 6737 7411; www.goodwoodparkhotel.com; $$$$; MRT: Orchard

Charming historical building dating back to 1900 that used to serve as a social club for the German community. Its suites open out to the swimming pool. Five acclaimed eateries, including a grill, Chinese restaurant and coffee lounge for local high tea.

SEE ALSO MONUMENTS, P.80

Grand Hyatt

10 Scotts Road; tel: 6738 1234; singapore.grand.hyatt.com; $$$$; MRT: Orchard; map p.134 B1

Minimalist, almost stark décor, comfortable rooms and excellent service. Its eateries – including the stylish **mezza9** with an elegant **martini bar**, and Straits Kitchen serving local fare – are very popular. Its free-form pool with lush gardens is a haven in this busy neck of the woods.

SEE ALSO NIGHTLIFE, P.96; RESTAURANTS, P.108

Mandarin Orchard Singapore

333 Orchard Road; tel: 6737 4411; www.meritushotels.com; $$$; MRT: Orchard or Somerset; map p.135 C4

Serious shoppers would do well to stay here as all the major malls and boutiques are within walking distance. Its **Chatterbox** coffee house is noted for its rendition of a Singaporean favourite: Hainanese chicken rice.

SEE ALSO RESTAURANTS, P.109

Marriott

320 Orchard Road; tel: 6735 5800; www.marriott.com; $$$$; MRT: Orchard; map p.134 C4

The pagoda-roofed landmark is perfect for shoppers and partiers. Its Crossroads alfresco café is the place to watch the world pass by, while the TANGS department store is just next door.

Above: drinks in the lounge at the Royal Plaza on Scotts.

Orchard Hotel
442 Orchard Road; tel: 6734 7766; www.orchardhotel.com.sg; $$$; MRT: Orchard; map p.134 B1
Deluxe rooms in the Orchard and Claymore wings are well-refurbished. The lobby coffee shop serves both buffet and à la carte meals; Hua Ting restaurant is one of the best in town for Cantonese cuisine and dim sum.

The Regent
1 Cuscaden Road; tel: 6733 8888; www.regenthotels.com; $$$; MRT: Orchard; map p.134 A1
Large, well-appointed rooms and excellent service. Highly recommended are the Italian restaurant serving quality antipasti buffet, Cantonese fine dining offering good dim sum and an established Japanese restaurant specialising in tempura. The Orchard

Price categories are for a double room for one night without breakfast and taxes:
$$$$ = over S$300
$$$ = S$200–300
$$ = S$100–200
$ = under S$100

MRT station is a 10-15 minute walk away and there is a bus stop right in front of the entrance.
SEE ALSO RESTAURANTS, P.109

Royal Plaza on Scotts
25 Scotts Road; tel: 6737 7966; www.royalplaza.com.sg; $$$; MRT: Orchard; map p.134 B1
Owned by the Sultan of Brunei, this business hotel has an excellent location for shoppers. Perks include a complimentary mini-bar and free internet in all rooms and proximity to the adjacent DFS Galleria mall and Orchard Road.

Shangri-La
22 Orange Grove Road; tel: 6737 3644; www.shangri-la.com; $$$$; MRT: Orchard; map p.134 A2
Its three towers are set amid luxuriant gardens. The plush Valley Wing is where visiting heads of state and other VIPs have stayed. There are superb Cantonese, Japanese and buffet restaurants, and a stylish pool-side Mediterranean-style café. Orchard MRT station is a good 15-minute walk away, though.

YMCA International House
1 Orchard Road; tel: 6336 6000; www.ymcaih.com.sg; $$; MRT: Dhoby Ghaut; map p.136 A3
Situated at the top end of Orchard Road, this has a rooftop swimming pool and fitness centre. Choose from guest rooms with attached bathrooms or four-person dormitories.

Little India

Albert Court Village
180 Albert Street; tel: 6339 3939; www.albertcourt.com.sg; $$; MRT: Little India; map p.136 A4
A boutique hotel adjacent to Little India. The interior décor exudes nostalgic charm, furnished with Peranakan teak carvings and old brassware. The comforts, however, are thoroughly modern.

Parkroyal on Kitchener Road
181 Kitchener Road; tel: 6428 3000; www.parkroyalhotels.com; $$$; MRT: Farrer Park; map p.133 D2
This hotel caters to corporate travellers with the usual business mod cons. But leisure travellers will not be disappointed with its spacious rooms and great location close to Serangoon Road.

Perak Hotel
12 Perak Road; tel: 6299 7733; www.peraklodge.com; $$; MRT: Little India; map p.133 C1
This occupies a restored shophouse. Lovely atmosphere with friendly staff, plus a courtyard with a fish pond. All rooms come with electronic room safes and breakfast.

If you find yourself at the airport but with no place to spend the night in Singapore, head to the Singapore Hotel Association counters at Terminals 1 and 2, where staff at their four counters can help. Two of those counters are open 24 hours.

Sentosa

Amara Sanctuary Resort Sentosa
1 Larkhill Road; tel: 6825 3888; www.amarasanctuary.com; $$$; MRT: HarbourFront, then resort shuttle bus from VivoCity
A brand-new resort nestled on a hillside, this is surrounded by 3.5 hectares (8.6 acres) of gardens and natural tropical rainforest. Design-wise it is an exotic blend of colonial architecture and modern concepts. The beautiful guest rooms, suites and villas provide plush comfort and state-of-the-art facilities.

Capella
1 The Knolls, Sentosa; tel: 6377 8888; www.capellasingapore.com; $$$$; MRT: HarbourFront, then resort shuttle bus from VivoCity
This temple of luxury boasts the biggest designer names from architect Lord Norman Foster to fashion designer Peter Som in its 'company of creators'. Play on the championship golf course that's just a stone's throw away, or sink into the sumptuous guest rooms and villas that overlook the South China Sea.

The Sentosa
2 Bukit Manis Road; tel: 6275 0331; www.thesentosa.com; $$$$; MRT: HarbourFront, then resort shuttle bus from VivoCity
This resort-style hotel on a forested hill is so stunning, you might be tempted to park yourself here and not venture into the city. Features hotel-style rooms and suites and villas with private pools. **The Cliff** serves superb seafood, and the sea-facing bar is perfect for sunset cocktails. Be sure to book a massage at its **Spa Botanica**.
SEE ALSO PAMPERING, P.98; RESTAURANTS, P.111

Shangri-La's Rasa Sentosa Resort
101 Siloso Road; tel: 6275 0100; www.shangri-la.com; $$$$; MRT: HarbourFront, then resort shuttle bus from HarbourFront Centre
Singapore's only beachfront hotel overlooks the South China Sea. It serves a fine buffet breakfast and has good restaurants. Not the most convenient place to stay at, but it offers plenty of recreational activities, from sailing to cycling. Ideal for families.
SEE ALSO RESTAURANTS, P.110

Resorts World Sentosa
Tel: 6577 8888; www.rwsentosa.com; $$$$; MRT: HarbourFront, then take Sentosa Express at VivoCity to Waterfront Station or bus RWS8 outside HarbourFront MRT station
At Resorts World Sentosa, travellers can choose between six hotels with six unique themes, from high end with 24-hour butler service to family friendly accommodations. The hotels are: Crockfords Tower, Hotel Michael, Hard Rock Hotel, Festive Hotel, Hotel Equarius and Beach Villas.

SEE ALSO CHILDREN, P.38; RESTAURANTS, P.110

The East Coast

Changi Village
1 Netheravon Road; tel: 6379 7111; www.changivillage.com.sg; $$; MRT: Tanah Merah; bus 2 or 9
A multimillion-dollar renovation has transformed this former transit hotel into a chic resort. Free shuttle service from the airport to the city. Changi Beach and Changi Village nearby are great places to chill out at.

Grand Mercure Roxy
50 East Coast Road; tel: 6344 8000; www.grandmercureroxy.com.sg; $$; bus 16, 31, 135 or 196
Value-for-money four-star hotel with the Parkway Parade Shopping Centre just opposite. It is also a short walk to the East Coast beach. Spacious rooms with a contemporary look, café and Chinese restaurant. No MRT station nearby, but buses across the street service the city.

Below: the lobby at the Amara Sanctuary Resort Sentosa.

75

Literature

BESTSEL

Singapore's literature is published in its four main languages: English, Chinese, Malay and Tamil. Most of the country's literary works portray and explore various aspects of Singapore society. Given the small domestic market, it cannot be said that local literature has a huge following. Yet that doesn't mean that Singaporean's aren't voracious readers. Major bookshops like Kinokuniya continue to see a healthy crowd. Like their outlook in life, Singaporeans' tastes in books are international; weekly bestseller lists include books by authors like JK Rowling and Mitch Albom.

Poets and Authors

Many recognise Singapore's first-generation writers as those who emerged with the country's independence in 1965. Names like Edwin Thumboo, Arthur Yap, Goh Poh Seng, Lee Tzu Pheng and Chandran Nair published mainly poetry in English. Today's Singaporean poets are a new generation under the age of 40, including Alvin Pang, Cyril Wong, Felix Cheong and Alfian Sa'at. They have published works both in Singapore and internationally.

Goh Poh Seng's *If We Dream Too Long* (1972) is widely recognised as the first true Singaporean novel.

Catherine Lim is Singapore's most widely read author – largely due to her first two books of short stories, *Little Ironies: Stories of Singapore* (1978) and *Or Else, the Lightning God and Other Stories* (1980), being GCSE set texts.

Over the last few years, the leading non-fiction author has been Singapore's former Prime Minister Lee Kwan Yew. Considered the founder of modern Singapore, Lee has

written two books, which sold out within days of release.

Another Singaporean non-fiction best-seller was 2009's *Men In White*, by Sonny Yap, Leong Weng Kam and Richard Lim, all staff at the main local newspaper *The Straits Times*.

Further Reading

GENERAL

The Air-Conditioned Nation: Essays on the Politics of Comfort and Control, by Cherian George (Landmark, 2000). Insights into what makes Singapore tick.

Complete Notes from Singapore: The Omnibus Edition, by Neil Humphreys (Marshall Cavendish Editions, 2007). A British humourist writes on Singapore's idiosyncrasies.

From Third World To First: The Singapore Story: 1965–2000, by Lee Kuan Yew (HarperCollins, 2000). The man responsible for Singapore's transformation tells his story.

Lee Kuan Yew: Hard Truths to Keep Singapore Going, by Han Fook Kwang, Zuraidah Ibrahim, Chua Mui Hoong, Lydia Lim, Ignatius Low, Rachel Lin, Robin Chan

(Straits Times Press, 2011). This tome compiled by local writers is based on 32 hours of interviews at the Istana with Singapore's influential former Prime Minister. It features a politically incorrect, controversial, thought-provoking leader and a devoted husband, father and grandfather.

Singapore The Encyclopedia, by various authors (Editions Didier Millet, 2006). Everything you've always wanted to know about Singapore is in here.

FICTION AND POETRY

One Fierce Hour, by Alfian Sa'at (Landmark, 1998). Highly charged poems about life in Singapore by this acclaimed poet and playwright.

Raffles Place Ragtime, by Philip Jeyaretnam (Times Books International, 1988). About love and ambition in Singapore.

The Shrimp People, by Rex Shelley (Times Books International, 1991). An evocative tale on Singapore's Eurasians that won the National Book Prize.

Left: browsing in Kinokuniya.

language bookstore chain.

{prologue} @ ION Orchard
2 Orchard Turn #04-16; tel: 6465 1477; www.prologue.com.sg ; daily 10.30am–10pm; MRT: Orchard; map p. 134 R4
Browse the latest English books and magazines, followed by a coffee at the adjacent Epilogue Café.

Select Books
51 Armenian Street; tel: 6337 9319; www.selectbooks.com.sg; Mon–Sat 9.30am–6.30pm, Sun and public hols 10am–4pm; MRT: City Hall; map p. 136 A2
Since 1976, this bookstore has been specialising in books and journals on the Asia region. Categories include architecture, art, business, literature, politics and economics, religion, travel and many more.

Sunny Bookstore
06-11/12 Plaza Singapura, 68 Orchard Road; tel: 733 1583; daily 11am–9.30pm; MRT: Dhoby Ghaut Orchard; map p.135 E3
Filled with brand-new and secondhand titles from every literary genre.

Times Bookstore
04-08/09/10/11 Centrepoint, 176 Orchard Road; tel: 6734 9022; www.timesbookstores.com.sg; daily 10.30am–9.30pm; MRT: Somerset; map p.135 D4
This household name has a wide selection of locally published tomes, reference books, paperbacks and magazines.

Woods in the Books
No.3 Yong Siak Street, Tiong Bahru, tel: 6222 9980 and Millenia Walk, 9 Raffles Boulevard 02-32, tel: 6337 3385; www.woodsinthebooks.sg; Mon–Sat 11am–8.30pm, Sun 11am–8pm; MRT: Tiong Bahru and Promenade; map p.136 C2
This quiet bookstore specialises in picture books for children and adults.

Bookstores

Books Actually
9 Yong Siak Street; tel: 6222 9195; www.booksactually.com; Mon 11am–6pm, Tues–Fri 11am–9pm, Sat 10am–9pm, Sun 10am–6pm; MRT: Tiong Bahru
This small, independent bookstore mainly focuses on fiction, including poetry, and rare/antique editions, but non-fiction such as biography, current affairs, sciences, travel, food, music and film is available. The store also offers the largest collection of Singapore literary publications.

Books Kinokuniya
03-09/10/15 Ngee Ann City; tel: 6737 5021; www.kinokuniya. com.sg; Sun–Fri 10am–9.30pm, Sat 10am–10pm; MRT: Orchard; map p.134 C4
This huge store has just about every English-language title imaginable and the biggest selection of magazines in town. Look out for books in Chinese, French and German.

Earshot
1/F, The Arts House, 1 Old Parliament Lane; tel: 6338 8220; www.theartshouse.com.sg; daily 11.30am–7pm; MRT: Raffles Place; map p.139 D4
This bookshop-music store-café carries many local works.

Harris Book Company
04-25/26/27/28 313@Somerset, 313 Orchard Road; tel: 6514 6755; daily 10.30am–10.30pm; MRT: Somerset; map p.135 D3
English-language bookstore specialising in comics and periodicals.

MPH
B1-21 Raffles City Shopping Centre, 252 North Bridge Road; tel: 6336 4232; www.mph.com.sg; daily 10am–10pm; MRT: City Hall; map p.136 B2
The flagship store of a reliable and trusted English-

Below: Select Books.

Monuments

By international standards, Singapore's monuments are small and can barely boast grandeur along the lines of, say, the Eiffel Tower in Paris or the Statue of Liberty in New York City. But what Singapore's monuments lack in size, they make up for with charm and character. From the grande dames of hotels, the Raffles and Goodwood Park, to the quaint Cavenagh Bridge, to the Gothic-style convent now reinvented as the nightlife hub Chijmes, each has a unique story to tell. Let these eclectic structures lead you through the city's history, culture and development.

Anderson Bridge

Singapore River; MRT: Raffles Place; map p.139 D4

Anderson Bridge was built in 1910 when it became apparent that the adjacent Cavenagh Bridge could not cope with increasing traffic. It was named after Sir John Anderson, governor of the Straits Settlement. During the Japanese Occupation (1942–5), the severed heads of criminals were hung on the bridge as a warning to discourage people from breaking the law.

Cavenagh Bridge

Singapore River; MRT: Raffles Place; map p.139 D4

Cavenagh Bridge is the oldest suspension bridge in Singapore. It was constructed in Scotland and assembled here by Indian convict labourers in 1869. The bridge was named in honour of Major General Cavenagh, the last India-appointed governor. Originally planned as a drawbridge, it was found upon completion to be suitable only as a fixed structure. It is now a pedestrian bridge.

Chijmes

30 Victoria Street; tel: 6337 7810; www.chijmes.com.sg; MRT: City Hall; map p.136 B2

This neo-Gothic-style former Convent of the Holy Infant Jesus (CHIJ) school building was painstakingly restored with the help of conservationist Didier Reppelin. The name Chijmes (pronounced 'chimes') was adopted to incorporate the initials of the convent, church and school that had stood here since its founding in 1854. The convent also ran an orphanage; its **Gate of Hope** was where babies would be left by their unmarried mothers.

Chijmes is today a collection of restaurants, pubs and handicraft shops. Don't miss the Belgian-crafted stained-glass windows in the chapel, which is now renamed **Chijmes Hall** and a venue for concerts and weddings. The **Fountain Court**, flanked by pubs and restaurants with alfresco dining areas, reverberates with life when there are free outdoor concerts. Alfresco dining in its softly lit courtyard is a delight.

Below: the Gothic-inspired Chijmes is a nightlife destination.

Left: the water of the Fountain of Wealth is said to bring good luck to whoever touches it.

Fountain, commissioned by the Municipal Council and built in gratitude for a donation 'towards the cost of the Singapore Water Works' given in 1857 by the trader and public benefactor Tan Kim Seng (1805–64). This Victorian cast-iron fountain has been part of Singapore's urban landscape since 19 May 1882. During Tan's lifetime, one of the major problems of the town was its inadequate water supply. Tan donated a generous sum of $13,000 to support the construction of a system to provide piped water to the town. The ambitious plans were only approved after his death in 1864.

Esplanade Park

Along Connaught Drive; free; MRT: City Hall or Esplanade; map p.136 B1

The Esplanade Park and the tree-lined **Queen Elizabeth Walk** was formerly a seafront promenade where Europeans spent their leisure time strolling or playing cricket during colonial times.

At the park's southern end is the **Lim Bo Seng Memorial**, with its four bronze lions. It is dedicated to local hero and martyr Lim Bo Seng (1909–44), an active member of an underground resistance movement against the Japanese in World War II.

Further along is the **Cenotaph**, built to remember the soldiers who died fighting in the two World Wars. Standing at nearly 20m (66ft) tall, it is made from smooth granite, and the words 'Our Glorious Dead' are engraved on its surface. The structure was erected in memory of 124 British men who gave their lives in World War I. Their names are cast on a metal plate that sits before the foundation stone laid by Sir Lawrence Guillemard, governor of the Straits Settlement, on 15 November 1920. After World War II, more inscriptions were made on the reverse side of the stone.

At the park's northern end is the **Tan Kim Seng**

Below: the Cenotaph honours the heroes of two World Wars.

Fountain of Wealth

Suntec City Mall, 3 Temasek Boulevard; tel: 6825 2668; www.sunteccitymall.com; free; MRT: City Hall or Promenade; map p.136 C2

The water of the gigantic Fountain of Wealth in the centre of Suntec City supposedly brings good fortune to those who touch it. Others perform a special ritual to harness the forces of the excellent *feng shui* that surrounds both the Fountain and Suntec City.

The massive bronze structure, which covers

The entire **Suntec City** development is inspired by *feng shui* principles. Based on the human hand, it has four 45-storey towers representing the four fingers while a shorter 18-storey tower is the thumb. The fountain, with its water symbolising wealth, is held in the palm of the hand.

1,683sq m (18,115sq ft), is listed in the Guinness World Records as the world's largest and was inspired by the Hindu *mandala*. The fountain is switched on daily 10am–10pm. There is also a free nightly laser show at 8pm and 9pm.

Goodwood Park Hotel

22 Scotts Road; tel: 6737 7411; www.goodwoodparkhotel.com; MRT: Orchard

This castle-like hotel was built in 1900 as the Teutonia Club for German residents in Singapore. Designed by colonial architect R.A.J. Bidwell, it has an interesting history. During World War II, the Japanese used the building as a military headquarters, and in 1945, the British turned its premises into a war crimes court. It is now a luxury hotel.
SEE HOTELS, P.73

Istana

Orchard Road; www.istana.gov. sg; MRT: Dhoby Ghaut; map p.132 A1

The Istana is the official residence of Singapore's president. The palace and its sprawling gardens are strictly off-limits to the public, except on National Day and certain public holidays when the gates are thrown open to curious sightseers.

The Istana was completed in 1869 by the colonial engineer J.F.A. McNair and served as the residence of the British governor until the island became self-governing in 1959. Facing the Istana squarely is the **Istana Park**, dominated by an imposing steel sculpture that is flanked by gardens of heliconia and lotus-filled ponds. The café is a pleasant stop for a drink.

Merlion Park

By the Esplanade Bridge, next to One Fullerton; free; MRT: Raffles Place; map p.139 E4

The Merlion Park is the home of the Merlion statue, the city's tourism mascot inspired by the creature Prince Sang Nila Utama saw when he arrived in Singapore (then known as Temasek) in the 13th century. Believing it to be a *singa* (lion), he renamed the island Singapura, meaning 'Lion City'. Once located at the original Merlion Park by the Esplanade Bridge, the

Merlion became a popular tourist attraction for visitors. Today the Merlion is found just 120m (394ft) away from its original site, adjacent to One Fullerton. Built from cement fondue by the late Singaporean craftsman Lim Nang Seng, the Merlion statue measures 8.6m (28ft) high and weighs 70 tonnes.

Parliament House

1 Parliament Place; tel: 6332 6677; www.parliament.gov.sg; tours by appointment only; MRT: City Hall or Clarke Quay; map p.139 D4

The new Parliament House was completed in 1999, right next door to the old Parliament House, which is now an arts hub called **The Arts House**. The new building is five times larger than the old one, and retains the colonial architectural style to preserve a sense of history. Porcelain dating back to the Ming and Yuan dynasties was found on the site during construction and is now displayed in the new complex.
SEE ALSO THEATRE, P.121

Raffles Hotel

1 Beach Road; tel: 6337 1886; www.raffles.com; MRT: City Hall; map p.136 B2

> Travelling scribes who have laid their hats at the **Raffles** include Somerset Maugham and Rudyard Kipling, who described it as a place 'where food is as excellent as the rooms are bad. Let the traveller take note. Feed at Raffles and sleep at the Hotel de l'Europe'. The latter was demolished in 1934 to make way for the Supreme Court building. The Raffles has since earned itself a stellar reputation.

Below: the Goodwood Park Hotel is styled after a Bavarian castle.

Above: the Raffles Hotel.

Nearly all visitors to Singapore end up at the Raffles at one point or another, usually to try the world-famous Singapore Sling in the **Long Bar** (invented here in 1915) or to walk through the lush gardens. Enter via its cast-iron porticoed entrance on Beach Road – the hotel originally faced the beach before it was reclaimed – which leads into the lobby with marbled floors embellished with plush Persian carpets.

Opened in 1887 by the Sarkies Brothers, this 'Grand Old Lady of the East' has seen its fair share of kings and queens, presidents and prime ministers, movie actors and giants of literature, as well as ordinary people attracted to this icon of tropical elegance and style.

The Raffles' history is a chequered one. It was briefly used by the Japanese forces in World War II when it was renamed Syonan Ryokan (Light of the South Hotel). In the early 1990s the hotel underwent a major facelift that involved years of tracking down original plans and finding skilled craftsmen to repair and re-create the original fittings. The result is a resounding success and the Raffles can once again take her place among the great hotels of the world.

The hotel also houses a **shopping arcade** and the **Jubilee Hall.**
SEE ALSO HOTELS, P.72; SHOPPING, P.116; THEATRE, P.121

Raffles' Landing Site
Northern bank of the Singapore River; free; MRT: Raffles Place; map p.139 D4
The founder of modern Singapore, Sir Thomas Stamford Raffles, is said to have landed on this very spot on 29 January 1819. To mark this momentous event, a white marble statue of him was erected on what is now the northern bank of the Singapore River.

This white stone statue, circa 1972, is a replica cast from the original bronze statue created in 1887. The bronze statue was relocated outside the Victoria Concert Hall in 1919 to mark the 100th anniversary of Singapore's founding.

War Memorial Park
Beach Road; free; MRT: City Hall or Esplanade; map p.136 B2
The War Memorial Park is dedicated to the thousands of civilians who suffered and died in Singapore in World War II. Popularly known as the 'Chopsticks Monument', the memorial consists of four interlinked tapering columns representing each of the four main ethnic groups. Beneath the 61-m columns are urns containing the remains of some of those who died. It was gazetted as a national monument in 2013.

Below: the War Memorial honours civilians.

Watch the ceremony of the changing of the sentry guards that takes place on the first Sunday of every month at 6pm at the **Istana**'s gates. But forget about getting a glimpse of the palace building from the gates. The grounds are massive and all you will see is an endless expanse of green. Interestingly, Singapore's current president, S.R. Nathan, prefers to live in his own humbler abode in eastern Singapore. He uses the Istana for receiving foreign dignitaries and for hosting state functions.

Museums and Galleries

For a small country, Singapore has a disproportionally large number of museums and galleries; visitors will be spoilt for choice. There are history museums that capture and catalogue the stories of the early days of the island and Southeast Asia through artefacts and war relics; art and design museums and commercial galleries that showcase cutting-edge creativity; and idiosyncratic repositories that display the quirky and niche tastes of the people, such as the Mint Museum of Toys.

Art Retreat

10 Ubi Crescent, Lobby C, 01-45/46/47 Ubi Techpark; tel: 6749 0880; www.artretreat museum.com; free; Tue–Sat 11am–6pm, guided tours by appointment; MRT: Eunos or Paya Lebar; bus: 63

This private museum could well be the best-kept secret of Singapore's art scene, and is well worth an excursion to the suburbs. One of its two galleries hosts exhibitions of works selected from its solid collection of Southeast Asian art by renowned artists such as Affandi, S. Sudjojono, Lee Man Fong and Chen Wen Hsi, and paintings by European masters like Russel Flint, Edvard Munch and Karel Appel. The other gallery is solely dedicated to the brilliance of the much-admired Chinese master Wu Guanzhong. Other than the permanent collection, the main gallery also features temporary exhibitions from other collections.

ArtScience Museum

10 Bayfront Avenue, Marina Bay Sands; tel: 6688 8868; en.marinabaysands.com/Singa-pore-Museum/; daily 10am–10pm; entrance charge; MRT: Bayfront or Promenade or Marina Bay; map p. 139 E3

The world's first ArtScience Museum is housed in an iconic all-white lotus-inspired structure that is hard to miss. It covers 21 gallery spaces and has showcased major international touring exhibitions such as *Titanic: The Artifact Exhibition*, *Dali: Mind of a Genius* and *Andy Warhol: 15 Minutes Eternal*.
SEE ALSO ARCHITECTURE, P.29

Asian Civilisations Museum

1 Empress Place; tel: 6332 2982; www.acm.org.sg;

Below: a recreated Chinese scholar's studio, with a 19th-century wooden couch bed from Fujian, at the Asian Civilisations Museum.

The National Art Gallery will open in 2015, housed in two historic buildings – the City Hall and the former Supreme Court – right in the heart of the Civic District. It's yet another step in the right direction in Singapore's vision to establish itself as a regional and international hub for visual arts. For more information, go to nationalartgallery.sg.

Left: Gallery 2.1 at the Singapore Art Museum.

Mon 1–7pm, Tue–Thur & Sat–Sun 9am–7pm, Fri 9am–9pm; entrance charge; MRT: Raffles Place; map p.139 D4

From prehistoric agricultural tools to fabric displays and bronze artefacts, the exhibits in the 11 galleries at this museum reveal the cultural and historical diversity of West, South and Southeast Asia, as well as China. In the **China Gallery**, learn about the Middle Kingdom from the displays – the Chinese deities and fragile Dehua porcelain are the highlights, while the **West Asia Gallery** impresses with Qur'an-inspired calligraphic art. The **South Asia galleries** hold religious statuary and architectural motifs of the Indian subcontinent.

Even visitors who are not history buffs will find the snazzy interactive zones and videos highly entertaining. To fully appreciate the museum, take the free one-hour guided tour (Mon 2pm, Tue–Fri 11am and 2pm, Fri 7pm, Sat–Sun 11am, 2pm and 3pm; not available end Dec–early Jan and selected public holidays).

Baba House

157 Neil Road; tel: 6227 5731; www.nus.edu.sg/museum/baba; guided tours by appointment; MRT: Outram Park; map p.138 A2

Opened in 2008, this treasury of Peranakan history and material culture is nestled among a cluster of conservation terrace houses. The three-storey building it is housed in was built in the 1860s and is perhaps the last Peranakan house still owned by its original owners. Its opulent interior bears intricately carved wooden windows, doors, timber brackets and partition screens.

The exhibition space hosts heritage art shows and yearly Peranakan festivals. The museum even has a live-in *bibik* (Peranakan colloquialism for matron) housekeeper and tour guide.

Changi Chapel and Museum

1000 Upper Changi Road North; tel: 6214 2451; www.changi museum.sg; daily 9.30am–5pm; free; MRT: Tanah Merah, then bus: 2 or MRT: Tampines,

then bus: 29

The historic Changi Chapel and Museum, formerly located at Changi Prison, moved to this new site in 2001. The museum focuses on the memories and lives of both POWs and civilian internees who survived the Japanese Occupation (1942–5) with a collection of wartime memorabilia, including drawings by W.R.M. Haxworth and photographs by George Aspinall, which were taken and developed under great danger.

Particularly compelling are the **Changi Murals**. Painted by British POW Stanley Warren, the five murals, each with a Biblical significance, are replicas of the restored originals at Changi Prison.

The chapel, a symbolic replica of the one at Changi Prison, is housed in the courtyard. There are also videos and rare books depicting life during the war years.

Chinatown Heritage Centre

48 Pagoda Street; tel: 6221 9556; www.chinatownheritage centre.sg; daily 9am–8pm;

Below: notes left in remembrance of POWs at the Changi Museum.

Above: antique fire engine at the Civil Defence Heritage Gallery.

entrance charge; MRT: Chinatown; map p.138 C3

The Chinatown Heritage Centre was opened in 2002 to give Chinatown a sense of history. Occupying three restored shophouses on Pagoda Street, the museum showcases the lifestyles, traditions and rituals of the people who lived and worked there in 15 galleries. The dark and cramped living quarters of early Chinatown are realistically re-created using authentic furniture, utensils and other paraphernalia.

Civil Defence Heritage Gallery

Central Fire Station, 62 Hill Street; tel: 6332 2996; www.scdf.gov.sg; Tue–Sun 10am–5pm; free; MRT: Clarke Quay or City Hall; map p.136 A1

Housed in Singapore's oldest fire station, the Civil Defence Heritage Gallery traces Singapore's civil defence development from the 1900s. The museum has displays of antique fire engines and interactive stations depicting what fire fighters and rescuers undergo in a rescue operation. Register for a guided tour and you'll get to climb up the hose tower, the lookout point for fire fighters in the early days.

SEE ALSO ARCHITECTURE, P.26

Fort Siloso

33 Allanbrooke Road, Sentosa; tel: 1800-736 8672; www.sentosa.com.sg; daily 10am–6pm; MRT: HarbourFront, then Sentosa Express from VivoCity

Singapore's only preserved coastal fort on Sentosa's western tip is another of the island's must-see sights.

At Fort Siloso the British built numerous guns and tunnels for the defence of Singapore, which proved to be ineffective in World War II as the Japanese invaded from the Malay peninsula and not from the sea.

The interactive displays along the underground passages, the cannons and guns, and the video games tell the fort's history from its construction through to its fall in World War II. Also here are the **Surrender Chambers**, which bring to life Singapore's formal surrender to the Japanese in 1942 with a mix of gripping audio-visual footage, artefacts and realistic wax figurines.

Fuk Tak Chi Museum

76 Telok Ayer Street, Far East Square; tel: 6532 7868; daily 10am–10pm; free; MRT: Raffles Place; map p.139 C3

Dating from 1824, this is Singapore's oldest temple, set up by the Hakkas and Cantonese. The museum has a collection of 200 artefacts, including a Chinese gold belt, abacus board and a rental expiry notice from early Chinatown residents.

Images of Singapore

40 Imbiah Road, Sentosa; tel: 1800-736 8672; www.sentosa.com.sg; daily 9am–7pm; entrance charge; MRT: HarbourFront, then Sentosa Express from VivoCity

A museum that explores four experiences – Four Winds of Singapore, Celebration City, Singapore Adventure and Singapore Celebrates – Images of Singapore. These take you through Singapore's history and give a sneak preview of the country's rich cultural diversity through multimedia shows and walk-through settings.

Labrador Nature Reserve

Labrador Villa Road, off Pasir Panjang Road; tel: 1800-471 7300; www.nparks.gov.sg; 24 hours (park is lit 7am–midnight); free; MRT: Labrador Park

Labrador Park houses World War II gun batteries, along with bunkers and other relics that have been restored. Storyboards posted in the 17-ha park explain the development of the battery and its fortification. The Bunker Path winds around underground chambers, gun emplacements, an 1892 ammunition storeroom, a six-pounder quick-fire gun and remains of an old fort wall.

In addition, an aerial staircase built into the edge

of the secondary forest offers a panoramic view of the sea.

Malay Heritage Centre

85 Sultan Gate; tel: 6391 0450; www.malayheritage.org.cg; Malay Heritage Centre Museum Tue–Sun 10am–6pm, Malay Heritage Centre Compound Tue–Sun 8am–8pm, Fri–Sat 8am–10pm; entrance charge; MRT: Bugis; map p.137 C4

The old royal palace of Istana Kampong Gelam was built in the early 1840s by Sultan Ali Iskandar Shah on the site of his father Sultan Hussein's original wooden construction. Erected on stilts, the original building was styled after a Malay palace with a verandah on the upper floor. Restored in 2004, the palace has been converted into a Malay Heritage Centre with nine galleries chronicling Malay history and culture. Exhibits include artefacts unearthed during restoration, such as earthen pots and rifles belonging to World War II Malay soldiers.

There are daily cultural programmes at the centre as well as guided tours (prebooking is required).

Marina Bay City Gallery

11 Marina Bay Boulevard; tel: 6592 5336; www.marina-bay.sg ; Tues–Fri 10am–8pm, Sat–Sun 10am–9pm; free; MRT: Marina Bay or Bayfront; map p.139 E2

Find out how the reclaimed Marina Bay transformed into Singapore's centrepiece filled with a dazzling new waterfront, major attractions and financial centre. Look out for interactive exhibits in this two storey gallery.

Maritime Experiential Museum

8 Sentosa Gateway, Resorts World Sentosa; tel: 6577 8888; www.rwsentosa.com; Museum: Mon–Thu 10am–7pm, Fri–Sun 10am–9pm, Typhoon Theatre Mon–Thu 10am–6pm, Fri–Sun 10am–8pm; MRT: HarbourFront, then take the Sentosa Express from VivoCity and get off at Waterfront Station

The only museum in Singapore where you can discover the island's past as a trading port and experience Asia's rich maritime history.

There are life-sized ship replicas and don't miss Typhoon Theatre, where you'll get to 'board' a ship and experience a nasty storm.

SEE ALSO CHILDREN, P.38

Of interest to nature lovers is Labrador Nature Reserve's rich variety of flora and fauna, including the white-crested laughing thrush, the yellow-vented bulbul and the regal white-bellied sea eagle.

Memories at Old Ford Factory

351 Upper Bukit Timah Road; tel: 6332 8198; moff.nas.sg; Mon–Sat 9am–5.30pm, Sun 12pm–5.30pm; entrance charge; MRT: Bukit Batok, then bus 173

Opened in 1941 as the first Ford vehicle assembly plant in Southeast Asia, this building served as the venue for the formal surrender of Malaya by the British General Officer Commanding Malaya, Lt.-Gen. Arthur Ernest Percival, to the Japanese Commander of the 25th Army, Gen. Yamashita Tomoyuki.

Find out everything you've wanted to know about the Japanese Occupation as you walk through the gallery.

Mint Museum of Toys

26 Seah Street; tel: 6339 0660; www.emint.com; daily 9.30am–6.30pm; entrance charge; MRT: City Hall; map p.136 B2

A treasure trove of toys put together by a private collector, this is a definite draw for both adults and children. Rare collections of Popeye the Sailor, Felix the Cat and superheroes from Batman to Superman are lovingly kept in this museum across the street from the Raffles Hotel.

The museum is owned by Chang Yang Fa, who started collecting the toys when he was six years old. He has accumulated some 50,000 pieces, estimated to be worth S$5 million, from auctions and curio shops around the world.

Below: wax figures and British-built artillery at Fort Siloso.

85

National Museum of Singapore

93 Stamford Road; tel: 6332 3659; www.nationalmuseum.sg; Singapore History Gallery daily 10am–6pm, Singapore Living Galleries daily 10am–8pm; entrance charge; MRT: Dhoby Ghaut or City Hall; map p.136 A2

Billing itself as 'Singapore's oldest museum with the youngest and most innovative soul', the National Museum reopened in late 2006 after a three-year, S$132 million facelift, its Neo-Palladian and Renaissance architectural elements restored and its approaches to chronicling Singapore's history reinvigorated.

Stories of Singapore's history are told in the **Singapore History Gallery**; look out for the 11 national treasures, ranging from the Singapore Stone, a rock with inscriptions dating back to the 10th century, to 14th-century Majapahit gold ornaments excavated from Fort Canning Hill.

The **Singapore Living Galleries** celebrate the creativity of Singaporeans through the themes of food, fashion, film and photography. Past temporary exhibitions (separate charge) have included Greek masterpieces from the Louvre and paintings commissioned by the British Resident William Farquhar that record the flora and fauna of the region.

The museum also has a line-up of performing and visual arts programmes, as well as audio guides to help you discover its wonderful architectural details, including the 15-m- (49-ft-) high glass rotunda that illuminates like a lantern at night, with images that depict scenes from Singapore's history.

NUS Museums

National University of Singapore, 50 Kent Ridge Crescent; tel: 6516 8817; www.nus.edu.sg/cfa/museum/index.php; Tue–Sat 10am–7.30pm, Sun 10am–6pm; free; MRT: Clementi, then bus: 96

The NUS Museums feature three well-curated galleries. The impressive **Lee Kong Chian Art Museum**, named after the first Chancellor of the former University of Singapore, is noted for its collection of Chinese art spanning some 7,000 years of civilisation and culture. There are close to 4,000 pieces of art-

work, which include paintings and calligraphic works as well as ceramics, bronzes and sculptures. The **South and Southeast Asian Gallery** mirrors classical traditions as well as modern trends and comprises ceramics, textiles, sculpture and paintings. Be sure to stop at the **Ng Eng Teng Gallery**, which houses the sculptures of the late Ng Eng Teng, who was known for his whimsical renditions of the human form.

Peranakan Museum

39 Armenian Street; tel:6332 7591; www.peranakan museum.sg; Mon 1–7pm, Tue–Sun 9am–7pm; entrance charge; MRT: City Hall or Bras Basah

This one-of-a-kind museum takes pride of place in the beautiful former Tao Nan Chinese School building, constructed in 1912. It showcases the hybrid culture that has evolved through intermarriage between Chinese men and Malay women from the 17th century onwards. Galleries on three floors unveil the finest and most comprehensive collections of Peranakan culture and heritage.

red dot design museum

28 Maxwell Road; tel: 6327 8027; museum.red-dot.sg; Mon, Tue and Fri 11am–6pm, Sat, Sun 11am–8pm, open one Fri a month 5pm–12am; entrance charge; MRT: Tanjong Pagar; map p.138 C2

Located in the historical red dot Traffic building, this museum is the only one of its kind in Singapore and the second red dot design museum in the world (the first is in Germany), run by the German body that presents the prestigious red dot design award. Its stark, industrial-looking

Below: the Fashion Gallery at the National Museum.

Above: the red dot design museum is housed in the traffic-stopping-red red dot Traffic building.

On the first weekend of the month, the red dot design museum hosts MAAD, a weekend market that boasts original works by Singaporean designers. The market is curated by a committee of established artists and designers so only the most original and creative works are presented. Check www.maad.sg for details. *(See also Shopping, p.116)*

interior is a fittingly cool background to the interactive installations and exhibits of the slickest, most acclaimed products from around the world.

Reflections at Bukit Chandu

31-K Pepys Road; tel: 6375 2510; www.s1942.org.sg; Tue–Sun 9am–5pm; entrance charge; MRT: HarbourFront, then bus: 10, 30 or 143

This World War II site is dedicated to the heroes of the Malay Regiment, made up of the British, Australian and Malay soldiers, who fought 13,000 Japanese soldiers at the Battle of Pasir Panjang in 1942. Five galleries showcase artefacts and multimedia interactive shows and provide rich insight into the war, while the *Sounds of Battle* video in the theatre practically transports you onto the battlefield with realistic sound effects of machine-gun firing and human cries.

Royal Selangor Pewter Centre

01-01 3A, River Valley Road, Clarke Quay; tel: 6268 9600; www.royalselangor.com.sg; daily 9am–9pm; entrance charge; MRT: Clarke Quay; map p.135 E1

Get an introduction to pewter, an alloy made of copper, antimony and tin, by taking a tour of the collection of 75 pewterware pieces here. If what you see, from tobacco boxes to pewter-making tools, suitably impresses, take the School of Hard Knocks course to fashion your own pewter souvenir (separate charge).

Sculpture Square

155 Middle Road; tel: 6333 1055; www.sculpturesq.com.sg; Mon–Sat 11am–6pm; free; MRT: Bugis; map p.136 B3

The building was constructed in 1870 as a church and then a girls' school. Its chapel, with arch windows and circular vents, is one of the few Gothic-style buildings still standing in Singapore. It is now the pillar-free Chapel Gallery with a dramatic 9-m- (29.5-ft-) high ceiling.

Sculpture Square is the only space in Singapore solely devoted to contemporary three-dimensional art, with an active schedule of exhibitions all year round. Its shaded courtyard and cool garden are good spots to take a breather from the city.

Below: Ng Eng Teng Gallery exhibits at the NUS Museums.

Plan well and you could enjoy some museum visits free of charge or at a big discount. The Asian Civilisations Museum offers a discount on admission every Friday 7–9pm. The National Museum has free admission to the Singapore Living Galleries daily 6–8pm, while the Singapore Art Museum charges no admission 6–9pm on Friday. Check www.nhb. gov.sg for more details.

Singapore Art Museum

71 Bras Basah Road; tel: 6332 3222; www.singaporeart museum.sg; Mon–Sun 10am–7pm, Fri 10am–9pm; entrance charge; MRT: Dhoby Ghaut or City Hall; map p.136 A3

Institutional and private collectors in Singapore avidly amass art from the region, and the Singapore Art Museum is one of them. This powerhouse of 20th-century Southeast Asian art showcases an excellent sampling of works by the region's leading names, such as Affandi, Hendra Gunawan and Georgette Chen. It also ranks among the finest contemporary art museums in the region; past temporary exhibitions have included works from the Guggenheim Museum in New York and the Louvre in Paris.

The museum is housed in a colonial-era structure built in the early 1800s, which was formerly occupied by St Joseph's Institution, a school set up by missionaries. Even if not for the artworks, the museum is worth visiting just to see the splendidly restored chapel and the school hall, now called the Glass Hall. The latter features a colourful glass sculpture by American artist Dale Chihuly.

Singapore City Gallery

45 Maxwell Road, URA Centre; tel: 6321 8321; www.ura.gov.sg/

gallery or www.singaporecity gallery.sg; Mon–Sat 9am–5pm; free; MRT: Chinatown or Tanjong Pagar; map p.138 C2

If you've wondered about what makes this city tick, then a trip to this gallery to understand the city planners' work is in order. Its highlight is an enormous scaled and detailed 11x11-m (36x36-ft) architectural model of Singapore's central area. Spread over two storeys are the rest of the gallery's 50 exhibits, including a multimedia exhibit that charts Singapore's architectural development over the past 180 years. You can also survey the vision the planners have for this island in the 21st century.

Singapore Philatelic Museum

23B Coleman Street; tel: 6337 3888; www.spm.org.sg; Mon 1–7pm, Tue–Sun 9.30am–7pm; entrance charge; MRT: Clarke Quay or City Hall; map p.136 A2

This museum is housed in the former Anglo Chinese School, which was restored in 1995. Although small, the interactive museum has regular thematic exhibitions inspired by stamps, first-day covers and postcards. Peruse Singapore's early stamps and

stamp archival materials such as artworks and proofs.

Singapore Tyler Print Institute

41 Robertson Quay; tel: 6336 3663; www.stpi.com.sg; Tue–Sat 10am–6pm; free; MRT: Clarke Quay, then taxi; bus: 32, 54, 64, 123, 143, 139, 186 or 195; map p.135 D1

Housed in a restored 19th-century warehouse, this is dedicated to printmaking, papermaking and paper-based art. STPI collaborates with leading and emerging artists from around the world to explore new techniques and aesthetics of printmaking and to create works on paper. Artists who have worked and presented at the gallery include Donald Sultan (US), Zhu Wei (China), Liu Kuo-Sung (Taiwan), as well as local Chinese ink painter Chua Ek Kay, watercolourist Ong Kim Seng and photographer Russell Wong.

Sun Yat Sen Nanyang Memorial Hall

12 Tai Gin Road; tel: 6256 7377; www.wanqingyuan.org.sg/ENG/; Tue–Sun 9am–5pm; entrance charge; MRT: Novena, then bus: 21 or 131

Below: the Singapore Art Museum.

Right: the statue of Dr Sun Yat Sen in front of the Sun Yat Sen Nanyang Memorial Hall.

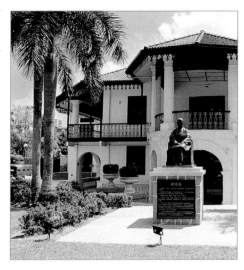

In 1906 Dr Sun Yat Sen, the leader of China's nationalist movement, arrived in Singapore to rally support for his cause among the overseas Chinese in Nanyang (meaning 'Southern Seas' in Chinese and referring to Southeast Asia). He was given a villa for his use, where he plotted the overthrow of the Qing dynasty. The bungalow later became known as the Sun Yat Sen Villa. It was the headquarters of the Singapore branch of the Kuomintang.

This two-storey Victorian-style bungalow, built in 1900, is now the Sun Yat Sen Nanyang Memorial Hall. Architecturally it represents a prevalent type of residence that existed in Singapore in the 19th century. A statue of Dr Sun sits in front of the building in the garden.

Six exhibition halls spread over two storeys feature exhibits such as a set of life-sized wax figures showing Dr Sun holding a secret meeting at the villa. Dr Sun's revolutionary activities in Southeast Asia are also told through some 400 photographs.

Art Galleries

Art-2 Gallery

01-03 Old Hill Street Police Station Building, 140 Hill Street; tel: 6338 8713; www.art2.com.sg; Mon–Sat 11am–7pm; MRT: Clarke Quay or City Hall; map p.136 A1

This focuses on sculptures, ceramics, paintings and prints from Singapore and around the region.

Art Forum

82 Cairnhill Road; tel: 6737 3448; www.artforum.com.sg; Mon–Sat 10am–6pm; MRT: Newton

Well-established gallery in an old-style shophouse, with a focus on contemporary Southeast Asian art.

Art Seasons Gallery

5 Gemmill Lane; tel: 6221 1800; http://artseasons.museum.com; Mon–Fri 11am–8pm, Sat noon–6pm; MRT: Chinatown; map p.139 C3

Concentrates on contemporary talents from China.

Gilman Barracks

9 Lock Road; www.gillmanbarracks.com; Tues–Sat 11am–8pm, Sun 10am–6pm (various opening times for various galleries, check website for info); free; MRT: Labrador Park

Formerly a military compound for the British army, this is now an up-and-coming contemporary art destination in Singapore. Set amid lush greenery, there are 13 local and international art galleries including Mizuma Gallery and Tomio Koyama Gallery from Japan and ShangART Gallery from China. They are housed in different buildings, so browse around and then have a bite at one of the food outlets. The Centre for Contemporary Art Singapore (CCA) will open here in 2013.

Night and Day

139 A/C Selegie Road; tel: 6884 5523; www.nightandday.sg; by appointment only; MRT: Dhoby Ghaut; map p. 136 A4

When Night and Day first started in 2007, artists and patrons were invited to 'vandalise' the walls with graffiti. It was founded as a platform for local artists to showcase their talent. There is also a chill-out bar on the second floor.

Opera Gallery

03-05 ION Orchard, 2 Orchard Turn; tel: 6735 2618; www.operagallery.com; Mon–Fri 11am–8pm, Sat–Sun 10am–8pm; MRT: Orchard; map p.134 C4

Arguably the best gallery in Singapore to view paintings by 19th-century European masters.

Soobin Art International

04-90/95 Ubi Techpark Lobby E, 10 Ubi Crescent; tel: 6837 2777; www.soobinart.com.sg; Mon–Sat 11am–6pm; MRT: Paya Lebar then taxi; map 136 A1

Soobin is especially strong in contemporary Chinese works. Artists who have shown here previously include Shen Xiaotong and Yue Minjun.

89

Music

With its small domestic market and local musicians competing with international acts from the US and the UK, Singapore does not have a big contemporary music scene, although indie bands such as Electrico and The Observatory are quietly thriving. Classical music, introduced by Europeans in the 19th century, has managed to gain a healthy following over the years, while the island's jazz scene is enlivened by first-rate jazz bars graced by visiting international musicians. Meanwhile, annual music festivals like Baybeats and Mosaic have become destination events.

Classical and Opera

The **Singapore Symphony Orchestra** (SSO), the country's first professional orchestra, was formed in 1979. Its repertoire tends to be mainstream, with most concerts comprising standard works. But the works of many Asian composers have also been given a fair share of airing, and naturally, local musicians and the works of Singaporean composers feature prominently in its seasons too.

SSO performs over 50 symphonic concerts a year, both in Singapore and around the world, and also holds free outdoor concerts in parks such as the Singapore Botanic Gardens.

Aiming to break new ground by extending classical music to a wider audience is the **T'ang Quartet**. Not your usual classical musicians, these four lads are hip and adventurous when it comes to programming, including contemporary and Asian works as well as chamber favourites in their repertoire. The quartet has performed in community events and schools besides formal concert halls, and has been lauded internationally. *The Boston Globe* called it 'astounding' and *The Times*

praised its 'enthusiasm, energy and commitment'.

Opera was largely performed by visiting international companies until 1991, when the **Singapore Lyric Opera** was formed. It performs one to two works per year.

Classical Venues

Esplanade Concert Hall
Esplanade – Theatres on the Bay, 1 Esplanade Drive; tel: 6828 8377; www.esplanade.com; MRT: City Hall/Esplanade; map p.136 B1
This 1,600-seat hall offers exceptional acoustics. SSO plays its regular season here.
SEE ALSO ARCHITECTURE, P.27; DANCE, P.47; THEATRE, P.121
Shaw Foundation Symphony Stage
Singapore Botanic Gardens, 1 Cluny Road; tel: 6471 7138; www.sbg.org.sg; MRT: Botanic Gardens
This floating amphitheatre on Symphony Lake offers open-air concerts of various genres, from jazz and Latin to classical and pop. The audience sit by the

Below: the T'ang Quartet is breaking new ground.

Left: live performance at Singapore Mosaic Festival.

The Harry's chain of bars has various locations around the city. There is live music here as well as at the Boat Quay outlet (tel: 6538 3029), which is packed to the rafters every day. The band ChromaZone performs Thursday to Saturday. Sunday sees fantastic jam sessions.

The Sultan Jazz Club
2F Sultan Hotel, 101 Jalan Sultan; tel: 6723 7117; www.sultanjazzclub.com;
Tues–Sun 9pm–1am;
MRT: Bugis
Located in Sultan Hotel in the Kampong Glam conservation area, this venue sees local and international jazz singers performing, and the weekly Sunday jam session is worth a visit too.

Music Stores

HMV
04-23/24 313@Somerset, 313 Orchard Road; tel: 6733 1822; www.hmv.com.sg;
MRT: Somerset; map p.135 D3
The largest music shop in Singapore stocks just about every genre of music.
(Also at 02-323 Marina Square, 6 Raffles Boulevard;
tel: 6238 7218.)

Straits Records
24 Bali Lane; mobile tel: 9681 6341; MRT: Bugis; map p.136 C3
Local music gets great support here. There is also a good collection of indie, hip hop and other alternative genres.

That CD Shop
02-10/15 Pacific Plaza, 9 Scotts Road; tel: 6238 7254; MRT: Orchard; map p.134 B1
Jazz, lounge and chill-out tunes get plenty of airplay here. (Also at B1-87/88 Raffles City; tel: 6336 5885 and B1-01 Great World City; tel: 6738 0894.)

---

water's edge.
Singapore Conference Hall
7 Shenton Way; tel: 6557 4019; www.sch.org.sg; MRT: Tanjong Pagar; map p.139 C1
This mainly hosts concerts by Singapore's only professional Chinese orchestra, the Singapore Chinese Orchestra.

Contemporary Venues

SEE ALSO NIGHTLIFE, P.97

Jazz Venues

Crazy Elephant
01-03/04 3E River Valley Road, Clarke Quay; tel: 6337 7859; www.crazyelephant.com; Sun–Thur 5pm–2am, Fri–Sat 5pm–3am, shows Sun 10pm; MRT: Clarke Quay;

Above: the Shaw Foundation Symphony Stage in the Singapore Botanic Gardens.

map p.135 E1
Its blues-crazy patrons include big names like Deep Purple and Robbie Williams. Live bands perform nightly, with a mix of blues and rock taking centre-stage. Sundays are for free jam sessions.

Harry's@The Esplanade
01-05/07 Esplanade Mall, 8 Raffles Avenue; tel: 6344 0132; www.harrys.com.sg; Mon–Thur noon–1am, Fri–Sat noon–2am, Sunday noon–1am; MRT: City Hall/Esplanade; map p.136 B1

Nightlife

In the last few years, Singapore's nightlife scene has undergone a remarkable transformation. No longer bland and boring, as was once the common description, it is now hip and happening. Whether it is a night of pub-crawling or one of non-stop dancing you are searching for, the options are plentiful. There are chill-out bars set in balmy alfresco locales, roof-top bars with stunning views, chic lounges for design-conscious partiers, bars and pubs with world-class bands performing nightly, and dance clubs that have been called some of the best in the world.

Bars and Pubs

Balaclava Live
05 02 Orchard ION (entrance through 5th level car park); tel: 6634 8377; www.imaginings. com.sg; Mon–Thu 5pm–1am, Fri–Sat 5pm–2am; MRT: Orchard; map p.134 B4
Relocated from Suntec City, Balaclava Live continues to offer great drinks, bar food and live music by resident band Shagies.

Bar Opiume
1 Empress Place, Asian Civilisa-tions Museum; tel: 6339 2876; www.indochine.com.sg;

Mon–Thur 5pm–2am, Fri–Sat 5pm–3am, Sun 5pm–1am; MRT: Raffles Place; map p.139 D4
Located at the Asian Civilisations Museum, this prosecco and vodka bar draws a hip crowd with its spacious interior and huge terrace. Ideal for taking in the shimmering CBD skyline and watching the river boats go by.

Bar Stories
55/57A Haji Lane; tel: 6298 0838; Mon–Thurs 3pm–1am, Fri–Sat 3pm–2am, Sun 3pm–1am;

MRT: Rugis;
map p.136 C3
If you prefer to ensconce yourself in the hip Haji Lane, away from the pulsing club-bing spots, head to this quirky bar above a furniture store. Soak in the charm of this Arab quarter and sip specially concocted

Left: crowds pack the bar at trendy KPO.

Night spots are scattered all over the island, but there are a few key areas where you could spend an entire night hopping from one venue to another. Along the Singapore River, there are bars and pubs at **Boat Quay** and more fashionable options at **Clarke Quay**. **Robertson Quay** has plenty of watering holes and some clubs. **Orchard Road** is rife with classy hotel bars, while **Emerald Hill** offers charming pubs that draw creative types. In **Tanglin Village** are trendy alfresco bars and clubs in colonial-era bungalows.

mojitos, martinis and caipirinhas.

Brewerkz Restaurant and Microbrewery
01-05/06 Riverside Point, 30 Merchant Road; tel: 6438 7438; www.brewerkz.com; Mon–Thu, Sun noon–midnight, Fri–Sat noon–1am; MRT: Clarke Quay; map p.138 C4

Handcrafted beer fresh from its onsite microbrewery and hearty American cuisine in an industrial-like setting. A brewmaster creates seven varieties of beer, including the bestselling India Pale Ale. There are also interesting seasonable beers. Try the mussels with beer sauce.

Ice Cold Beer
9 Emerald Hill Road; tel: 6735 9929; www.emeraldhillgroup. com; Sun–Thur 5pm–2am, Fri–Sat noon–3am; MRT: Somerset; map p.135 D4
The name says it all – this is the place to savour a variety of ice-cold beers. Their jumbo-sized hot dogs are the perfect accompaniment.

Jigger & Pony
101 Amoy Street; tel: 6223 9101; www.jiggerandpony.com; Mon–Thu 6pm–1am, Fri–Sat 6pm–3am; MRT: Raffles Place; map p.139 C3
Another small bar that attracts a large crowd. Jigger & Pony pays tribute to great classic cocktails of the 19th

century, but its impressive list of 24 cocktails also includes some modern concoctions. The team ensures that quality ingredients and premium spirits are used and topped with meticulous Japanese bartending techniques.

Kazbar
01-03 Capital Square 3, 25 Church Street; tel: 6438 2975; www.kazbar.com; Mon–Fri noon–1am, Sat 5.30pm–1am; MRT: Raffles Place; map p.139 C3
Popular with oil traders and advertising types, this stylish lounge is decked in Middle Eastern style with cosy alcoves and a tented divan. Knock back a Kazbar Special cocktail and dine on authentic Moroccan cuisine.

KPO
1 Killiney Road; tel: 6733 3648; www.imaginings.com.sg; Mon–Thu 3pm–1am, Fri–Sat 3pm–2am; MRT: Somerset; map p.135 D3
So named because it sits on the junctions of Killiney, Penang and Orchard roads.

Far left: Lantern. **Near left:** KU DÉ TA.

It is also housed in the premises of the Killiney post office. Its glass walls and steel architecture draw sophisticated yuppies. This two-storey bar feels like a modern home and boasts a balcony where one can watch the traffic go by with a cold drink in hand.

KU DÉ TA

L57-01 North Sky Park Marina Bay Sands, 10 Bayfront Ave; tel: 6688 7688; www.marinabay sands.com; Mon–Tues, Thurs–Fri noon–1am, Wed, Sat–Sun noon–2am; MRT: Marina Bay or Bayfront; map p.139 E3

Perched on top of Marina Bay Sand's SkyPark, the highlight at KU DÉ TA has to be its 360 degree view of the city's amazing skyline. It consists of a restaurant with a breezy open-air bar, a club lounge and a poolside terrace. Order cocktails, wines and Modern Asian bites and soak in the view, or join the trendy set at the dance floor.

Lantern

The Fullerton Bay Hotel, 80 Collyer Quay; tel: 6597 5299; www.fullertonbayhotel.com; Sun–Thu 8am–1am, Fri–Sat 8am–2am; MRT: Raffles Place; map p.139 D3

This chic and sexy rooftop bar by the hotel pool is great on balmy evenings. Munch on gourmet snacks, sip champagne and enjoy the gorgeous view of Marina Bay.

Level 33

33-01 Marina Bay Financial Centre Tower 1, 8 Marina Boulevard; tel: 6834 3133; www.level33.com.sg; Sun–Thu noon–midnight, Fri–Sat noon–2am; MRT: Raffles Place; map p.139 D2

The world's highest urban craft brewery serving freshly brewed beer and hearty sharing platters. Executives head up after work to take in the stunning views of Marina Bay and the city's skyline.

Loof

03-07 Odeon Towers Extension Rooftop, 331 North Bridge Road; tel: 6338 8035; www.loof.com.sg; Mon–Thur 5pm–1am, Fri–Sat 5pm–3am; MRT: City Hall; map p.136 B2

This playful rooftop bar attracts a laid-back crowd. Lounge around amidst lush foliage, and sip Southeast Asian inspired cocktails. Local bar bites are served too.

Molly Malone's

56 Circular Road, Boat Quay; tel: 6536 2029; www.mollymalone.com; Mon 11am–midnight, Tues–Sat 11am– 2am; MRT: Raffles Place; map p.139 C4

Like a scene straight out of Dublin, this offers Guinness and Kilkenny on tap, as well as decent pub grub and foot-stomping Irish music.

One Rochester

1 Rochester Park, off Buona Vista Road; tel: 6773 0070; www.onerochester.com; Mon–Thu 6pm–11pm, Fri–Sat 6pm–12.30am, Sat–Sun 10.30am–4.30pm (brunch); MRT: Buona Vista

Set in a black-and-white colonial-era bungalow, this has four rooms with individual themes: a living room, play room, library and bar. The action happens mainly outside on the deck. Choose from over 200 bottles of wine, a list of sakes, martinis and lovely bar food.

Orgo

04-01 Roof Terrace, Esplanade–Theaters on the Bay, 8 Raffles Avenue; tel: 6336 9366; www.orgo.sg; daily 6pm–2am; MRT: Esplanade; map p.139 E4

Set on the roof terrace of Esplanade, Orgo is a chill-out gem offering lovely views of sunsets. A highlight here

Right: a slice of the Middle East at Kazbar.

is the Japanese master mixologist who concocts original martinis using fresh ingredients such as peaches, chillies and shiso leaves.

Tanjong Beach Club
120 Tanjong Beach Walk; tel: 6270 1355; www.tanjongbeach-club.com; Tues–Fri 11am–11pm, Sat–Sun 10am–midnight; MRT: HarbourFront, then Sentosa Express from VivoCity

A superb place to unwind by the beach. Special cocktails feature local ingredients. Try the Tanjong Sling made of vodka, elderflower cordial, lychee, kaffir lime and fresh ginger. Check out the full moon party held three times a year.
SEE ALSO BEACHES AND ISLANDS, P.34

The Wine Company @ Dempsey
Block 14D Dempsey Road, Tanglin Village; tel: 6479 9341; www.thewinecompany.com.sg; Mon–Thur 3pm–midnight, Fri 3pm–1am, Sat noon–1am, Sun noon–11pm; MRT: Orchard, then taxi; bus: 7, 105, 123 or 174

Hidden away in an old army barracks, this has a wonderfully cosy courtyard where guests can eat and drink under the stars. Excellent South African wines.

Clubs

Attica/Attica Too
01-03 Clarke Quay, 3A River Valley Road; tel: 6333 9973; www.attica.com.sg; Attica: Sun–Tue 5pm–2am, Wed, Fri, Sat 5pm–3am; Attica Too: Fri–Sat 11pm–6am; MRT: Clarke Quay; map p.135 E1

The cool and gorgeous congregate at Attica's lush, open courtyard with a fountain to groove to Latin, jazz and funk. At Attica Too upstairs, the sound is

Above: the exclusive Avalon.

more Euro-trashy, with a crowd to match.

Avalon
B2-05 South Crystal Pavilion, Marina Bay Sands, 2 Bayfront Avenue; tel: 6688 7448; www.avalon.sg; Wed, Fri, Sat, Sun 10pm–6am; MRT: Marina Bay or Bayfront; map p.139 E3

One of the latest glitzy party hotspots in town where you can potentially rub shoulders with high profile celebrities.

> Singaporeans love happy hour (usually 5–9pm) when establishments offer drinks at deep discounts. But if you want truly cheap beer, head to a hawker centre or *kopitiam* (basic coffee shop), where you can drink local and imported beers and ales for a song.

Housed in the Crystal Pavilion on the waters of Marina Bay, the mega club offers a two-level nightclub experience with state-of-the-art lighting and sound. Look out for world-class music acts such as Ludacris, Steve Aoki and The Chemical Brothers.

Butter Factory
02-02/03/04 One Fullerton, 1 Fullerton Road; tel: 6333 8243; www.thebutterfactory.com; Wed 10pm–4am, Thur 10pm–3am, Fri–Sat 10pm–5am; MRT: Raffles Place; map p.135 D1

This imaginative party spot combines cutting edge electronic music, design, art and fashion. The dance floor is fashioned as a 'swimming pool' complete with life

95

Above: the Post Bar is popular with Raffles Place suits.

buoys and ladders. Expect to see celebs, models and other beautiful people among the civilian jeans-and-tee clubbers.

Mink
GF Pan Pacific Singapore, 7 Raffles Boulevard; tel: 6734 0205; Wed 10pm–4am, Fri–Sat 10pm–5am; MRT Promenade
Mingle and sip champagne with the well-heeled and jetsetters at this luxurious club/lounge which offers plush private booths, dance podiums and premium bottle service. Access the venue through the rear exit of The Royal Room just next door. Look out for theme nights featuring pole dancers, live musicians and vocalists.

Pangaea
B2-05 Crystal Pavilion South, Marina Bay Sands, 10 Bayfront Ave; tel: 6688 7448; www.pangaea.sg; Wed–Sat 10pm–dawn; MRT Marina Bay
This Ultra-Lounge, by founder Michael Ault, has outlets in New York City, Miami, London and Spain. Make your way to the exclusive club via the underwater tunnel connected to The Shoppes at Marina Bay

Sands. Besides resident and international DJs who entertain the crowd, look forward to exciting parties that attract the ultra-hip set. Special drinks are injected with fresh ingredients and local flavours.

St James Power Station
3 Sentosa Gateway; tel: 6270 7676; www.stjamespowerstation.com; opening hours vary for different venues; MRT: HarbourFront
There are more than a dozen concept venues in this huge former power station. The main space is the **Powerhouse**, a hip dance club, while **Bossa Movida** features Brazilian music in Bossa Nova style by Banda Morena, and the **Bellini Room** serves jazz and martinis. The **Gallery Bar** has a bird's-eye view of the other outlets.

Zouk/Velvet Underground
Jiak Kim Street; tel: 6738 2988; www.zoukclub.com; Zouk: Wed and Fri–Sat 10pm–late, Velvet Underground: 9pm–late; MRT: Clarke Quay, then taxi; bus: 16 or 195; map p.135 C1
Zouk is one of Singapore's most enduring clubs with regular appearances by guest

www.e-clubbing.com offers news, reviews and forums on some of the best clubs in Singapore.

celebrity DJs. Its brand of trance and techno is always a hit with the younger crowd, while the adjoining **Velvet Underground** caters to a more mature audience. It is widely regarded as one of the best dance clubs in the world.

Hotel Bars
eM by the River
01-05 The Gallery Hotel, 1 Nanson Road; tel: 6836 9691; www.em-n-em.com; Mon–Thur 9am–2am, Fri 9am–3am, Sat 8am–3am, Sun 8am–2am; MRT: Clarke Quay, then taxi; bus: 51, 64, 123 or 186; map p.135 D1
From breakfast till supper, sit alfresco and enjoy the breeze and riverside views at this chilled-out bar. Pair your drinks with savoury bar snacks.

Martini Bar
Grand Hyatt, 10 Scotts Road; tel: 6738 1234; www.singapore.grand.hyatt.com; daily noon–2am; MRT: Orchard; map p.134 B1
Located in the **mezza9** restaurant, this glass-walled space is great for pre- or post-prandial drinks. There are over 30 handcrafted martinis, which guests can enjoy on a sumptuous sofa or at the bar overlooking Scotts Road.
SEE ALSO HOTELS, P.73; RESTAURANTS, P.108

New Asia Bar
71/F, Swissôtel The Stamford, 2 Stamford Road; tel: 9177 7307; www.newasiabar.com.sg; Wed–Thu 3pm–2am, last Thurs of the month 3pm–4am, Fri–Sat

Right: live music at Timbre.

3pm–3am, Sun–Tues 3pm–1am;
MRT: City Hall; map p.136 B2
Located on the 71st floor of
the Swissôtel, this venue
draws affluent locals, expats
and business travellers with
its spectacular views and
happy-hour prices. The
weekday crowd tends to
gather during happy hour (3–
9pm), while on weekends,
the vibe is clubby with some
action on the small dance
floor. International guest DJs
are showcased on the last
Thursday of every month.
SEE ALSO HOTELS, P.72

Post Bar
The Fullerton Hotel, 1 Fullerton
Square; tel: 6877 8135; www.
fullertonhotel.com; Mon–Fri
noon–2am, Sat 5pm–2am, Sun
3pm–2am; MRT: Raffles Place;
map p.139 D4
Famous for the city's best
caipirinha, this is all trendy
chic with its high ceilings and
beige décor. A sophisticated
crowd, mostly from the CBD,
plies the room, where drinks
are pricey (try the signature
Fullerton Sling) and the dress
code is elegant.
SEE ALSO HOTELS, P.70

Live Music

The Arena
01-08 Clarke Quay, 3B River

Right: Singapore is shaking off
its staid image and boasts some
great dance clubs.

Valley Road; tel: 6338 3158;
www.thearenalive.com.sg;
Tue–Sat 10pm–4am; MRT:
Clarke Quay; map
p.135 E1
This R&B, hip hop club
keeps the music fresh by
changing its headline live act
every two months. Besides
resident DJs, the venue has
hosted international bands
from the US, UK, Australia
and Asia.

Timbre @ Substation
45 Armenian Street; tel: 6338
8030; www.timbre.com.sg;
Mon–Thu, Sun 6pm–1am,
Fri–Sat 6pm–2.30am; MRT: City
Hall; map p.136 A2
An atmospheric nook set in
the garden of The Substa-
tion arts centre, overhung
with trees. This is one of the
best places to hear local
musicians, who take to the
stage nightly. The food
and drinks aren't half bad
either. So popular is this
original Timbre that there
are now four more Singa-
pore outlets, including
Timbre Mobile which
changes its location every
four months.

Wala Wala Café Bar
31 Lorong Mambong, Holland
Village; tel: 6462 4288;
www.imaginings.com.sg;
Mon–Thur 4pm–1am, Fri
4pm–2am, Sat 3pm–2am,
Sun 3pm–1am;
MRT: Buona Vista
A renowned name in
Singapore for high quality
live music. This laid-back
café bar has local rock,
pop-rock and acoustic
bands and musicians
playing nightly.

Pampering

It is sometimes said that Singaporeans are not the most stylish bunch. Say what you like about their sartorial sense, but when it comes to looking good, Singaporeans are big spenders. There are hardly any home-grown beauty and skincare brands; imported labels dominate the beauty counters in department stores. Beauty salons and slimming centres are around every corner, as are all manner of spas – big, boutique, luxury, budget, traditional, modern, Javanese, Thai – you name it, this city probably has it. Aesthetic and medical spas are also popular, especially in the age of non-invasive cosmetic surgery.

Spas

Amrita Spa & Wellness
Swissôtel Merchant Court, 20 Merchant Road; tel: 6239 1780; www.swissotel.com/hotels/singapore-merchant-court/spa-fitness/amrita-spa-wellness/; daily 10am–10pm; MRT: Clarke Quay; map p.138 C4
With eight spacious treatment rooms, a fitness centre, a manicure station, a landscaped garden and a freeform pool. The menu is extensive; when in doubt, simply go for a signature Spa Ritual package.

Aramsa Garden Spa
Bishan Park II, 1382 Ang Mo Kio Avenue 1; tel: 6456 6556; www. aramsaspas.com; Mon–Thu 11am–10pm, Fri–Sun 10am–11pm; MRT: Ang Mo Kio, then taxi or bus: 133, 136 or 262, or MRT: Bishan, then bus: 410
The only spa that's set amid the lush greenery of a park. Its individual spa suites are beautifully appointed and some even have sunken bathtubs in private gardens. Try the 2.5-hour Botanical Energy Package that includes a floral exfoliation, re-mineralising mud therapy and shiatsu focus massage.

Espa
Resorts World Sentosa, 8 Sentosa Gateway; tel: 6577 8880; www.rwsentosa.com/language/en-US/Homepage/ThingsToDo/FSPA; MRT: HarbourFront, then the Sentosa shuttle bus from VivoCity
This sprawling spa includes treatment pavilions, private beach villas and garden spa suites. Try Singapore's first Turkish Hammam, rock saunas, or choose from the menu of natural therapies.

St Gregory
5/F, Marina Mandarin, 6 Raffles Boulevard; tel: 6845 1161; www.stgregoryspa.com; daily 10am–10pm; MRT: City Hall/Esplanade; map p.136 B1
The only spa in Singapore to be awarded Leading Spa status by Leading Hotels of the World. It also houses the sole mineral-water swimming pool in the country. Try the Traditional Chinese Tui Na Massage.

Spa Botanica
The Sentosa, 2 Bukit Manis Road, Sentosa; tel: 6371 1318; www.spabotanica.com; daily 10am–10pm; MRT: HarbourFront, then the Sentosa shuttle bus from VivoCity
Hidden away from the rigours

Below: meditating in the Spa Botanica's labyrinth.

Left: water therapy – enjoy a relaxing outdoor rainforest shower at the Aramsa Spa.

03-17 Mandarin Gallery, 333A Orchard Road; tel: 6734 6038; www.hollywoodsecrets.com.sg; daily 9am–9pm; MRT: Somerset; map p.135 C4

This chain of one-stop beauty centres offers everything under one roof – manicures, pedicures, hair services, facial treatments and photography. The service is always good.

Pacific Specialist Practice
20-01 The Paragon, 290 Orchard Road; tel: 6887 1288; www.pac healthholdings.com; call for appointment; MRT: Orchard; map p.135 C4

The who's who of Singapore's society come here for their non-invasive aesthetic treatments. There's everything from mesotherapy to obstetrics and gynaecology services. And if you are shy about the fact that you are getting 'work done', discreet alcoves in the waiting room ensure you won't be easily spotted.

SK-II Boutique Spa by Senze Salus
31 Scotts Road; tel: 6836 9168; www.senzesalus.com; Mon–Fri 10am–9pm, Sat–Sun 10am– 7pm; MRT: Newton

The SK-II brand of skincare from Japan enjoys a huge following in Singapore. This spin-off face spa utilises the powers of its product range in pampering facials set in an elegant black-and-white colonial-era house. Many women emerge from here swearing the results are immediately evident.

Although known for spices and saris, Little India is also a beauty hub with boutiques offering everything from henna tattoos to Ayurvedic massage to the ancient beauty art of threading.

Late-night spas are starting to gain ground in Singapore. **Spa Lifestyle Inc** (www.spalifestyleinc.com), tucked away in the trendy Siglap neighbourhood, stays open until 2am. **Aramsa – The Garden Spa** *(see left),* set in an idyllic park in Bishan, opens until 11pm from Fridays to Sundays.

of everyday life, Spa Botanica offers back-to-nature luxury, surrounded by verdant greenery. There are private Balinese-style pavilions, a mud pool and a labyrinth where you can literally get lost in thought. Choose from a large menu of treatments including Tibetan oil and clay massages and aromatherapy facials.

Spa Esprit at Paragon
290 Orchard Road, 05-10 Paragon; tel: 6836 0500; www.spa-esprit.com; daily 10am–9pm; MRT: Orchard; map p.135 C4

Therapeutic grade essential oils are used here, with four distinct blends created especially to calm, revitalise, invigorate and ground your senses. Also has a branch at Dempsey

Road (tel: 6479 0070).

Willow Stream Spa
80 Bras Basah Road, Fairmont Singapore; tel: 6339 7777; www.fairmont.com/singapore/willow-stream/; daily 9am–10pm; MRT: City Hall

Authentic and energising spa treatments are what you will get here. Opt for a session in one of its 35 treatment rooms, including three couples suites, with private jacuzzi and aromatherapy steam room.

Beauty
Hollywood Secrets

Below: the float pool with waterfalls at the Spa Botanica.

Parks and Gardens

For an urban jungle, Singapore has plenty of green space – excellent respites from the assaults of city life. Then again, Singapore isn't called the Garden City for nothing. Seeing one park a day during your visit could be a nice way to unwind after a day of indulging in the trappings of the city. Larger parks like Gardens by the Bay and the Botanic Gardens can be explored over an entire morning, while smaller ones like the Mandai Orchid Garden can be tail-end stops to stock up on exotic souvenirs.

Chinese Garden

1 Chinese Garden Road; tel: 6261 3632; main garden daily 6am–11pm, free; Bonsai Garden and Garden of Abundance daily 9am–6pm; MRT: Chinese Garden

This is a collection of theme gardens in the style of the Summer Palace in Beijing. The lovely twin pagodas afford nice views of the lake. Another attraction here is the Garden of Abundance, a Suzhou-style *penjing* (bonsai) garden with more than 1,000 bonsai, including a pair of 200-year-old *Podocarpus* trees shaped like lions. A good time to visit the garden is September/October, when it is lit at night by pretty lanterns for the **Mid Autumn Festival** celebrations.

SEE ALSO FESTIVALS & EVENTS, P.58

Fort Canning Park

Canning Rise; tel: 1800-471 7300; www.nparks.gov.sg; free; MRT: City Hall or Dhoby Ghaut; map p.136 A2

Once known as Bukit Larangan (Forbidden Hill), this was the site of grand palaces, protected by high walls and swamps. Raffles built his residence here in 1822 and renamed it Government Hill. He chose the location for its good vantage to watch enemy movements at sea. It was later renamed Fort Canning after Viceroy Canning of India. In 1860 the British built a fort on the hill.

This lovely oasis is today a historical park with well-marked trails. Its two Gothic-style gates lead to the old cemetery used from 1823 to 1867, which was exhumed in 1970. The park also holds an older tomb said to contain the remains of Iskandar Shah, the last ruler of pre-colonial Singapore. It has been consecrated as a Muslim shrine.

Gardens by the Bay

18 Marina Gardens Drive; tel: 6420 6848; www.gardensbythebay.com.sg; Bay South Outdoor Gardens daily 5am–2am free, Conservatories daily 9am–9pm; Supertree Grove daily 5am–2am free; OCBC Skyway daily 9am–9pm; MRT: Marina Bay or Bayfront; map p.139 E2

The most iconic structures at Gardens by the Bay are the

Above: remains of the old gates at Fort Canning Park.

two conservatories: Flower Dome and Cloud Forest. The former replicates the cool-dry climate of Mediterranean regions. Walk around in 22 degree C and smell the flowers, herbs and plants. The Cloud Forest boasts the world's tallest indoor waterfall, tropical plants, and a 35-metre-tall mountain covered in lush vegetation. Outdoors, more than a dozen of the towering Supertrees (up to 16 storeys high) offer shade in the day and glittering light displays at night. Walk along the OCBC Skyway which connects two of the Supertrees and enjoy views of the lush area. Other attractions here include the Heritage Gardens that tell you how the plants of

Left: Supertree Grove at Gardens by the Bay.

www.sbg.org.sg; daily 5am–midnight; free; MRT: Botanic Gardens Station

Singapore's oldest park, set up in 1859, this renowned living museum of tropical plants is home to over 2,000 species of trees and shrubs, which have been integrated into the beautiful 52-hectare (129-acre) landscape. This is one of the two primary forests left in the city – Bukit Timah Nature Reserve *(see p.128)* is the other.

The main **Tanglin Core** features a lake with swans, an 1860s bandstand and bronze sculptures by Sydney Harpley. The **Central Core** has the **National Orchid Garden** (daily 8.30am–7pm; entrance charge) with over 1,000 orchid species, and the **Palm Valley** with the **Symphony Lake**, where regular concerts are held. The **Bukit Timah Core** is home to the Eco Lake and spice gardens. Parents will welcome the **Jacob Ballas Children's Garden** (Tues–Sun 8am–7pm; free).

The open-air café **Casa Verde** is a lovely spot for a bite, and the fine dining **Au Jardin** is one of the most established French restaurants in Singapore.

SEE ALSO CHILDREN, P.36; MUSIC, P.90; RESTAURANTS, P.108

the island are linked to its culture. Bay East Garden is where you should go for some serenity and amazing views of the Marina Bay skyline.

Kranji Commonwealth War Cemetery

9 Woodlands Road; tel: 6269 6158; daily 7am–6pm; free; MRT: Kranji

This peaceful park honours the men from Britain, Australia, Canada, India, Malaya, New Zealand and other commonwealth countries who died in World War II. Marked graves of 4,000 servicemen stand in neat rows. Another 24,000 names of soldiers whose bodies were never recovered are inscribed on 12 columns.

Mandai Orchid Garden

200 Mandai Lake Road; tel: 6269 1036; www.mandai.com. sg; Mon 8am–6pm, Tue–Sun 8am–7pm; MRT: Ang Mo Kio, then bus: 138 or MRT: Choa Chu Kang, then bus: 927

Set on a hillside, this lush garden has a fine display of colourful orchids. Visitors can make their selections to take away, boxed for their flights.

Padang

In front of City Hall, across St Andrew's Road; free; MRT: City Hall; map p.136 B1

This well-manicured lawn was the focal point of the colonials. Flannelled cricketers played here and the British took a turn on cool evenings in their horse-drawn carriages, gossiping at 'Scandal Point'. After the Japanese captured Singapore in 1942, European civilians were rounded up here and marched to Changi Prison. Now the Padang serves as the venue of myriad sporting and national events.

Singapore Botanic Gardens

1 Cluny Road; tel: 6471 7361;

Below: blooms at the Mandai Orchid Garden.

Restaurants

What can be said about Singaporeans and eating that hasn't already been said? With the kind of gastronomic culture this island enjoys, it is no surprise that there are restaurants around every corner, each as lauded as the other. This section gives a round-up of the many eateries in the city, offering names that consistently serve great food at various price points. Included are some of the best fine-dining restaurants in Singapore's hotels, acclaimed culinary addresses helmed by innovative restaurateurs and chefs, and decades-old family eateries beloved by Singaporeans.

Singapore River

FRENCH

Absinthe

71/72 Boat Quay; tel: 6222 9068; www.absinthe.sg; Mon–Fri noon–2.30pm and daily 6.30–11pm; $$ (set lunch) $$$$ (à la carte); MRT: Raffles Place; map p.139 D4

This elegant French restaurant relocated from its original location at Bukit Pasoh to Boat Quay. Chef Francois Mermilliod continues to attract his regulars with well-executed and unassuming French fare. The wine list is predominantly French. Ask the sommelier for wine recommendations.

FUSION

Coriander Leaf

02-03 Block 3A Merchant's Court, River Valley Road; tel: 6732 3354; www.corianderleaf.com; Mon–Fri noon–2pm and 6.30–10pm, Sat 6.30–10.30pm; $$$; MRT: Clarke Quay; map p.135 E1

The pan-Asian and Mediterranean menu is given a creative Western spin. Try the mezze platter and the spice-rubbed rack of lamb. Runs cookery classes as well.

SEE ALSO FOOD AND DRINK, P.65

INDIAN

Kinara

57 Boat Quay; tel: 6533 0412; www.thekinaragroup.com; daily noon–2.30pm and 6–11pm; $$; MRT: Raffles Place; map p.139 D4

Warm, friendly staff serve hearty North Indian cuisine in a beautiful space decorated with antique furniture from Rajasthan. The roasted leg of lamb, marinated for over 24 hours, is a must-try.

SPANISH

Catalunya

The Fullerton Pavilion, 82 Collyer Quay; tel: 6534 0188; www.catalunya.sg; daily noon–2am; $$$$; MRT: Raffles Place or Marina Bay; map p.139 D3

The former culinary team of elBulli arrived on Singapore's shores to set up this fabulous

Below: chinoiserie-chic at Peach Blossoms.

Prices for a three-course dinner per person without drinks and taxes:
$$$$ = S$60 and above
$$$ = S$40–$60
$$ = S$20–$40
$ = under S$20

Left: dine amid the lush greenery of the Botanic Gardens at Au Jardin.

Hall; map p.136 C1

This stalwart offers fine Cantonese cuisine prepared by an experienced Hong Kong chef. The business crowd entertain here for weekday lunch, and families flock here for dim sum buffet on weekends.

Summer Pavilion

The Ritz-Carlton, Millenia Singapore, 7 Raffles Avenue; tel: 6337 8888; www.ritzcarlton.com; daily 11.30am–2.30pm and 6.30–10pm; $$$$; MRT: Promenade; map p.137 C1

An elegant restaurant that overlooks a peaceful garden setting. Noteworthy Cantonese specialities include baked marinated silver cod fish with champagne sauce and poached fish noodles soup with lobster. The creative dim sum is worth trying too.

SEE ALSO HOTELS, P.71

INDIAN

Rang Mahal

3/F, Pan Pacific Hotel, 7 Raffles Boulevard; tel: 6333 1788; www.rangmahal.com.sg; Mon–Fri, Sun noon–2.30pm, daily 6.30–10.30pm; $$$ (buffet lunch) $$$$ (à la carte);

Below: savoury *bouchees* at Rang Mahal.

contemporary Spanish restaurant, built in a specially designed glass enclosed dome floating on the waters of Marina Bay. Feast on exquisite avant-garde and authentic northeastern Spanish dishes while gazing at the 360-degree panoramic views.

Marina Bay

AMERICAN

Morton's of Chicago

4/F, Mandarin Oriental, 5 Raffles Avenue; tel: 6339 3740; www.mortons.com; Mon–Sat 5.30–11pm, Sun 5–10pm; $$$$; MRT: City Hall; map p.136 C1

The dark-wood interiors, attentive waiters, 24-ounce Porterhouse and premium wine list are all part of the Morton experience. Start with a martini at the bar, with filet mignon steak sandwiches.

Cut

B1-71 Galleria Level, The Shoppes at Marina Bay Sands, 2 Bayfront Avenue; tel: 6688 8517; www.marinabaysands.com; Sun–Thu 6–10pm, Fri–Sat 6–11pm; $$$$; MRT: Marina Bay or Bayfront; map 139 E3

Celebrity chef Wolfgang Puck's outpost is a must for

all steak lovers. This place is famous for its perfectly grilled cuts of *wagyu* and superb wine list. The Cut Bar & Lounge is great for pre- and post-dinner drinks. Sip some of the best cocktails in town and munch on bar bites such as mini Kobe sliders and main lobster Louis rolls.

CHINESE

My Humble House

02-27/29 Esplanade Mall, 8 Raffles Avenue; tel: 6423 1881; www.tunglok.com; daily 11.45am–3pm and 6.30–10.30pm; $$$ (set lunch) $$$$ (à la carte); MRT: City Hall or Esplanade; map p.136 B1

This modern Chinese restaurant has been around for more than a decade. The creative menu, which reads like a poetic work of art, includes signatures such as 'Dance of the Wind' or double-boiled seafood consommé.

Peach Blossoms

5/F, Marina Mandarin, 6 Raffles Boulevard; tel: 6845 1111; www.meritushotels.com; Mon–Fri noon–2.30pm, Sat–Sun 11am–2.30pm and daily 6.30–10.30pm; $$$$; MRT: City

Above: dazzling city views from the Equinox complex.

MRT: City Hall; map p.136 C1
This elegant restaurant has been around since 1971. Dine on classic northern, southern and coastal Indian specialities in a chic, modern interior. Whether it's a new twist to a traditional dish (tandoori salmon) or a classic favourite (*murg hazari*, or stuffed chicken), you can be assured of a memorable meal. The lunch buffet is fantastic value for money.
SEE ALSO HOTELS, P.71

ITALIAN
Osteria Mozza
B1 Galleria Level 42-46, Marina Bay Sands, 2 Bayfront Avenue; tel: 6688 8868; www.osteria-mozza.com; Sun noon–2pm, daily 5pm–11pm; $$$$; MRT: Marina Bay or Bayfront; map p.139 E3
Celebrity chef Mario Batali's outpost is crowded almost

Prices for a three-course dinner per person without drinks and taxes:
$$$$ = S$60 and above
$$$ = S$40–$60
$$ = S$20–$40
$ = under S$20

every day of the week. Choose from a variety of fresh antipasti and about 20 types of mozzarella. Recommended mains include grilled quail wrapped in pancetta with sage and honey, pan-roasted Iberico pork chop with fennel and sambuca and grilled whole snapper. The adjacent pizzeria serves some of the best pizzas in town.

JAPANESE
Keyaki
4/F, Pan Pacific Hotel, 7 Raffles Boulevard; tel: 6826 8240; www.singapore.panpacific.com; daily noon–2.30pm and 6.30–10.30pm; $$$ (set lunch) $$$$ (à la carte); MRT: City Hall; map p.136 C1
To get to the restaurant, you stroll past a Zen garden and fish pond before smiling, soft-spoken waitresses greet you at the entrance. Take your pick from kaiseki, robatayaki, sashimi, teppanyaki and shabu shabu. Round up with sake in the garden.
SEE ALSO HOTELS, P.71
Waku Ghin
L2-02 The Shoppes, Atrium, Marina Bay Sands; tel: 6688 8507; www.marin-

abaysands.com; daily 6pm and 8.30pm (two seatings); $$$$; MRT: Marina Bay or Bayfront; map p.139 E3
One of the most expensive restaurants in Singapore with prices starting from $400 per head. There are only 25 seats so booking is necessary. Renowned chef Tetsuya Wakuda offers nothing but the best. Diners can enjoy a 10-course degustation menu created using seasonal produce from Japan such as marinated botan shrimp with sea urchin and caviar as well as *wagyu* with wasabi and citrus soy.
SEE ALSO HOTELS, P.71

MEDITERRANEAN
Pollen
01-09 Flower Dome, Gardens By The Bay, 18 Marina Gardens Drive; tel: 6604 9988; www.pollen.com.sg; daily noon–2.30pm and 6.30–10.30pm; $$$$; MRT: Marina Bay or Bayfront; map p.139 E2
This is the only restaurant located in the unique climate-controlled Flower Dome. UK chef Jason Atherton and his team prepare modern Mediterranean cuisine and classics from the chef's flag-ship restaurant in London, Pollen Street Social. Escape from the heat and humidity and dine in 22 degrees C temperature amid temperate trees, herbs and vegetation. End your meal at the dessert bar followed by a stroll through the garden.
SEE ALSO PARKS & GARDENS, P.100

The Civic District
CHINESE
Lei Garden
01-24 Chijmes, 30 Victoria Street; tel: 6339 3822; daily 11.30am–3pm and 6–11pm; $$ (set lunch) $$$ (à la carte); MRT: City Hall; map p.136 B2

For a detailed guide to the best restaurants in Singapore, pick up a copy of Singapore Tatler's *Singapore's Best Restaurants* or the local food magazine *Appetite* from a major bookstore.

Regulars flock to this restaurant for its well-made dim sum and Cantonese dishes such as double-boiled soups and fresh seafood dishes.

ITALIAN
Garibaldi

01-02, 36 Purvis Street; tel: 6837 1468;
www.garibaldi.com.sg; daily noon–3pm and 6.30–11pm;
$$$$; MRT: City Hall;
map p.136 B2

This established restaurant helmed by chef Roberto Galetti is one of those outfits that continue to appeal to diners with an authentic menu using the best ingredients from Italy. Its adjoining bar serves great pre- and post- dinner cocktails.

MODERN EUROPEAN
Equinox

1 and 69–72/F, Swissôtel The Stamford, 2 Stamford Road; tel: 6837 3322; www.equinoxcomplex.com; Mon–Sat noon–2.30pm, Sun 11am–2.30pm, daily 3.30–5pm and 6.30–11pm;

$$$ (set lunch) $$$$ (à la carte); MRT: City Hall; map p.136 B2

At this complex of five restaurants and bars, start with drinks at the **New Asia Bar** on the 71st level while taking in stunning city views. Then descend one level to the swanky modern French restaurant **Jaan**, helmed by Julien Royer, who has been feted as the most exciting chef in the city.
SEE ALSO NIGHTLIFE, P.96

Wild Rocket at Mount Emily

Hangout@Mt.Emily, 10A Upper Wilkie Road; tel: 6339 9448; www.wildrocket.com.sg;
Tue–Sat noon–3pm and 6.30–11pm, Sun 11.30am–3pm and 6.30–10.30pm; $$$; MRT: Dhoby Ghaut; map p.136 A4

Lawyer-turned-chef Willin Low helms this breezy, stylish restaurant in a lovely hilltop location, scoring with refreshing Asian spins on European-style cuisine. Must-orders are the signature laksa pesto spaghetti with quail eggs, the juicy rib-eye and the divine strawberry cheesecake. End with drinks at **Wild Oats** bar next door (tel: 6336 5413).
SEE ALSO HOTELS, P71

PERANAKAN
True Blue

49 Armenian Street; tel:

6440 0449; www.truebluecuisine.com; daily 11.30am–2.30pm and 6–9.30pm; $$$$; MRT: City Hall; map p.136 A2

The food here is consistently good, but the portions are small and pricing expensive. Ask for the *ayam buah keluak* (chicken with Indonesian black nuts) and beef rendang. While waiting for your food, feast your eyes on owner Benjamin Seck's personal collection of Straits Chinese antiques.

THAI
Yhingthai Palace

36 Purvis Street; tel: 6337 9429; daily 11.30am–2pm and 6–10pm; $$; MRT: City Hall; map p.136 B2

There's nothing palatial about this place; in fact, the décor is uninspiring and it can be noisy. But it pleases with a bill of Thai-Chinese fare at reasonable prices. The olive fried rice and Thai fish cakes are particular favourites, as is the grilled squid salad drenched in a piquant sauce.

Chinatown and the CBD

CHINESE
Majestic Restaurant

1/F, New Majestic Hotel, 31–37 Bukit Pasoh Road; tel: 6511 4718; www.restaurantmajestic.com; daily 11.45am–3pm and 6.30–11pm; $$$$ (à la carte); MRT: Outram Park; map p.138 B2

Arguably the hippest culinary address this side of town, this restaurant pairs refined modern Cantonese cuisine with an idiosyncratic décor. Savour elegant fare such as grilled rack of lamb in Chinese honey sauce with pan-fried carrot cake and braised lobster in a milk and lime sauce while you contemplate the view of swimmers in the pool above through ceiling portholes.
SEE ALSO HOTELS, P.73

Below: the minimalist interior of Majestic Restaurant.

Silk Road

2/F, Amara Hotel, 165 Tanjong Pagar Road; tel: 6227 3848; www.silkroadrestaurants.com; daily 11am–3pm and 6–10pm; $$ (set lunch) $$$$ (à la carte); MRT: Tanjong Pagar; map p.138 B1

Delicious Chinese regional dishes from Beijing, Liaoning, Shaanxi and Sichuan cuisines. Everything else here is also refined, from the poem by Tang poet Li Bai carved onto the warm, contemporary décor.

Swee Kee Fishhead Noodle House

96 Amoy Street; tel: 6224 9920; www.ka-soh.com.sg; daily 11.45am–2.30pm and 5.30–10.45pm; $$; MRT: Raffles Place; map p.139 C3

The stern-looking waitresses will tell you their menu has not changed since the 1970s. So reliable it is that celebrities and politicians are known to drop by regularly for the creamy fish-head soup, prawn-paste chicken and pork ribs in a 'secret' sauce.

FRENCH
Restaurant Andre

41 Bukit Pasoh Road; tel: 6534 8880; restaurantandre.com; Tue–Fri noon–2pm, Tues–Sun 7–10pm; $$$$; MRT: Outram; map p.138 B2

Chef Andre Chiang from Taiwan has made waves in the dining scene since he arrived in Singapore. After leaving Jaan at Swissôtel, he opened his own restaurant at the Bukit Pasoh enclave. The culinary maestro has been wowing diners with his version of French nouvelle cuisine injected with a Mediterranean touch. Voted number five on Asia's 50 Best Restaurants 2013 list.

ITALIAN
Buko Nero

126 Tanjong Pagar Road; tel: 6324 6225; Tue–Thurs 6.30–9.30pm, Fri–Sat noon-2pm, 6.30–9.30pm; $$ (set lunch) $$$ (à la carte); MRT: Tanjong Pagar; map p.138 B2

The regularly changing menu reflects an Italian-Asian marriage, with signatures such as tofu and vegetable tower, spaghetti with spicy crabmeat and prawns, and Horlicks ice cream. The seven-table restaurant is always full. Call in advance for dinner.

Oso Ristorante

46 Bukit Pasoh Road; tel: 6327 8378; www.oso.sg; Mon–Fri noon–2.30pm, Mon–Sat 6.30–10.30pm; $$$$; MRT: Outram Park; map p.138 B2

This chic, cosy restaurant is recognised as one of the best in Singapore. It has a climate-controlled cheese and wine room, and the menu changes monthly. Order the rigatoni with rabbit and truffle puree.

JAPANESE
Marutama Ra-Men

03-90 The Central, 6 Eu Tong Sen Street; tel: 6534 8090; $$; daily 11am–10pm; MRT: Clarke Quay; map p.138 C4

The snaking queues that form outside its doors at mealtimes are evidence of this small restaurant's popularity. Its speciality is ramen served with one of four soup bases (chicken, spicy chicken, prawn or nuts). Don't forego the delicious side dishes like *kakuni* (thick wedges of stewed pork belly) and *dashimaki tamago* (a thick, pillowy omelette).

MODERN EUROPEAN
Ember

Hotel 1929, 50 Keong Saik Road; tel: 6347 1928; www.hotel1929.com; Mon–Fri 11.30am–2pm, Mon–Sat 6.30–10pm; $$$ (set lunch) $$$$ (à la carte); MRT: Tanjong Pagar; map p.138 B3

Chef-owner Sebastian Ng is one of Singapore's most talented young chefs. His modern European cuisine is delightfully robust yet refined, and sometimes comes with Asian accents. Everything is good really, but you should definitely have the slow-roasted lamb loin.

SEE ALSO HOTELS, P.72

PERANAKAN
The Blue Ginger

97 Tanjong Pagar Road; tel: 6222 3928; www.theblueginger.com; daily noon–2.30pm and 6.30–10.30pm; $$$; MRT: Tanjong Pagar; map p.138 B2

Left: some of the finest modern European food is at Ember.

Above: the Crustacean Bar, The Line, The Shangri-La.

This stylish, authentic Peranakan restaurant has been around for more than a decade. It serves satisfying offerings such as *ayam buah keluak* (stewed chicken with black nuts), *otak otak* (spicy fish mousse) and the must-have durian *cendol* (a dessert with green jelly).

THAI
Thanying
2/F, Amara Hotel, 165 Tanjong Pagar Road; tel: 6222 4688; singapore.amarahotels.com/thanying; daily 11.30am–3pm, 6.30–11pm; $$$ (à la carte); MRT: Tanjong Pagar; map p.138 B1
A loyal following for its royal Thai cuisine. Whether it's the green curry or crispy grouper, every dish served in the elegant teak-panelled dining room is beautifully presented. The extensive menu is complemented by a Thai dessert buffet.
SEE ALSO HOTELS, P.72

Orchard Road

CHINESE
Crystal Jade Palace
04-19 Ngee Ann City, 391

Prices for a three-course dinner per person without drinks and taxes:
$$$$ = S$60 and above
$$$ = S$40–$60
$$ = S$20–$40
$ = under S$20

Orchard Road; tel: 6735 2388; www.crystaljade.com; Mon–Fri 11.30am–11pm, Sat 11am–3pm and 6–11pm, Sun 10.30am–3pm and 6–11pm; $$ (set lunch) $$$ (à la carte); MRT: Orchard; map p.134 C4
Crisp, contemporary décor – apart from the kitschy etched-glass windows. Excellent roast meat and seafood. Also runs **Crystal Jade La Mian Xiao Long Bao** (tel: 6238 1661) and **Crystal Jade Kitchen** (tel: 6238 1411) in the same building.
Din Tai Fung
B1-03/06 The Paragon, 290 Orchard Road; tel: 6836 8336; www.dintaifung.com.sg; Mon–Fri 11am–10pm, Sat–Sun 10am–10pm; $$; MRT: Orchard Road; map p.135 C4
You notice the flurry of activity at the open-concept kitchen before you realise diners are watching the chefs in action and lining up for their *xiao long bao*, or steamed pork dumplings, that have exactly 18 pleats each. Fans sing praises of the chicken soup and humble fried rice, too.
Imperial Treasure Nan Bei
05-12/13 Ngee Ann City, 391 Orchard Road; tel: 6738 1238; Sun–Fri 11am–10pm, Sat 10.30am–10pm; $$$; MRT: Orchard; map p.134 C4
The Imperial Treasure empire promises high standards in both food and service. This

outlet boasts top-grade Cantonese dishes, from roast goose and dim sum to comforting double-boiled chicken soup. The equally lauded **Imperial Treasure Teochew Cuisine**, one level down, serves fine Chaozhou dishes in plush surroundings (04-20A/21; tel: 6736 2118).
Jiang Nan Chun
Four Seasons Hotel Singapore, 190 Orchard Boulevard; tel: 6734 1110/6831 7220; www.fourseasons.com; daily 11.30am–2.30pm and 6–10.30pm; $$$$; MRT: Orchard; map p.134 C4
This top-notch Cantonese restaurant serves refined dishes such as double-boiled herbal soups and special creations by the talented chef from Hong Kong.

Below: Au Jardin's trout with egg confit.

Singaporeans make a beeline for luxurious hotel buffets. Offering some of the best are **Kopi Tiam** (tel: 6431 6156) at Swissôtel the Stamford, serving a wide variety of local dishes from Hainanese chicken rice to roti pratá; **The Line** (tel: 6213 4275) at The Shangri-La, which has a substantial spread of international and local fare; and **Straits Kitchen** (tel: 6732 1234) at Grand Hyatt offering high quality hawker-style and local cuisine such as satay, biryani and *char kway teow*.

107

Above: stroll past a lush ginger garden to get to Halia in the Botanic Gardens.

The dim sum is especially outstanding. The Weekend Oriental Brunch welcomes guests to dine on unlimited servings of the chef's specialities and dim sum.
SEE ALSO HOTELS, P.73

FRENCH
Au Jardin
EJH Corner House, Singapore Botanic Gardens Vistors Centre, 1 Cluny Road; tel: 6466 8812; www.lesamis.com.sg; Tue–Fri noon–2pm, Tue–Sun 7–10.15pm, Sun 11am–1pm; $$$$; MRT: Botanic Gardens
'Au Jardin', meaning 'in the garden', is set in a restored

The laid-back enclave of **Tanglin Village** is the latest hotspot for wining and dining. Tropical trees and colonial architecture lend a charming air to the achingly hip establishments housed in bungalows. Check out **Long Beach** (Block 25 Dempsey Road; tel: 6323 2222; www.longbeachseafood.com.sg) for its lip-smacking black pepper crab; **Sammy's Curry** (Block 25 Dempsey Road; tel: 6472 2080; www.samyscurry.com) for its famous fish head curry and other fiery dishes served on banana leaves; and **PS Café** (Block 28B Harding Road; tel: 6479 3343; pscafe.com) for delicious cakes. *(See also Nightlife, p.93, 95)*

1920s bungalow in the Botanic Gardens. The contemporary French flavours at this highly acclaimed restaurant are peerless. Highly recommended are the dégustation menus which you can pair with exquisite wines. Ask the sommelier for recommendations.
SEE ALSO PARK AND GARDENS, P.101

Les Amis
02-16 Shaw Centre, 1 Scotts Road; tel: 6733 2225; www.lesamis.com.sg; Mon–Sat noon–2pm, 7–9.30pm; $$$$; MRT: Orchard; map p.134 C4
Flagship of the Les Amis Group that exudes elegance and opulence; think chandeliers and velvety upholstery. Still boasting one of the city's best wine lists, this chi-chi restaurant understandably draws well-heeled regulars who appreciate contemporary French cuisine that's both delicate and flavourful.

INDONESIAN
The Rice Table
02-09/10 International Building, 360 Orchard Road; tel: 6835 3783; www.ricetable.com.sg; daily noon–3pm and 6–9.15pm; $ (set lunch) $$ (set dinner); MRT: Orchard; map p.134 B4
For one price, you order as many authentic Dutch Rijsttafel dishes as your stomach will allow. Try the *tahu telor*, a tower of bean

curd with shredded cucumber and sweet sauce, the tender spicy beef *rendang* (dry curry) and grilled chicken. Don't be shy to ask for seconds.

INTERNATIONAL
Halia
Ginger Garden, Singapore Botanic Gardens, 1 Cluny Road; tel: 8444 1148; www.halia.com.sg; Mon–Fri noon–5pm, daily 6.30–11pm; Sat–Sun 10am–4pm (brunch), 3–5pm (tea); $$ (set lunch) $$$ (à la carte); MRT: Botanic Gardens
To get to Halia ('ginger' in Malay), you walk past a ginger garden to find the restaurant nestled amid lush tropical foliage. It's so tranquil you will forget the city is just metres away. Dine on European-style dishes with light Asian touches as well as some ginger-inspired creations.
mezza9
Grand Hyatt, 10 Scotts Road; tel: 6732 1234; www.singapore.grand.hyatt.com; daily noon–3pm and 6–11pm, Sunday 11.30am–3pm; $$$$; MRT: Orchard; map p.134 B1
Conceptualised by international design firm 'Super Potato', this restaurant features show kitchens for sushi, yakitori, seafood, Western and Chinese dishes as well as deli and dessert counters and a **martini bar**. It's so

cleverly designed you can sit anywhere and still watch the chefs in action.
SEE ALSO HOTELS, P.73

PS Café
Level 2 Palais SC, 390 Orchard Road; tel: 9834 8232; pscafe.com; daily 11.30am–4pm; Mon, Thu, Sun 6pm–midnight, Fri–Sat 6pm–1am; $$$; MRT: Orchard; map p.135 C4
This trendy and perennially busy café has inspired East-West fusion dishes, sandwiches and scrumptious desserts. Favourites include the PS Caesar Salad and banana mango crumble. Another must-visit outlet, **PS Café**, is in Tanglin Village *(see box, below left)*.

ITALIAN
Basilico
Level 2 Regent Singapore, 1 Cuscaden Road; tel: 6725 3232; www.regenthotels.com; Mon–Sat noon–2.30pm, Sun noon–3pm, daily 6.30–10pm; $$; MRT: Orchard, bus 36; map p.134 A4
This restaurant facing the pool offers a la carte and buffet options. The consistently good Italian cuisine with superb antipasti and dessert spreads will easily tempt you for seconds or thirds.
SEE ALSO HOTELS, P.74

JAPANESE
Akashi
01/01A, Orchard Parade Hotel, 1 Tanglin Road; tel: 6732 4438; www.akashigroup.com.sg; daily 11.30am–3pm and 6–11pm; $$$; MRT: Orchard, then taxi; bus: 7, 105, 123 or 174; map p.134 A1
It's a good sign that Akashi is well patronised by the expat Japanese community. The constant buzz, efficient service, and the food, especially the California roll, *ebi miso yaki* (grilled miso prawns) and

smooth *tara inaniwa udon* noodles, all keep its regulars returning for more.

MODERN EUROPEAN
Iggy's
Level 3 The Hilton Hotel, 581 Orchard Road; tel: 6732 2234; www.iggys.com.sg; Mon–Fri noon–1.30pm, Mon–Sat 7–9.30pm; $$$$; MRT: Orchard; map p.134 A1
British *Restaurant* magazine has been ranking Iggy's as one of the world's top 100 restaurants since 2007. Call ahead to enjoy degustation menus of inventive dishes, such as cappellini in scampi oil and scallop sashimi with foie gras and *yuzu*.

SINGAPOREAN
Chatterbox
Mandarin Orchard, 333 Orchard Road; tel: 6831 6288/91; www.chatterbox.com.sg; Sun–Thur 11am–1am, Fri–Sat 11am–2am; $$; MRT: Orchard; map p.135 C4
This coffee house is famed for its iconic but expensive chicken rice, often voted as the best in Singapore. Also check out the other local fare such as *nasi lemak* (rice cooked in coconut milk), lobster laksa and *bak kut teh* (pork rib soup).
SEE ALSO HOTELS, P.73

Below: flaky *roti prata* is a firm breakfast favourite.

Prices for a three-course dinner per person without drinks and taxes:
$$$$ = S$60 and above
$$$ = S$40–$60
$$ = S$20–$40
$ = under S$20

VEGETARIAN
Lingzhi
05-01 Liat Towers, 541 Orchard Road; tel: 6734 3788; www.lingzhivegetarian.com; daily 11am–3pm and 6–10pm; $$; MRT: Orchard; map p.134 B4
The vegetarian cuisine here is so good some would gladly give up meat for life. The goodness of soy, mushrooms, nuts and vegetables is creatively employed and the beautifully presented dishes complement the restaurant's understated elegance.

Little India and Kampong Glam
INDIAN
Ananda Bhavan
01-10 Block 663 Buffalo Road; tel: 6291 1943; www.anandabhavan.com; daily 7am–10pm; $; MRT: Little India; map p.132 C1
Established in 1924, this is the oldest Indian restaurant in Singapore. You order, take a queue number and wait for it to be called to collect your scrumptious South Indian meal. While waiting, read all about the virtues of vegetarianism posted on the wall. One of the vignettes reads 'the strength of an elephant is sustained on a vegetarian diet'. (Also at 58 Serangoon Road; tel: 6396 5454.)
Banana Leaf Apolo
54/56 Race Course Road; tel: 6293 8682; daily 10.30am–10.30pm; $$; MRT: Little India; map p.132 C1
Never mind the unimaginative, fluorescent-lit space. The busy restaurant fills up quickly. It is the place for

109

Above: pizza at Trapizza.

spicy South Indian food served on banana leaves. Everything looks good and the efficient waiters are ever ready to help if you need recommendations. Must-tries: masala prawns and chicken. (Also at 01-32 Little India Arcade, 48 Serangoon Road; tel: 6297 1595.)

Komala Vilas
76/78 Serangoon Road; tel: 6293 6980; www.komalavilas.com.sg; daily 7am–10.30pm; $; MRT: Little India; map p.133 C1
This boisterous, charming Little India institution is the place for saffron rice accompanied by an array of vegetable curries, vadai (savoury fritters), and Indian breads such as wholewheat bhattura and chappati and rice flour-based dosai. Sauces and dips are replenished as desired and you should definitely eat with your fingers. (Also at 12/14 Serangoon Road; tel: 6293 3664.)

Muthu's Curry
138 Race Course Road; tel: 6392 1722; www.muthuscurry.com; daily 10.30am–10.30pm; $$; MRT: Farrer Park; map p.132 C1
Singaporeans are passionate about fish-head curry, and this inevitably comes up as one of the top places to sample the dish. It has

served its award-winning version since 1969. The chicken, mutton and prawn dishes are also always good bets.

Singapore Zam Zam Restaurant
697–699 North Bridge Road; tel: 6298 6320; daily 8am–11pm; $; MRT: Bugis; map p.136 C4
A rough-and-ready place serving Indian Muslim specialities. The fragrant mutton or chicken briyani (saffron rice) is robustly spicy, as are the prata (flaky bread) and murtabak (flaky bread stuffed with minced meat) dipped in curry.

MALAY
Hajjah Maimunah Restaurant
11 & 15 Jalan Pisang; tel: 6294 8732; www.hjmaimunah.com; Mon–Sat 7am–8pm; $; MRT: Bugis; map p.136 C1
This self-service restaurant is always packed to the gills. Just point to the dishes you'd like and they will be served with fluffy rice. The tender and spicy beef rendang (dry curry) and sotong bakar (grilled squid) are heavenly.

Sentosa

FRENCH
L'Atelier de Joël Robuchon
8 Sentosa Gateway, Hotel Michael, Resorts World Sentosa; tel: 6577 7788; www.rwsentosa.com; daily 6–10.30pm, Sun noon–2pm; $$$$; MRT: HarbourFront, then the Sentosa shuttle bus from VivoCity
With a team of stellar chefs trained by Monsieur Robuchon, diners are assured of only the finest food and service. Like all the other L'Atelier restaurants, this one is decked out in red and black, and fitted with a huge open kitchen. Request a seat at the bar counter and

interact with the waiters and chefs while you dine on the menu's innovative tasting portions.

ITALIAN
il Lido
Sentosa Golf Club, 27 Bukit Manis Road; tel: 6866 1977; www.il-lido.com; daily noon–2.30pm and 6.30–10.30pm; $$$ (set lunch) $$$$ (à la carte); MRT: HarbourFront, then Sentosa Express from VivoCity
The setting is the drawcard at il Lido. The best time to go is in the evenings. Ask for a table at the balcony and enjoy the beautiful sunset view. The unfussy Italian menu includes homemade pastas, fine meats and fish. The adjacent **il Lido Lounge Bar**'s designer décor, champagne and chill-out music make for a posh finale to the evening.

Trapizza
Rasa Sentosa Resort, Siloso Beach; tel: 6376 2662; www.shangri-la.com; Mon–Fri 11am–10pm, Sat–Sun 11am–11pm; $$$; MRT: HarbourFront, then Sentosa Express from VivoCity or Shangri-La's Rasa Sentosa shuttle bus from HarbourFront Centre
This casual Italian-style family restaurant sits on Siloso Beach next to a trapeze. On a hot day, nothing beats a scoop of their mango sorbet and a mug of cold beer. Wait for the sun to set and wind down with hearty salads, delicious pastas and excellent pizzas from the wood-

Prices for a three-course dinner per person without drinks and taxes:
$$$$= S$60 and above
$$$= S$40–S$60
$$= S$20–S$40
$= under S$20

Fashionable eating and drinking establishments have gathered in far-flung enclaves in recent years. One example is Sentosa Cove's **Quayside Isle** – an ultra stylish stretch by the waters (next to W Hotel). It offers a whole range of fashionable eateries and bars, luring in the trendy set and anyone who doesn't mind the drive out of the city centre. who do not mind the trek out of the city centre.

fired oven. If you prefer to slurp up hearty Asian noodles, head up to **8 Noodles** on Level 3 (daily 11am–11pm. tel: 6371 1966).
SEE ALSO HOTELS, P.75

SEAFOOD
Ocean Restaurant by Cat Cora
22 Sentosa Gateway, Marine Life Park, S.E.A. Aquarium; tel: 6577 6869; www.rwsentosa.com; daily 11am–10.30pm; $$$$; MRT: HarbourFront, then the Sentosa shuttle bus from VivoCity
Resorts World Sentosa and Cat Cora, renowned chef from the US, have unveiled their latest dining concept at the world's largest aquarium. As you gaze into the man-made deep-blue, feast on sustainably sourced seafood. The dishes are light, simple and healthy, with a focus on the freshest produce from the region.
The Cliff
The Sentosa, 2 Bukit Manis Road; tel: 6371 1425; www.thecliff.sg; daily 6.30–10pm; $$$$; MRT: HarbourFront, then the Sentosa shuttle bus from VivoCity
One of Singapore's most beautiful and romantic restaurants, The Cliff sits at the edge of a cliff and offers a view of lovely, lush

surroundings and the South China Sea. In fact, the artful and sensuous Yasuhiro Koichi-designed restaurant and the elegant contemporary seafood-inspired dishes seem a perfect marriage. There are eight varieties of oysters, which can be prepared in five different ways.
SEE ALSO HOTELS, P.75

SPANISH
Sabio by the Sea
01-02, 31 Ocean Way (next to W Hotel Singapore); tel: 6690 7568; Mon–Thurs noon–10pm, Fri–Sat noon–midnight, Sun 10.30m–10pm; $$$; bus: from Beach Station, take Sentosa Bus 3 to Sentosa Cove
The folks behind popular Sabio tapas bar at Duxton Hill opened up their second outlet at the ultra-trendy waterside enclave at Sentosa Cove. Sip signature sangrias and share modern tapas, grilled meats and fish cooked in charcoal ovens flown-in from Spain.

Southern and Western Singapore

CHINESE
Min Jiang at One North
5 Rochester Park; tel: 6774 0122; www.goodwoodparkhotel.com; daily 11.30am–2.30pm and 6.30–10.30pm; $$$; MRT: Buona Vista
Long acclaimed for its refined food at Goodwood Park Hotel (tel: 6737 7411), Min Jiang's second home is in a conserved colonial-style bungalow in Rochester Park. The repertoire here extends beyond Sichuan fare. There are dishes from various Chinese regions, and the highlight is the Peking duck with eight different condiments. It's also the first Chinese restaurant in Singapore to have a Peking duck oven – a chef was specially flown in from China to oversee the whole building process.
Tung Lok Signatures
01-57 VivoCity, 1 HarbourFront Walk; tel: 6376 9555; www.tunglok.com; Mon–Sat 11.30am–3pm, Sun 11am–3.30pm, daily

Below: The Cliff is one of the most romantic dining spots.

Singapore's coffee scene has been booming over the past couple of years. These days you can find independent roasters and expert baristas serving perfectly brewed coffee in many places. One of the more popular joints is **Chye Seng Huat Hardware** (150 Tyrwhitt Road; tel: 6396 0609; www.cshhcoffee.com; Tue–Fri 9am–7pm, Sat–Sun 9am–10pm; MRT: Farrer Park). Complement your cup of java with a range of cakes and light bites. Besides an on-site roaster, there's also a private coffee tasting room.

6–10.30pm; $$$$; MRT: HarbourFront
You will not be disappointed when the name is 'Tung Lok'. This outlet, done up in minimalist white décor, serves the most memorable dishes from the group's stable of outstanding Hunanese, Cantonese and seafood restaurants. There are classic Chinese dishes, healthy double-boiled soups and exquisite dim sum.

FRENCH
Chez Petit Salut
01-54 Block 44 Chip Bee Gardens, Jalan Merah Saga, Holland Village; tel: 6474 9788; www.aupetitsalut.com; Mon–Sat 11.30am–2.30pm and 6.30–10.30pm; $$ (set lunch) $$$ (à la carte); MRT: Buona Vista or Holland Village
This casual bistro offers diners hearty French cuisine paired with wines. Favourites include coq au vin, duck pate and cassoulet.

ITALIAN
Da Paolo Ristorante
01-56 Block 44 Chip Bee Gardens, Jalan Merah Saga, Holland Village; tel: 6479 6522; www.dapaolo.com.sg; daily 11.30am–2.30pm and 6.30–10.30pm; $$ (set lunch) $$$$ (à la carte); MRT: Buona Vista or Holland Village
Despite Da Paolo's expansion in recent years, its outlets are as stylish as ever. This outlet oozes sophistication yet remains laid-back. Chef-owner Paolo Scarpa's pastas are always excellent – you

won't go wrong with any of the pasta dishes on the menu.

MEDITERRANEAN
Original Sin
01-62 Block 43 Chip Bee Gardens, Jalan Merah Saga, Holland Village; tel: 6475 5605; www.originalsin.com.sg; daily 11.30am–2.30pm and 6–10.30pm; $$ (set lunch) $$$ (à la carte); MRT: Buona Vista or Holland Village
Whether you're on an ovo-lacto diet, a vegan or just plain health-conscious, chef-owner Marisa Bertocchi ensures there's something imaginative for everyone. Her mezze platter, moussaka, Sicilian pizza and tiramisu would win over even the most hardened meat lover.

MEXICAN
Cha Cha Cha
32 Lorong Mambong, Holland Village; tel: 6462 1650; daily 11.30am–11pm; $$; MRT: Buona Vista or Holland Village
This is a subdued little spot where you will find good south-of-the-border food – chimichangas, fajitas, burritos – along with a relaxed atmosphere and great margaritas.

The East Coast
INDIAN
Vansh
01-04 Singapore Indoor Stadium, 2 Stadium Walk; tel: 6345 4466; www.vansh.com.sg; daily noon–2.30pm and 6–10.30pm; $$ (set lunch) $$$$ (à la carte); MRT: Stadium or Kallang, then taxi
The setting is so bold, yet so sexy, you may just want to sip the Kamasutra cocktail horizontally – on the low lounge chairs around the open

Left: a sexy décor at Vansh to go with its modern Indian cuisine.

tandoor kitchen. Modern Indian cuisine means everything is individually plated and creatively presented.

PERANAKAN
Guan Hoe Soon
38/40 Joo Chiat Place; tel: 6344 2761; www.guanhoesoon.com; Wed–Mon 11am–2.30pm and 6–9.30pm; $$; MRT: Paya Lebar, then taxi or MRT: Bedok, then bus: 33

Singapore's oldest Peranakan restaurant was a mere coffee shop when it was founded in 1953. Despite some attempts at modernisation in the 1980s, its old-world ambience is still palpable. You can't go wrong with traditional dishes such as *satay babi* (pork satay curry), *nogh hiang* (sausage) and *ayam tempra* (chicken stew).

SEAFOOD
East Coast Seafood Centre
1202–1206 East Coast Parkway, near car park E1; $$$; MRT: Bedok, then bus: 31, 196 or 197

A collection of casual seafood restaurants, located by the beach, which fill up at weekends. These are good spots for Singapore-style seafood, including **Red House** (tel: 6442 3112), **Jumbo** (tel: 6442 3435) and **Long Beach** (tel: 6448 3636).
Hua Yu Wee
462 Upper East Coast Road; tel: 6442 9313; daily 5.30–11.30pm; $$; MRT: Tanah Merah, then bus: 14

Chinese families flock in droves to this old, nondescript restaurant for its Singapore-style seafood. Its chilli and pepper crabs, butter prawns and seafood rolls are highly recommended.

SINGAPOREAN
Marine Parade Laksa
Nan Sin Food Centre, 57/59 East

Above: chilli crab is a must-try in Singapore.

Coast Road; daily 9am–6pm, closed alternate Tue; $; MRT: Paya Lebar, then taxi or MRT: Tanah Merah, then bus: 12

Laksa is noodles in a curry-like, coconut-based soup. This particular stall is said to have pioneered *Katong laksa*, the now-famous variety that has even warranted a story in *The New York Times*. You can ask for clams (or without) and you eat the short noodles with your spoon – no chopsticks required.

Central and Northern Singapore
PERANAKAN
Ivins
21 Binjai Park; tel: 6468 3060; daily 11.30am–3pm and 5–9pm; $ (set lunch) $$ (à la carte); bus: 151, 154, 157 or 170

Delicious Peranakan fare at down-to-earth prices. A lavish meal of chilli prawns, spring rolls, honey pork and stewed chicken with Indonesian black nuts can be had for a song.
Violet's Kitchen
881 Bukit Timah Road; tel: 6468 5430; www.violetoon-skitchen.com; Tues–Thu 11.30am–10pm, Fri–Sun 11.30am–11pm; $$; MRT:

Botanic Gardens and taxi, bus: 48, 52 or 157

Culinary doyen Violet Oon, together with her son and daughter, opened this small, casual chic restaurant serving her well-known signatures such as braised oxtail stew, shepherd's pie, laksa and several Peranakan favourites. Homemade jams and cookies are available too.

SINGAPOREAN
The Roti Prata House
246M Upper Thomson Road; tel: 6459 5260; daily 24 hours; $; MRT: Ang Mo Kio, then taxi; bus: 132 or 165

Enjoy your *roti prata* bread crispy or paper thin, with cheese or filled with chicken, mutton, sardines or vegetables.

Then work off the calories at the MacRitchie Reservoir Park, just 15 minutes' walk away.

Prices for a three-course dinner per person without drinks and taxes:
$$$$ = S$60 and above
$$$ = S$40–$60
$$ = S$20–$40
$ = under S$20

Shopping

For Singaporeans, shopping is right up there with eating – they love it; they live for it. This might explain the large number of malls in the city, both downtown and in the suburbs. Orchard Road and Marina Bay are Singapore's style headquarters, filled with mall-crawling shoppers any time of the day and week. Beyond the malls and department stores are idiosyncratic shops hidden in little enclaves such as Ann Siang Hill, just a stone's throw from Chinatown, and Haji and Bali lanes in Kampong Glam. In the flea markets and ethnic neighbourhoods, cultural finds and arts and crafts quietly wait to be discovered.

Department Stores

DFS Galleria

25 Scotts Road; tel: 6229 8100; www.dfsgalleria.com; Sun–Thur 10am–10pm, Fri–Sat 10am–10.30pm; MRT: Orchard; map p.134 B1

Shop duty-free at this temple to consumerism, with high-end clothing, kitschy tourist souvenirs and fine wines.

Mustafa Centre

145 Syed Alwi Road; tel: 6295 5855; www.mustafa.com.sg;

Below: malls selling clothes.

daily 24 hours; MRT: Farrer Park; map p.133 D2

An institution in Singapore, selling just about everything under the sun. Luggage, jewellery, electronics, power tools, you name it – if no one else stocks it, Mustafa probably does. The prices here are great, too. But be warned: like everywhere in Little India, this place is packed on Sunday.

Robinsons

05-05 Centrepoint, 176 Orchard Road; tel: 6733 0888; www.robinsons.com.sg; daily 10.30am–10pm; MRT: Somerset; map p.135 D3

Robinsons dates back to the 1850s. When its owners tried to sell it in 2003, infuriated shoppers petitioned against the sale – such is the loyalty it enjoys. It has the nicest sales staff around, and its biannual sales are eagerly awaited. Its new flagship store will open at The Heeren Shops in 2013. (Also at Raffles City; tel: 6216 8388 and The Shoppes at Marina Bay Sands, tel: 6688 7622.)

TANGS

310 Orchard Road; tel: 6737 5500; www.tangs.com.sg;

Mon–Thur, Sat 10.30am–9.30pm, Fri 10.30am–11pm, Sun 11am–8.30pm; MRT: Orchard; map p.134 C4

This well-loved icon was founded by C.K. Tang, who made his fortune by peddling China-made lace from house to house in the early 1900s. It is particularly noted for its cult skincare labels and kitchen gadgets. (Also at VivoCity; tel: 6303 8688.)

Yue Hwa

70 Eu Tong Sen Street; tel: 6538 4222; www.yuehwa.com.sg; Sun–Fri 11am–9pm, Sat 11am–10pm; MRT: Chinatown; map p.138 B3

All things Chinese, from silk products to herbs and health tonics, can be found here.

Shopping Malls

313@Somerset

313 Orchard Road; tel: 6496 9313; www.313somerset.com.sg; Sun–Thu 10am–10pm, Fri–Sat 10am–11pm; MRT: Somerset; map p.135 D3

Recently built, this mall offers a decidedly girl-oriented shopping experience with three floors of American

Left: colourful fabrics in Little India.

malls, ION Orchard is laid out like the Borobudur of shopping with mass labels and eateries built four floors underground, while the bigger designer names are spread across four floors up from the street level.

Marina Square
6 Raffles Boulevard; tel: 6339 8787; www.marinasquare. com.sg; daily 10am–10pm; MRT: City Hall/Esplanade; map p.136 C1
This shiny mall has plenty of hip boutiques, eateries and a cineplex. Check out Cathay Photo on the second floor for affordable photo equipment.

Ngee Ann City
391 Orchard Road; tel: 6506 0461; www.ngeeanncity. com.sg; daily 10am–9.30pm; MRT: Orchard; map p.134 C4
Locals like to refer to it as 'Taka' (its anchor tenant is Takashimaya Shopping Centre), and love the **Books Kinokuniya** store on the third level and the food hall in the basement.
SEE ALSO LITERATURE, P.77

The Paragon
290 Orchard Road; tel: 6738 5535; www.paragonsc.com.sg; daily 10am–9pm;
MRT: Orchard; map p.135 C4
Sleek high-fashion boutiques from Gucci to Prada, younger brands like Miss Sixty and home-grown label Project Shop, with a gourmet supermarket and eateries in the mix.

Plaza Singapura
68 Orchard Road; tel: 6332 9298; www.plazasingapura. com.sg; daily 10am–10pm; MRT: Dhoby Ghaut; map p.135 E3
Major stores here include John Little, Marks & Spencer and

All of Singapore (and the region) comes out to shop during the Great Singapore Sale from end May to early July. *See Festivals and Events, p.58.*

label Forever 21 and a host of other ladies' boutiques including Spanish label Zara. It also boasts a Food Republic food court on the 5th floor and many smaller eateries in the basement.

Bugis Junction
200 Victoria Street; tel: 6557 6557; www.bugisjunction-mall. com.sg; daily 10am–10pm; MRT: Bugis; map p.136 B3
Bugis Street was once famous for the transvestites and transsexuals who plied

the area. Today it has been transformed into this mall of glassed-in shophouses housing boutiques.

Far East Plaza
14 Scotts Road; tel: 6732 6266; www.fareast-plaza.com; daily 10am–10pm; MRT: Orchard; map p.134 B1
Don't let the slightly decrepit exterior put you off; shops here sell great streetwear. There is a host of tattoo parlours and cheap and good food on the upper levels.

ION Orchard
2 Orchard Turn; tel: 6238 8228; www.ionorchard.com; daily 10am–10pm; MRT: Orchard; map p.134 C4
One of Singapore's glitzy

Left: exploring VivoCity could take days.

Above: fashion-shopping hot spot Wisma Atria.

Spotlight. Golden Village cinemas operates a cineplex here too. The mall went through a massive revamp and its new-look was unveiled in late 2012. It's now combined with the adjacent **The Atrium@Orchard** offering about 320 options for shopping and dining.

Raffles Hotel Shopping Arcade
Raffles Hotel, 1 Beach Road; tel: 6337 1886; www.raffles.com; daily 10.30am–7pm; MRT: City Hall; map p.136 B2
Luxury labels (think Tiffany & Co., Swarovski, Louis Vuitton), bespoke tailors and antiques stores pepper this mall within the legendary Raffles Hotel.

Suntec City Mall
3 Temasek Boulevard; tel: 6825 2667; www.sunteccity.com.sg; daily 10am–10pm; MRT: Esplanade/Promenade;

You can lodge complaints against errant retailers with the **Singapore Tourism Board** (tel: 1800-736 2000; www.yoursingapore.com) or the **Small Claims Tribunal** (tel: 6435 5946; www.smallclaims.gov.sg).

map p.136 C2
It is easy to get lost in this veritable city with over 350 shops and a whole lot of restaurants and eateries. Until VivoCity was built, Suntec City was the largest mall on the island.

VivoCity
1 HarbourFront Walk; tel: 6377 6860; www.vivocity.com.sg; daily 10am–10pm; MRT: HarbourFront
This is so huge that most visitors never make it to the second floor on their first visit. Spread over one million square foot, it has a cineplex, a hypermart and hundreds of shops and restaurants, some of which overlook Sentosa.

Wisma Atria
435 Orchard Road; tel: 6235 8177; www.wismaonline.com; daily 10am–10pm; MRT: Orchard; map p.134 C4
Wisma Atria has European high-street boutiques aplenty – Warehouse, FCUK, the Gap and Mango. The futuristic-looking building was relaunched in 2012 after a year-long renovation that cost S$31 million.

Markets

Chinatown Night Market
Pagoda, Trengganu and Sago streets; Mon–Thur 5–11pm, Fri–Sat & eve of public holidays 5pm–1am; MRT: Chinatown; map p.138 B3/C3
Over 200 stalls selling trinkets, tourist souvenirs and traditional Chinese goods like calligraphy and masks.

MAAD
red dot Traffic, 28 Maxwell Road; tel: 6534 7209; www.maad.sg; one Friday night of every month 5pm–midnight; MRT: Tanjong Pagar; map p.138 C2
The Market of Artists and Designers is a bazaar with t-shirts, bags, home accessories and more crafted by

There are several brand new malls located away from the city centre. They include the futuristic **Star Vista** (www.thestarvista.com) in Buona Vista and **Jcube** (www.j-cube.com.sg) in Jurong East.

local emerging talents.
SEE ALSO MUSEUMS AND GALLERIES, P.86

Sungei Market (Thieves' Market)
Sungei Road; daily 11am–7pm; MRT: Bugis; map p.133 D1
Broken radios, chipped crockery and vinyl records might not be the sort of things you would want to buy, but this market, busiest at weekends, offers an insight into the city's underbelly.

Tanglin Mall
163 Tanglin Road; tel: 6736 4922; www.tanglinmall.com.sg; daily 10am–10pm; MRT: Orchard, then taxi, or bus: 7, 105, 123 or 174; map p.134 A1
Frequented by expats living in the Tanglin area. Stalls at the biggest flea market in Singapore sell rare toys, comics and secondhand clothes.

What to Buy

ANTIQUES
Lopburi Arts & Antiques
01-04 Tanglin Place, 91 Tanglin Road; tel: 6738 3834; daily 11am–7pm; MRT: Orchard, then taxi; map p.134 A1
Shipping and certificates of authenticity are provided for its Buddhist art and antiques.

Pagoda House
143/145 Tanglin Road, Tudor Court; tel: 6732 2177; www.pagodahouse.com; Mon–Sat 11am–7pm, Sun 11am–5pm; MRT: Orchard, then taxi; map p.134 A1
Specialises in antique furniture from Europe, North Asia and Southeast Asia. It also custom-makes furniture and

Above: Funan DigitaLife Mall.

offers a selection of home accessories and arts objects.

Renee Hoy Fine Arts
01-44 Tanglin Shopping Centre, 19 Tanglin Road; tel: 6235 1596; Mon–Sat 10.30am–6.30pm, Sun by appointment only; MRT: Orchard, then taxi; map p.134 A1
Antique furniture from China, Korea, Japan and other Asian countries. It takes orders for reproductions as well.

ELECTRONICS
Funan DigitaLife Mall
109 North Bridge Road; tel: 6336 8327; www.funan.com.sg; daily 10am–10pm; MRT: City Hall; map p.136 A1
Check out **South Asia Computer** (03-01; tel: 6337 0871) and **Challenger Superstore** (06-00; tel: 6339 9008) for computer accessories and MP3 players. For photographic equipment, try **John 3:16** (04-27; tel: 6337 2877).

Sim Lim Square
1 Rochor Canal Road; tel: 6338 3859; www.simlimsquare.com.sg; daily 10.30am–9pm; MRT: Bugis or Little India; map p.136 B4
A crowded mall dedicated to electronics. Compare prices and haggle – or you'll be ripped off. That said, there are some good deals to be had.

HOME ACCESSORIES AND SOUVENIRS
Crate & Barrel
04-21/22, Ion Orchard, 2

Orchard Turn; tel: 6634 4222; www.crateandbarrel.com; daily 10am–9pm; MRT: Orchard
Home furnishings that are stylish and eco-friendly.

Egg 3
01-10/12, 33 Erskine Road, tel: 6536 6977; eggthree.com; Mon–Sat 10am–8pm, Sun 10.30am–7pm; MRT: Chinatown; map p.138 C3
Quirky homeware and graphic T-shirts.

FrancFranc
02-41/42 ViviCity, 1 HarbourFront Walk; tel: 6376 8077; www.francfranc.com.sg; daily 11am–10pm; MRT: HarbourFront
This Japanese brand rolls out sylish, practical design items that accentuate space management.

Lim's Arts & Living
02-01 Holland Road Shopping Centre, 211 Holland Avenue; tel: 6467 1300; www.lims.com.sg; daily 10am–8.30pm; MRT: Holland Village or Buona Vista
A wide selection of ethnic items and handicrafts.

Risis
Singapore Botanic Gardens, 1 Cluny Road; tel: 6475 5104; www.risis.com.sg; daily 8.45am–5.45pm; MRT: Orchard, then taxi; bus: 7, 105, 123 or 174
Gold-plated orchid blooms are crafted into jewellery. (Also at Suntec City Mall; tel 6338 8250 and Centrepoint; tel: 6235 0988.)

Salad
25 Haji Lane; tel: 6299 5805; Mon–Sat 1–8pm;

MRT: Bugis; map p.136 C3
Stocks slightly pricey home accessories like mirrors and picture frames and a range of affordable clothes.

The Shop
The Arts House, 1 Old Parliament Lanc; tol: 6332 6907; www.theartshouse.com.sg; Mon–Sat 11am–8pm; MRT: City Hall; map p.139 D4
Inspired homemade products including homeware, jewellery, pottery and illustrations from local artists.

ORIENTAL CARPETS
Oriental carpets, from tribal rugs to silk carpets, come from China, India, Iran, Turkey or Pakistan. The following has good selections:

Amir & Sons
36 Kandahar Street; tel: 6734 9112; www.amirandsons.com; Mon–Sat 11am–6pm; MRT: Bugis; map p.137 C4

Eastern Carpets
03-21C Raffles City Shopping Centre, 252 North Bridge Road; tel: 6338 8135; www.eastern carpets.com.sg; daily 10.30am–9.30pm; MRT: City Hall; map p.136 B2

Jehan Gallery
03-08 Tan Boon Liat Building, 315 Outram Road; tel: 6334 4333; www.jehangallery.com; daily 10am–7pm; MRT: Outram Park

Below: a poster for the MAAD weekend market.

Sport

Perhaps it is the country's miniscule size and population, or the fact that its people place an intense focus on academic education for its younger generation, but Singapore doesn't have a robust sporting culture. Its athletes tend to be stronger in only a few activities, such as bowling, table tennis, swimming, *wushu* (Chinese martial arts) and sailing, and have made their countrymen proud by taking top honours at international competitions. Efforts to promote a healthier appetite for sport among the people have led to a sound infrastructure and an event-packed calendar, which visitors are welcome to enjoy.

Adventure

Forest Adventure

825 Bedok Reservoir Road, Bedok Reservoir Park; tel: 8100 7420; www.forestadventure. com.sg; Tue–Sun 10am–6pm; MRT: Bedok, then bus: 18 or 28
Drum up some of that city-slicker courage for this camp. Plunge into the two-hour 'Grand Course', where you climb, crawl, swing between trees, and swoop down on ziplines across water to fine views of the Bedok Reservoir. There's also a less challenging kids' course.

Golf

Several of Singapore's golf courses are world class, attracting big tournaments like the **Johnnie Walker Classic**. Private golf courses offer limited access to non-members but public courses have no visitor restrictions. Fees range from S$40 for a weekday nine-hole course to S$450 for a full weekend round on a championship course.

Green Fairways Golf Course

60 Fairways Drive; tel: 6468 7233; daily 6.30am–5.30pm (golf course), 7am–11pm (driving range); MRT: Orchard, then taxi
Only 10 minutes by taxi from Orchard Road, this has a 62-bay driving range and a nine-hole public course.

Raffles Country Club

450 Jalan Ahmad Ibrahim; tel: 6861 7655; www.rcc.org.sg; daily 7am–6.30pm; MRT: Joo Koon, then taxi
Widely regarded as the most scenic course in Singapore. Two 18-hole courses skirt a reservoir and offer lovely views of Malaysia.

Seletar Country Club

101 Seletar Club Road; tel: 6481 4812; www.seletarclub.com.sg; Mon 3pm–10pm, Tue–Sun 7am–10pm; MRT: Khatib, then taxi
This challenging 18-hole course has scenic Lower Seletar Reservoir as its backdrop.

Sentosa Golf Club

27 Bukit Manis Road, Sentosa; tel: 6275 0090; www.sentosa golf.com; MRT: HarbourFront, then taxi or Sentosa Express from VivoCity
Home to two of Singapore's best courses with views of the South China Sea. The Tanjong course and the more difficult Serapong course are impeccably maintained.

Hiking

Despite the heat, hiking is one of Singapore's most attractive outdoor pursuits. The **Bukit Timah Nature Reserve**, **Sungei Buloh Wetland Reserve**, **Central Catchment Nature Reserve** and **Pulau Ubin** are popular trekking areas.
SEE ALSO BEACHES AND ISLANDS, P.33; WALKS AND VIEWS, P.128, 131

Spectator Sport

Among the most followed

Below: sailing off Changi.

Left: beach volleyball action on Sentosa.

Ski360 Cableski Park
1206A East Coast Parkway; tel: 6442 7318; www.ski360degree. com; Mon, Tue, Thu 10am–7pm, Wed, Fri 12pm 0pm, Sat–Sun 9am–10pm; MRT: Bedok, then bus: 197 or 401 (weekends only)
Wakeboarders and water-skiers can practise on a 'track' pulled by cables here. It is a lot harder to learn wakeboarding this way, as the cables move at a predetermined speed, which may be too quick for learners. It's best to learn behind a boat.

Venues

Singapore Indoor Stadium
2 Stadium Walk; tel: 6344 2660; www.sportshub.com.sg/indoor-stadium; MRT: Stadium
This seats 13,000 and has played host to sporting events like the the the AVIVA Badminton Open. It is also the home venue of the Singapore Slingers, who play in the Australian National Basketball League. Being constructed in the vicinity is the new Sports Hub which houses the National Stadium. When ready in 2014, it will have the world's largest dome roof.

Below: hiking in Sungei Buloh Wetland Reserve.

Beach volleyball is gaining popularity in Singapore. The best place to play and watch it is the white-sand Siloso Beach on Sentosa island. The beach also hosts beach volleyball championships and clinics regularly. See www.sentosa. com.sg for event schedules.

---

are cricket, rugby and field hockey, matches of which you might chance to see at the **Padang** *(see p.101)*, especially at the weekends. The annual Singapore Cricket Club International Rugby 7s tournament (www.sccrugbysevens.com) is also held at the Padang.

Singapore also has its own football league, the **S-League** (www.sleague.com), in which local and international teams play at stadiums around the island.

The country is most famous for the **Singapore Formula 1** (www.singaporegp.sg), the only night race in the world. The Singapore Grand Prix happens every September and the F1 Pit Building and Paddock buzzes with fast cars, world famous drivers, celebrities and fans. Concerts showcasing the biggest pop stars are held during this period too.
SEE ALSO FESTIVALS & EVENTS, P.58

Watersport

Changi Sailing Club
32 Netheravon Road; tel: 6545 2876; www.csc.org.sg; MRT: Tampines, then bus: 29
Singapore's only sailing club that offers courses in dinghy, catamaran and keelboat sailing for non-members.

Marina Country Club
600 Ponggol Seventeenth Avenue; tel: 6385 6166; www.marinacountryclub.com.sg; MRT: Sengkang, then shuttle bus
The watersport that has captured popular interest is wakeboarding. Several operators here offer boat and board rentals. Try **Waketime** (tel: 6387 1997; www.waketime.com.sg).

SAFYC Sea Sports Centre
110 Tanah Merah Coast Road; tel: 6758 3032; www.safyc.org.sg; daily 9am–10pm; MRT: Tanah Merah, then taxi
Offers windsurfing, kayaking and laser sailing courses.

Theatre

Major foreign and local theatre works with an Asian focus often premiere in Singapore, especially at the Singapore Arts Festival. Long-running Broadway favourites like *Les Misérables*, *Oliver!* and *Phantom of the Opera* also frequently make appearances. All these are showcased alongside a very healthy local English-language theatre scene populated by professional and amateur companies. These perform foreign and locally written works, including those that attempt to push boundaries and test the state's OB (out-of-bound) markers for politics, sexual content and more.

Major Companies

ACTION Theatre
42 Waterloo Street; tel: 6837 0842; www.action.org.sg; MRT: Bras Basah; map p.136 A3
The creator of *Chang & Eng*, Singapore's longest-running home-grown musical. This company presents original works and has staged some of the country's most acclaimed plays in its 30 years of operation. On its premises is a 100-seat studio theatre.

The Necessary Stage
B1-02 Marine Parade Community Building, 278 Marine Parade Road; tel: 6440 8115; www.necessary.org; bus: 15, 31, 36, 48 or 76
For over 20 years, TNS has consistently created some of the island's most provocative works, depicting the marginalised and repressed. It also runs the annual M1 Singapore Fringe Festival, in which its theatre section features local and foreign companies. Smaller productions are held in its 80-seat black box.

Singapore Repertory Theatre
20 Merbau Road; tel: 6733 8166; www.srt.com.sg; MRT: Clarke Quay, then taxi; bus: 32, 64, 123, 143 or 195; map p.135 D1
SRT is most associated with Broadway-scale productions that have brought together talented Asian stars like David Henry Hwang and Lea Salonga and award-winning directors, playwrights and designers. Its star musical was *The Forbidden City: Portrait of an Empress*. SRT has presented world-famous actors in a variety of productions including *Richard III* featuring Kevin Spacey and *King Lear* and *The Seagull* starring Sir Ian McKellen. It has its own theatre, The DBS Arts Centre, on its premises.

TheatreWorks
72-13 Mohamed Sultan Road; tel: 6737 7213; www.theatreworks.org.sg; MRT: Clarke Quay, then taxi; bus: 32, 54, 139 or 195; map p.135 D1
Singapore's top theatre company thrives under the artistic direction of Ong Keng Sen, most known for his edgy productions that turn tradition on its head with a mosaic of cultural interpretations. The group has its own warehouse performance space near the Singapore River.

Toy Factory Productions
15A Smith Street; tel: 6222 1526; www.toyfactory.com.sg; MRT: Chinatown
One of the country's leading bilingual (English and Mandarin) theatre companies. Among its repertoire are sell-out favourites like *Titoudao*, which is inspired by the life story of its chief artistic director's mother who was a famous Chinese opera performer, as well as some of the most risque shows possible in Singapore, including the raunchy *Cabaret*, *Bent* and *Shopping and F*cking*.

Event listings can be found in the newspapers or in listings magazines like *I-S*, available free at many cafes and casual restaurants, or *TimeOut Singapore*, sold at major bookstores. For ticketing, check out **SISTIC** (tel: 6348 5555; www.sistic.com.sg) or **Tickets.com** (tel: 6296 2929; www.tdc.sg).

Left: a performance at the Singapore Repertory Theatre.

Jubilee Hall
1 Beach Road, Raffles Hotel; tel: 6412 1323; MRT: City Hall; map p.136 B2
It's easy to imagine what watching a performance in the Jubilee Hall was like in the old days with its chandeliers, red velvet curtains and ceiling cornices. It is limited to smaller performances.

The Substation
45 Armenian Street; tel: 6337 7535; www.substation.org; MRT: City Hall/Bras Basah; map p.136 A2
The late Kuo Pao Kun, doyen of Singapore theatre, turned this former power station into the country's first independent contemporary arts centre in 1990. The Substation is a real bare-bones kind of place, but therein lies the charm of its bohemian atmosphere. Small performances are held at its Guinness Theatre.

Theatres at Marina Bay Sands
Marina Bay Sands, 10 Bayfront Avenue; tel: 6688 8868; www.marinabaysands.com; MRT: Marina Bay; map p.139 E3
Headlining acts and major musicals such as *The Lion King*, *Wicked* and *Jersey Boys* have been staged in the two world-class theatres at Marina Bay Sands.

Wild Rice
65 Kerbau Road; tel: 6292 2695; www.wildrice.com.sg; MRT: Little India
'Glocal' works are inspired by Singapore society and universal issues. It has played to sell-out crowds at the New Zealand International Festival, with a distinctly Singaporean adaptation of Orwell's *Animal Farm*. Its founding artistic director Ivan Heng is something of an institution – an actor, writer and director, he has won international awards for his solo performances as *Emily of Emerald Hill*.

Venues

The Arts House
1 Old Parliament Lane; tel: 6332 6900; www.theartshouse.com.sg; MRT: City Hall; map p.139 D4
Housed in the former Parliament House, this stages a monthly programme of small performances and exhibitions.
SEE ALSO FILM, P.61

Drama Centre
100 Victoria Street, 05-01 National Library Building; tel: 6837 8400; www.dramacentre.com; MRT: Bugis; map p.136 B3
Once a decrepit venue, the Drama Centre has gained a fresh lease of life in its new location within the new National Library building. It now has a main space that seats 615 and a black box that can accommodate 120.

Esplanade Theatres
Esplanade – Theatres on the Bay, 1 Esplanade Drive; tel: 6828 8377; www.esplanade.com; MRT: Esplanade; map p.136 B1
The Esplanade's Theatre and Theatre Studio are the city's premier performance spaces for drama.
SEE ALSO ARCHITECTURE, P.27; DANCE, P.47; MUSIC, P.90

Right: Toy Factory's *Titoudao*.

Transport

Singapore is easily accessible from just about every city in the world. More than 80 airlines operate over 5,000 flights a week to the Singapore Changi Airport. The city is linked by rail to Malaysia and Thailand, and by cruise services to Southeast Asia. Singapore is also an excellent base from which to explore the Southeast Asian and Australasian region, especially with the proliferation of budget airlines in recent years. Within Singapore, a modern, efficient and clean public transport system helps visitors get to wherever they want with minimal fuss.

Getting There

BY AIR

Singapore Changi Airport is frequently rated the best in the world. It is so efficient that one can hop into a taxi – after clearing immigration and customs and retrieving bags – within 15 minutes of landing. Its terminals – Terminal 1 (T1), Terminal 2 (T2), Terminal 3 (T3) – handled more than 51.2 million passengers in 2012. A new terminal, Terminal 4, is expected to be ready in 2017.

The main terminals are linked to one other by the Sky Train.

The airport has been con-ceived for maximum comfort and convenience, with a wide range of services and shops. Everything from post offices to free broadband internet access to a transit hotel is available to make waiting time at the airport enjoyable.

If you need help, look out for the Information and Customer Service counters in the terminals or the 24-hour help phones. These phones will link you to the appropriate customer service officers.

For more information on airport services, contact **Changi Airport Customer Service** (tel: 6595 6868;

Singapore is an ideal jumping-off point to Southeast Asian destinations like Bali, Phuket, Koh Samui, Langkawi, and Siem Reap, many of which are served by Singapore Airlines' sister airline **SilkAir** (www.silkair.com). Budget carriers like **AirAsia** (www.airasia.com), **Jetstar Asia** (www.jetstar.com) and **Tiger Airways** (www. tigerairways.com) fly to regional tourism centres.

www.changiairport.com).
For information on flight arrival and departure times, dial tel: 1800-542 4422.

Flying from the UK and the US

The national carrier Singapore Airlines (www.singaporeair.com) is based at the Changi Airport and flies to over 60 cities in more than 30 countries.

There are regular daily flights out of London and major European cities direct to Singapore. Flying time is between 12 and 13 hours. Many UK and European travellers heading to Australia and New Zealand often use

Below: the Changi Airport's facilities, such as the orchid garden pictured here, keep passengers suitably entertained.

Left: Singapore's MRT system is reliable and speedy.

the world.

Tanah Merah Ferry Terminal (tel: 6545 2048), located near the Changi Airport, handles dual traffic to the resorts on Indonesia's Bintan island as well as Tanjung Pinang, its capital, and to Nongsa, on neighbouring Batam island. Ferries to Malaysia's Sebana Cove also depart from here.

Changi Ferry Terminal (tel: 6214 8031), also near the Changi Airport, handles regular ferry services to Tanjung Belungkor, on Malaysia's east coast.

Singapore as a transit point to break the long journey. From Singapore, it is another 4½ hours to Perth, 7½ hours to Sydney and Melbourne, and 10 hours to Auckland.

Flying from the US takes longer; a flight from Los Angeles or San Francisco, which crosses the Pacific Ocean, takes about 16 to 18 hours with a stop in Seoul, Taipei or Tokyo en route. From New York, flight time is about 22 hours, including transit time.

Singapore Airlines offers non-stop flights from Los Angeles and New York to Singapore. These flights typically shave two to four hours off flying time.

BY SEA

Most visitors arrive at the **Singapore Cruise Centre** (tel: 6513 2200; www.singapore cruise.com) located at the HarbourFront Centre. The facility is also used by several regional cruise operators, such as Star Cruises, and by many large cruise liners stopping over on their long voyages around

BY TRAIN

Coming by train through Malaysia and then across the Causeway at Woodlands in the north of Singapore is a leisurely way to arrive. Malaysia's **Keretapi Tanah Melayu** (KTM) has two lines: one links Singapore to Kuala Lumpur, Butterworth, Alor Setar and north across the Thai border to Bangkok, and the other branches off at Gemas and connects to Tumpat, near Kota Bharu on Malaysia's east coast.

Both Malaysian and Singapore immigration facilities are located at Woodlands and Tuas.

Below: travelling is a doddle at the efficient Changi Airport.

If money is no object, consider the Chronicles of Southeast Asia tour from **E&O Express** (tel: 6395 0678, www.orient-express.com), the ultimate re-creation of a bygone age of romantic Asian rail travel. The train carries a maximum of 125 passengers in 22 air-conditioned carriages, from Singapore to Bangkok, via Kuala Lumpur, Penang and the Bridge over the River Kwai.

BY COACH/BUS

There are good roads down the west and east coasts of Peninsular Malaysia, crossing either the Causeway in Woodlands or the Second Link in Tuas into Singapore. The Second Link is far less prone to the frequent congestion that the Woodlands checkpoint experiences.

Private air-conditioned buses run from Hat Yai in Thailand and many towns in Malaysia to Singapore. The ride from Hat Yai takes about 14 hours with stops for refreshments and arrives in Singapore at Golden Mile Complex on Beach Road. Call **Grassland** (tel: 6293 1166; www.grassland.com.sg) for bus tickets to Hat Yai.

Hasry (tel: 6294 9306; www.hasrytravel.com) has buses that connect Singapore to key Malaysian cities like Kuala Lumpur, Penang and Melaka. Buses arrive at and leave from its Lavender Street office.

Other coach operators such as **Five Stars** (Malaysia: tel: 1300 22 5555, Singapore tel: 6533 5555), **Plusliner** (Kuala Lumpur tel: 03-2070 1095, Singapore tel: 6238 9825; www.plusliner.com.my), **Aeroline** (Kuala Lumpur tel: 03-6258 8800, Singapore tel: 6258 8800; www.aeroline.com.my) and **Airebus** (Singapore tel: 6737 6535; www.airebus.net) offer the more luxurious and roomier 30-seater, double decker coaches. These link Kuala Lumpur and other major Malaysian cities to Singapore.

Getting Around

FROM THE AIRPORT

Changi Airport is linked to the city centre by the East Coast Parkway (ECP) and to other parts of Singapore by the Pan-Island (PIE) and Tampines (TPE) expressways.

There are four types of transport from the airport – taxi, bus, airport shuttle and MRT.

By Taxi

At the airport terminals, the taxi stands are situated on the same level as the arrival halls. A surcharge of S$3 (or S$5 from 5pm to midnight Fri–Sun) applies in addition to the fare shown on the taxi meter. Two other surcharges are added to the fare where applicable: for rides between midnight and 6am and for ERP (Electronic Road Pricing) tolls. The taxi trip to the city centre takes about 20–30 minutes and costs S$18–38, excluding surcharges.

By Bus

In the basements of the terminals are public bus depots. Buses depart between 6am and midnight daily, and information on bus routes is available at the bus stands. Service No. 36 gets you directly into the city. You'll need the exact fare as no change is given on board.

By Airport Shuttle

A shuttle bus service operates between the airport and major hotels in the city, with flexible alighting points within the

CBD. Tickets at S$9 for adults and S$6 for children are available at the shuttle counters located at the terminals.

By MRT

The MRT link to the Changi Airport is located underground next to Terminal 2 and Terminal 3. A ride to the city centre takes about 30 minutes and cost less than S$2. Note that trains do not go directly to the city so you have to switch lines at the Tanah Merah MRT station. The first train arrives at about 5.30am, and the last train departs at 11.18pm.

CITY TRANSPORT Information

A helpful source for information on the use of public transport is the **'Travel with Ease' Public Transport Guide for Tourists**, which is available at Singapore Visitors Centres and MRT stations. This guide gives travel directions to major tourist spots.

Ez-link Card

If you are going to be moving around a lot by public transport, it is convenient to buy an **ez-link card**, which is a stored-value card for use on the MRT, LRT and buses. This

Below: the city is served by an excellent MRT network and infrastructure of roads.

Above: the City Hall MRT interchange is always a bustle of activity at any time of the day.

card is available from all TransitLink offices in MRT stations and bus interchanges for S$12, of which S$5 is a non-refundable deposit. To use this card, tap it on the electronic reader located at MRT turnstiles or the entrances of buses. The electronic reader will automatically deduct the maximum fare. When exiting from an MRT station and bus, tap the card again against the electronic reader and the unused portion of the fare is credited back to your card. You can top up the value of your card when it runs low.

Singapore Tourist Pass

An excellent deal for tourists is the Singapore Tourist Pass (www.thesingaporetouristpass.com.sg). For just S$10 a day, you can use this pass (with 1-, 2- and 3-day options) for unlimited rides on the public transport system. Functioning like an ez-link card, it can be purchased at TransitLink Ticketing offices in selected MRT stations.

> Call TransitLink
> (tel: 1800-225 5663) for
> public transport information.

Buses

Around 11,000 buses operated by **Singapore Bus Service** (SBS) and **SMRT Buses** ply about 260 routes, covering practically every corner of the island. Buses (single and double deckers with or without air-conditioning) run from around 5.30am to 11.30pm, and some services have an extension of about half an hour for both starting and ending times at weekends and on public holidays.

Fares are cheap (maximum S$1.90 on air-conditioned buses) and calculated based on the number of sectors. Have loose change ready; bus drivers are generally helpful and will tell you the exact fare on boarding. Fare information is also clearly displayed at bus stops. Tickets are issued by automatic dispensers on board.

For convenience, buy an ez-link card or a tourist pass *(see left).*

Taxis

More than 23,000 taxis stalk the roads. Singapore's taxis are clean and generally in good condition. Most drivers speak or understand English.

All taxis are metered with a flagfall of S$3 to $5 for the first kilometre (0.6 miles) and 22 cents for every 400m thereafter or less for a trip of up to 10km (6.2 miles), or every 350m thereafter or less after 10km, or every 45 seconds or less of waiting time.

A string of surcharges apply: 50 percent extra from midnight to 5.59am; S$3 surcharge for trips hired in the CBD Mon–Sun and public holidays 5pm–midnight; 25 percent extra during peak hours (Mon–Fri 6–9.30am, Mon–Sun and

Below: bus numbers and bus-route information are clearly displayed at bus stops.

125

Above: all taxis in Singapore are metered, but watch out for the surcharges, which can add up.

public Holidays 6pm to midnight); for bookings *(see below)*; Electronic Road Pricing (ERP) fees; and trips from the airport. Tipping is not necessary.

Most taxi stands are found outside shopping centres, hotels and other public buildings. In the CBD and downtown areas, taxis can only pick up passengers at taxi stands, even when on call booking. Elsewhere, you can flag one down on the road. But be warned that during morning and evening rush hours and when it rains, it can be difficult to get one if you haven't booked ahead.

To book a taxi, contact:
Comfort/CityCab
Tel: 6552 1111
SMRT Taxi
Tel: 6555 8888
Premier Taxi
Tel: 6363 6888
Smart Cab
Tel: 6485 7777
Trans Cab
Tel: 6555 3333

Booking fees apply: S\$3.30–S\$5 for prime time (Mon–Fri 6–9.30am, Mon–Sun and public holidays 6pm–midnight) and S\$2.30–S\$2.50 for non-prime time (all other times).

DRIVING

Car rental is not cheap. Rates start from S\$175 for a 1.3-litre car to S\$295 for a two-litre car per day, including mileage but not insurance. These rates are only applicable for driving in Singapore; taking the car to Malaysia will cost extra.

Before you head out, stock up on parking coupons, available from petrol stations and convenience stores, and make sure you have a complete understanding of the Electronic Road Pricing (ERP) system *(see Environment, p.48)*. A valid driver's licence from your country of residence or an international driver's licence is required for driving in Singapore. Driving is on the left, and the wearing of seatbelts and the use of special child seats is compulsory. Speed limits are 60–70km/h (37–44 miles/h) in residential areas and 80–90km/h (50–56 miles/h) on expressways.

Contact any of the following car rental companies:
Avis
Tel: 1800-737 1668;
www.avis.com.sg
Hertz
Tel: 1800-734 4646 ;
www.hertz.com.sg

Tours

Original Singapore Walks
Tel: 6325 1631; www.singapore walks.com
There's no need for book-

Below: view the city skyline from a Singapore River cruise.

ings; just visit the website for tour schedules and turn up at the designated MRT station. These entertaining, guided walking tours are a great way to see Singapore's heritage areas, from Chinatown and Little India to Fort Canning Hill and the Changi Chapel and Museum. The *Tipple Exchange* tour, albeit more suitable for adults, deserves a mention. It is held at the Singapore River on Tuesday; guides tell stories of the river's glories and scandals at sunset over pints of beer.

Above: touring the city on trishaws.

Perspective Journeys
Mobile tel: 8127 2723; www.perspectivejourneys.com
Who better to give insight into Chinese culture in Singapore than an anthropologist? Mr C.W. Chan offers in-depth cultural tours like *Dreams of a Sojourner*, which traces the footsteps of Chinese immigrants, and one that looks at the various schools of Buddhism that coexist in Singapore. Tours last three to four hours.

SH Tours
Tel: 6734 9923; www.asiatours.com.sg
This offers a whole host of options, including a *feng shui* tour and an *Eastern*

Heartlands tour that visits Geylang Serai, Changi Chapel and Museum and Tampines town. If you want a guided glimpse of Singaporean suburban life, this is it. There are also city tours offered in German (six persons minimum).

Singapore River Criuse
Tel: 6336 6111; www.rivercruise.com.sg
Hop on an old bumboat and see the city from the water for a languid 30 minutes. Tickets are available from any of the 13 jetties along the Singapore River – River Valley, Robertson Quay, Clemenceau, Read Bridge, Clarke Quay, South Bridge, Boat Quay, Fullerton, Esplanade, Merlion Park, Bayfront South, Promenade and Marina Barrage. Boats run daily 9am to 11pm (last boat at 10.30pm).

Singapore Trolley
Tel: 6338 6877; www.singaporetrolley.com
A themed tour and attraction on a half-air-conditioned and half-open-air trolley bus. The three-hour tour covers the Civic District, Chinatown, Little India and Kampong Glam.

Tour East Singapore
Tel: 6735 1221; www.toureast.net
Tours include *Getting To Know Singapore*, *Let The Fun*

Begin, *Round Island Tour* and *Morning At The Zoo*. Whether it's history, culture, fun or a specific type of attraction you want to see, they have it for you.

Trishaw Tours
Alphaland Travel Services tel: 6336 1205; Singapore Explorer tel: 6339 6833; Trishaw Tours tel: 6344 1738; Triwheel Tours tel: 6336 9025
The quaint trishaw, a bicycle with a sidecar, has almost disappeared from Singapore's streets. Today it exists only for tourists who want to experience something of the old days. Most tours operate around Chinatown, Little India and the Civic District and last 30–45 minutes. Tickets cost S$25. Don't flag down a trishaw on the street unless you want to be ripped off.

Watertours
31 Marina Coastal Drive, #01-09 Marina South Pier; tel: 6533 9811; www.watertours.com.sg; MRT: Marina Bay
Hop on its ornate replica of a Ming-dynasty Chinese junk and take a leisurely cruise around Sentosa and the southern islands of St John's, Sisters' and Kusu.
Day cruises with high tea are at 10.30am and 3pm, while dining cruises set off at 3pm and 6.30pm.

Transit passengers at the Changi Airport who have a minimum of five hours' layover time before catching their connecting flight can book a two-hour **Free City Tour**. Bookings can be made at the Free Singapore Tours (FST) Registration Booth at Terminal 2 and Terminal 3. There are four **Heritage Tours** daily, starting at 9am, 11.30am, 2.30pm and 4pm, as well as one City Lights tour, at 6.30pm. Do register at least one hour before the tour commences.

Walks and Views

With Singapore's excellent transport system, it's easy to just hop on a bus, train or taxi and sightsee your way around the island. But if you don't mind the tropical heat and humidity, get out on foot, and the city will surprise you. A few of the walks recommended here involve more strenuous climbs and trails in delightful pockets of green in the suburbs, while others are simply idyllic strolls in charming neighbourhoods. It is best to embark on walks in the early morning or late evening, when the air is fresher and the weather is cooler. Wear good walking shoes and bring along plenty of water.

Bukit Timah Nature Reserve

Entrance at Hindhede Drive; tel: 6468 5736; www.nparks. gov.sg; daily 6am–7pm (night walks not encouraged); bus 67, 75, 170, 171, 173, 184, 852 or 961

Located 12km (7.5 miles) from the city, in the middle of the island, this is most easily reached by taxi. If you are taking the bus, alight along Upper Bukit Timah Road, opposite Bukit Timah Shopping Centre, or along Jalan Anak Bukit, opposite Courts furniture store, and walk to the end of Hindhede Drive. The reserve includes Singapore's highest hill, Bukit Timah, at a mere 164m (538ft), and protects 163 hectares (403 acres) of the nation's only virgin lowland rainforest.

Despite its diminutive size, the number of plant species in the reserve exceeds that found in all of North America. Make your way to the hilltop, which is a good place to wait for white-bellied sea eagles or brahminy kites. The besotted birdwatcher can take the challenge of identifying at least nine species of swifts and swallows. The view over the protected forest of several water reservoirs makes you forget you are in one of the world's most densely populated cities.

There are five walking trails, all clearly marked and with varying levels of difficulty, taking from 45 minutes to 2 hours to complete. There is also a challenging 6-km- (3.7-mile-) long mountain-bike trail for enthusiasts. Brochures and trail maps are available at the Visitor Centre. The hill gets crowded at weekends – if you're planning a trek, weekdays are your best bet.

Kampong Glam

MRT: Bugis

Start your stroll at **Arab Street**, where you can shop for *batiks*, baskets of every shape and size, leatherware, ethnic jewellery and alcohol-free perfume. At the end of Arab Street is **Beach Road**. Turn left past the fishing tackle shops – a reminder that this was once the seafront – and turn left again at **Bussorah Street**, which during the Ramadan fasting month

Below: a common tree shrew at Bukit Timah Nature Reserve.

Left: the Treetop Walk at the Central Catchment Reserve.

ria Street and you'll find the blue mosaic-tiled **Malabar Muslim Jama-Ath Mosque**, a quiet place of worship that is as old as Kampong Glam. The islands's oldest Muslim cemetery lies beneath fragrant frangipani trees a little further along **Victoria Street**, opposite Jalan Kledek.

Finally, end your walk at Singapore's very own Leaning Tower, the **Hajjah Fatimah Mosque**, built circa 1846, located behind Jalan Sultan and off Beach Road.

SEE ALSO CHURCHES, MOSQUES AND TEMPLES, P.41, 43, 44; MUSEUMS AND GALLERIES, P.85

before the Muslim celebration of Hari Raya Puasa is filled with street vendors peddling delicacies for Muslims breaking their fast at sunset. From here, gaze at the great golden dome of **Sultan Mosque**, which dates back to 1924.

Among the shops that sell Asian and Muslim-inspired crafts on Bussorah Street are also Arabic-style cafés and restaurants serving Middle Eastern cuisine, a magnet for young urban Malays in the evenings.

Two streets down, on **Haji Lane**, the hip quotient rises. There are arty venues like the indie film gallery **Pitch Black** (63 Haji Lane) and the style emporium-cum-ice cream parlour **Pluck**. The cool vibe continues on **Bali Lane**, where cafés like **Blu Jaz** (11 Bali Lane) have local musicians performing during dinner.

At the very heart of the district, at 85 Sultan Gate, is **Istana Kampong Gelam**, once the palace of the Malay royal family who ruled the island before Raffles arrived, which has now been converted into the **Malay**

> Arabic architectural influences are the most resplendent in Bussorah Street, which used to house *haj* pilgrims travelling to Mecca in the early days. Today the Arabic-style cafés and restaurants serving Middle Eastern cuisine attract a more secular crowd of patrons.

Heritage Centre.

Wander towards the corner of Jalan Sultan and Victo-

Katong

Eastern Singapore; MRT: Eunos, then taxi or MRT: Bedok, then bus: 31, 32, 40

Begin at the unofficial start of Katong, near the **Holy Family Church** (6 Chapel Road), where Catholics in the area have worshipped for decades. Walk down the same side of the street, towards **Katong Village** (86 East Coast Road). This former police station, built in

Below: basketware spills over onto the street in Arab Street.

Above: a morning walk in the MacRitchie Reservoir Park.

8.30am–5pm; free; MRT: Ang Mo Kio, then bus: 166
Several hiking routes in the **MacRitchie Reservoir Park**, which is located in the Central Catchment Nature Reserve, take visitors through mature secondary forest. Among these trails, the **HSBC Treetop Walk** is the most interesting. This free-standing suspension bridge is the first of its kind in Singapore and the region, connecting the two highest points of MacRitchie and offering a spectacular panorama of the forest canopy. The walkway is 250m (820ft) long, and its highest point is at 25m (82ft).

Getting to the Treetop Walk is a trek in itself. Enter through MacRitchie Reservoir Park via the **MacRitchie Nature Trail**. It's a 4.5km (2.8 mile) walk (about 1.5–2 hours) where you'll encounter interesting flora like the pitcher plant and ant plant, and catch a glimpse of the myriad forest birds and animals like the racket-tailed drongo, clouded monitor lizard and black bearded dragon. A round trip by this route, including the Treetop

Below: living room display at Rumah Bebe.

1928, is a hub of restaurants and pubs that come alive in the evening.

Across the road is **Katong Antique House** (No. 208), where Peranakan artefacts are on display (tel: 6345 8544; viewing by appointment only; free admission). This century-old shophouse has been home to five generations of Peranakan families. The gallery on level two showcases the owner's collection of porcelain, beaded slippers, *kebaya* (traditional embroidered blouses) and silver jewellery.

Further down the road, **Glory** (No.139) is best known for its pineapple tarts and traditional Peranakan confectionery, while **Kim Choo Kueh Chang** (No.109/111) sells delicious rice dumplings wrapped in fragrant pandan leaves. Two doors away is **Rumah Bebe** (No.113), a trove of Peranakan artefacts in a 1928 shophouse. Check out the lovely bridal chamber on level two. Peranakan culinary classes are also offered here. Peranakan fare is in fact Singapore's very own fusion cuisine, blending Chinese and Malay cooking styles and

ingredients with flair.

If you don't fancy a heavy meal, walk down towards Ceylon Road to the *Katong laksa* (rice noodles in curried coconut gravy) stalls situated at the start of the lane. The lively hawkers will yell for your custom.

The ornate **Sri Senpaga Vinayagar Temple** (daily 5.55am–11pm) sits at 19 Ceylon Road. An important place of worship for Hindus in the East Coast, it dates back to the 1850s. The present building, completed in 2003, features a five-tier, 21-m (69-ft) *rajagopuram* (royal entrance tower) sculpted according to Indian Chola traditions. The *dwarapalakas* (gatekeepers) at the base tier of the tower are not found anywhere else in Asia. The temple is also capped by a golden dome.

MacRitchie Reservoir Park, Central Catchment Nature Reserve

Enter via MacRitchie Reservoir or Venus Drive off Upper Thomson Road; tel: 1800 471 7300; www.nparks.gov.sg; Tue–Fri 9am–5pm, Sat, Sun and public holidays

Walk, takes about 3–5 hours (7–10km/4.3–6.2 miles), depending on your pace.

The shorter route to the Treetop Walk is a 2.5-km (1.5 mile) walk (approximately 1 hour) from **Venus Drive** off Upper Thomson Road, along a stream. A round trip by this route takes about 3 hours.

Do note that the walk has been graded as moderate to difficult, so it may not be suitable for young children and the elderly. As an alternative, try the boardwalk trails, which also offer rewarding experiences. They are accessible from the MacRitchie Reservoir Park.

Mount Faber
MRT: HarbourFront
Mount Faber offers both a lovely walking route and some of the island's best views. The sprawling rainforest-covered park, which surrounds Mount Faber, is one of the oldest in Singapore. During your walk, be sure to stop at the various lookout points for panoramic views of the city and the port area.

There are several well-defined footpaths that visitors can take, the best beginning at Kampong Bahru Road. A large stone sign marks the start of your

Get an unobstructed bird's-eye view of Singapore, Malaysia and Indonesia on a 37-minute ride on the 165-m- (541-ft-) high **Singapore Flyer** observation wheel. Located at Marina Bay, it is unabashedly touted as Singapore's version of the London Eye (tel: 6734 8829; www.singaporeflyer.com.sg; daily 8.30am–10.30pm; entrance charge).

10–15-minute walk up. Along the way, sneak a peek at the *keramat* (Muslim shrine) built in honour of Radin Ayu Mas, a Javanese princess who sacrificed herself to save her father. She is buried at the foot of Mount Faber.

The Jewel Box on the summit is worth a stopover. Wind down with fine food and drinks at one of its restaurants or bars and take in fantastic vistas. From here, you can also hop on a cable car ride to Sentosa, with a fine view of the harbour (tel: 6377 9688; www.mountfaber.com.sg; daily 8.30am–9pm; entrance charge).

Early mornings and evenings are the best times to take this walk. At daybreak, the song of birds and the cool morning air make for a delightful experience. At night, the view of lights twinkling in the distance is just dazzling, especially with a cold cocktail in hand.

Sungei Buloh Wetland Reserve
301 Neo Tiew Crescent; tel: 6794 1401; www.sbwr. org.sg; Mon–Sat 7.30am–7pm, Sun and public holidays

Below: the Singapore Flyer.

7am–7pm; free except on Sat, Sun, public and school holidays; MRT: Kranji, then taxi or bus: 925
On the extreme northwestern coast of Singapore is the Sungei Buloh Wetland Reserve, remarkable for its abundant and diverse birdlife – over 212 species of birds can be seen here. A boardwalk guides visitors through part of the reserve, with hides at regular intervals from where birds can be observed and platforms at vantage points. There are three trails, which last from one to five hours, including one through a mangrove. The Visitor Centre has more details on these and also screens an informative 10-minute audio-visual show at scheduled times.

The old ponds still remain, surrounded by mangroves. Plenty of fish and prawns still thrive, and with the farmers long gone, birds have a field day. Collared as well as white-throated kingfishers sit on the low stakes by the bunds waiting to swoop while cinnamon and yellow bitterns stalk the reedy edges.

But it is the migrating waders, of which more than 20 species have been sighted feeding on exposed mud beds, that are the stars of the reserve. From September to March, large flocks of plovers, sandpipers, stints, curlews, godwits and egrets gather to feed on the mud exposed by the ebbing tide.

With the rapid reclamation of other coastal areas in Singapore, this sanctuary now stands out as the last significant, sizeable feeding ground for migrating wading birds. It is the birds' last stopover on the migration path before the thrust to regions further south.

131

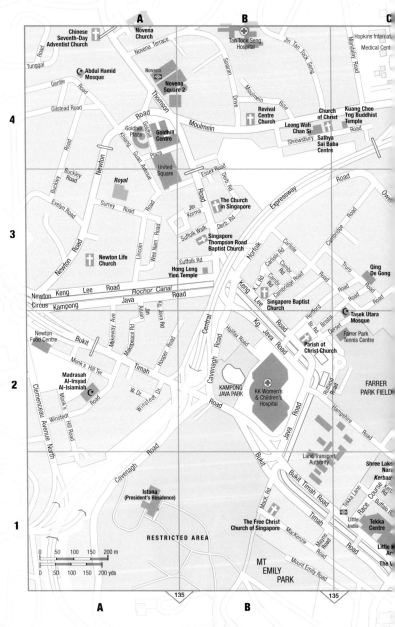

A

Chinese Seventh-Day Adventist Church

Novena Church

Tunggal Road

Novena Terrace

Abdul Hamid Mosque

Gentle Road

Novena

Gilstead Road

Novena Square 2

Thomson Road

Goldhill Plaza

Goldhill Centre

Goldhill Plaza

Goldhill Khiang

Guan Avenue

United Square

Buckley Road

Royal

Essex Road

Buckley Road

Evelyn Road

Surrey Road

Jln Korma

The Church in Singapore

Newton Road

Lincoln Road

Wee Nam Road

Suffolk Walk

Derb. Rd

Singapore Thompson Road Baptist Church

Newton Life Church

Suffolk Rd

Hong Leng Yien Temple

Newton Keng Lee Road Rochor Canal Road

Circus Kampong Java Road

Newton Food Centre

Bukit

Mekaway Ave

Jln

Kg Java Rd

Makepeace Rd

Hooper Road

Monk's Hill Ter.

Timah

Clemenceau Avenue North

Madrasah Al-Irsyad Al-Islamiah

Monk's Road

W. Dr.

Winstedt Dr.

Hill Road

Winstedt Road

Cavenagh Road

Istana (President's Residence)

RESTRICTED AREA

0   50   100   150   200 m

0   50   100   150   200 yds

B

Tan Tock Seng Hospital

Jln Tan Tock Seng

Sinaran Drive

Moulmein

Buse

Revival Centre Church

Moulmein Road

Essex Road

Derb. Rd

Expressway

Norfolk Road

Carlisle Rd

Cambr. Rd

Cambridge Road

Keng Lee Road

K.L. Rd

Cambr. Rd

Carlisle Rd

Singapore Baptist Church

Central Road

Halifax Road

Kg. Java Road

Hertford

Br. Rd.

Bristol

Dorset

Parish of Christ Church

Cavenagh Road

KAMPONG JAVA PARK

KK Women's & Children's Hospital

Rutland Road

Java Road

Land Transport Authority

Bukit Timah Road

MacK. Rd

The Free Christ Church of Singapore

MacKenzie Road

Mayne Road

Mount Emily Road

MT EMILY PARK

Race Course Road

Tekka Lane

Little India

Shree Laks Nara Kerbau

Kerb

Buffalo Rd

Tekka Centre

Little I Ar

The V

C

Hopkins Internat Medical Cent

Mandalay Road

Church of Christ

Kuang Chee Tng Buddhist Temple

Leong Wah Chan Si

Sathya Sai Baba Centre

Shrewsbury Road

Road

Owe

Road

Truro Road

Qing De Gong

Tasek Utara Mosque

Farrer Park Tennis Centre

Hampshire Road

FARRER PARK FIELD

135

132

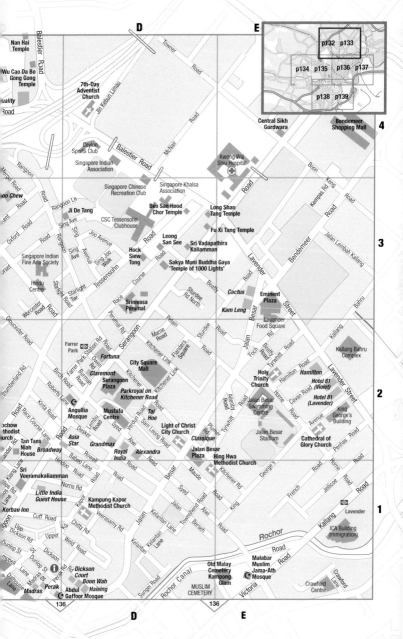

p132 | p133

p134 | p135 | p136 | p137

p138 | p139

Nan Hai Temple

Wu Cao Da Bo Gong Gong Temple

uality Road

Balestier Road

7th-Day Adventist Church

Jln Kebun Limau

Towner Road

McNair Road

Road

Central Sikh Gurdwara

Bendemeer Shopping Mall

4

Ceylon Sports Club

Singapore Indian Association

Balestier Road

Kwong Wai Shiu Hospital

Boon Keng Road

Rangoon Road

oo Chew

Rangoon Lane

Singapore Chinese Recreation Club

Singapore Khalsa Association

Kempas Rd

Road

Ji De Tang

Beo San Hood Chor Temple

Long Shan Tang Temple

Jalan Lembah Kallang

Bendemeer

3

scent Road

Oxford Road

Sing Ave

Rangoon Road

Sing Joo Walk

CSC Tessensohn Clubhouse

Fu Xi Tang Temple

Road

Hurset

Singapore Indian Fine Arts Society

Sing Ave

Sing Joo Avenue

Leong San See

Hock Siew Tong

Sri Vadapathira Kaliamman

Lavender

Starlight Ter.

Tessensohn Road

Sakya Muni Buddha Gaya 'Temple of 1000 Lights'

Road

Hindu Centre

Worcester Road

Race Course Road

Cactus

Eminent Plaza

Kallang

Bahru

Srinivasa Perumal

Sturdee Rd North

Kam Leng

Besar

Lavender Food Square

Gloucester Road

Farrer Park

Farrer Park Station Rd

Petain Road

Marne Road

Flanders Square

Sturdee Road

Jalan

Foch Rd

Beatty Road

Tyrwhitt Road

Kallang Bahru Complex

2

Fortuna

Owen Rd

Kitchener Link

Road

Holy Trinity Church

Hamilton Road

Lavender Street

umberland Rd

Birch Road

Claremont

Serangoon Plaza

City Square Mall

Parkroyal on Kitchener Road

Jalan Besar Swimming Centre

Allemby Road

Home Road

Cavan Road

Hotel 81 (Violet)

Hotel 81 (Lavender)

King George's Building

Kinta Road

Roberts Lane

Angullia Mosque

Mustafa Centre

Lambu Road

Tai Hoe

Jalan Besar Stadium

Plumer Road

Tyrwhitt Road

Penhas Road

ochow thodist urch

Asia Star

Grandmax

Desker Road

Verdun Road

Sam Leong Road

Light of Christ City Church

Classique

Cathedral of Glory Church

King

Road

Tan Tans Niah House

Broadway

Baboo Lane

Royal India

Alexandra

Syed Alwi Road

Jalan Besar Plaza

Hing Hwa Methodist Church

George's

Jellicoe Road

Penhas

Road

Sri Veeramakaliamman

Rowell Road

Hindoo Road

Maude Road

Road

1

Little India Guest House

Norris Rd

Kampung Kapor Methodist Church

Veerasamy Rd

Kapor Road

Syed Alwi Road

Kelantan Lane

King Street

Rochor

Road

French Road

Lavender

Kerbau Inn

Cuff Road

Chitty Rd

Weld Road

Jalan Berseh

Victoria Street

ICA Building (Immigration)

oon

Upp. Dickson Rd

Dunlop St

Dickson Road

Upper

Dunlop St

Kelantan Road

Kelantan Lane

Rochor Canal

Rochor Road

Crawford

Crawford Centre

ampbell

Dickson Court

Boon Wah

Haising

Old Malay Cemetery Kampong Glam

Malabar Muslim Jama-Ath Mosque

Madras

Perak

Abdul Gaffoor Mosque

MUSLIM CEMETERY

Lane

Dalhousie Lane

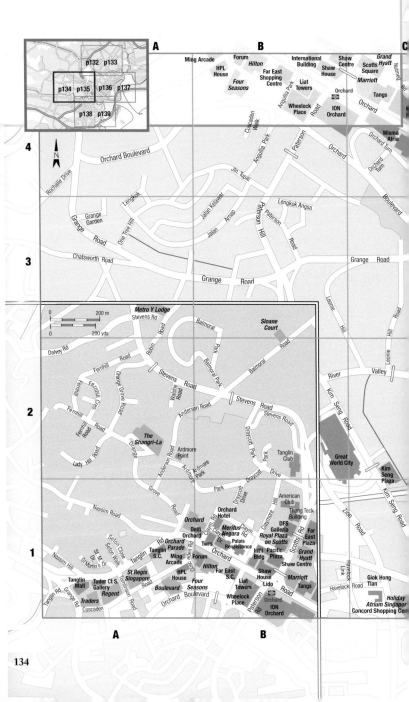

p132 p133

p134 p135 p136 p137

p138 p139

B

Ming Arcade
Forum
Hilton
International Building
Shaw Centre
Grand Hyatt
Scotts Square
HPL House
Far East Shopping Centre
Shaw House
Marriott
Four Seasons
Liat Towers
Orchard
Tangs
Wheelock Place
ION Orchard
Orchard
Wisma Atria

4

N

Orchard Boulevard

Rochalie Drive

Cuscaden Walk

Paterson

Orchard

Jln. Tupai

Anguilla Park

Orchard Turn

Lengkok

Grange Garden

One Tree Hill

Jalan Kelawar

Jalan Arnap

Lengkok Angsa

Paterson

Paterson Hill

Orchard Turn

Boulevard

Grange Road

Chatsworth Road

3

Grange Road

Grange Road

Leonie Hill

Leonie Hill Road

Metro Y Lodge
Stevens Rd
Balmoral
Sloane Court

0   200 m
0   200 yds

Robin Road

Park Road

Balmoral Park

Balmoral Road

River Valley

Dalvey Rd

Fernhill Road

Stevens Road

Fernhill Cres

Orange Grove Road

Walshe Road

Stevens Road

Kim Seng Road

2

Fernhill Road

Anderson Road

Stevens Road

Draycott Park

Park

River

Leonie Hill

The Shangri-La

Orange

Ardmore Point

Anderson Road

Arthmore Park

Draycott Park

Tanglin Club

Great World City

Kim Seng Plaza

Lady Hill

Grove

Park

Draycott Drive

Nassim Road

American Club

Orchard Hotel

Thong Teck Building

DFS Galleria

Kim Seng Road

Zion Road

Orchard
Delfi Orchard
Meritus Negara
Royal Plaza on Scotts
Far East Plaza

Claymore Hill

Scotts Rd

Orchard Parade S.C.
Tanglin S.C.
Ming Arcade
Twrs
Palais Renaissance
Int'l Bldg
Pacific Plaza
Grand Hyatt
Shaw Centre

Seton Close
Seton Walk
St. M.
St. Martin's Dr.

Tanglin Rd

Aden Rd

Forum
Orchard
Hilton
Far East S.C.
Liat Towers
Shaw House
Lido
Marriott
Tangs

1

Nassim Hill

St Regis Singapore

HPL House
Four Seasons
Boulevard
Wheelock Place

Paterson

ION Orchard
Orchard

Havelock Link

Giok Hong Tian

Tanglin Mall
Tudor Ct S.
Gallery
Regent
Traders

Tanglin Rd

Grange Rd

Tomlinson Road

Cuscaden

Orchard Boulevard

Paterson

Road

Havelock Road

Holiday Inn Singapore
Atrium Singapore
Concord Shopping Cen

A   **B**

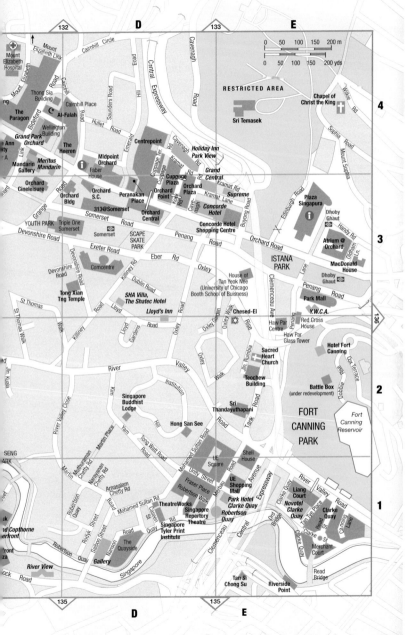

D
E

Malabar Muslim Jama-Ath Mosque

Crawford Centre

Crawford Lane

Crawford St

Crawford Road

Rochor

Nicoll Highway

Jalan Sultan

Jalan Klapa North

Bridge

Merdéka Bridge

Kallang Polo Club

Kallang Watersports Centre

Textile Centre

Sultan Plaza

Army Market

Beach Road

Golden Mile Complex

4

Aliwal Pk

Golden Sultan Theatre

Istana Kampung Gelam (Malay Heritage Centre)

Jalan Sultan

Hajjah Fatimah Mosque

Minto Rd

Golden Mile Food Centre

STM Video Theatre

Aliwal St

Sultan Gate

Pahang St

Keypoint

Beach Road

Java Rd

Golden Theatre

Bagdad St

Jalan Sultan

Golden Mile Tower

...py's

...St

The Concourse

Nicoll Highway

Golden Mile Tower

Avenue

MARINA PROMENADE

Plaza Parkroyal

Republic

The Plaza

Nicoll Highway

3

Road

Gateway

| 0 | 50 | 100 | 150 | 200 m |
| 0 | 50 | 100 | 150 | 200 yds |

...rad

Twr 3

Twr 4

Republic

MARINA

East Coast Parkway

2

...emasek

Centennial Tower

Gardens by the Bay (East) Visitor Centre

N

...illenia Walk

Millenia Tower

Promenade

Boulevard

PROMENADE

F1 Pit Lane and Paddock

Formula 1 Track

GARDENS BY THE BAY (EAST)

MARINA BAY GOLF COURSE

Boulevard

...itz-Carlton Millenia

Avenue

Sheares Bridge

Benjamin

1

Raffles

PROMENADE

PARK

Formula 1 Track

Singapore Flyer

The Helix Bridge

D

E

p132 p133

p134 p135 p136 p137

p138 p139

A · **B** · **C**

River View
Havelock
Road
Havelock

Holiday Inn
Atrium Singapore &
Concord Shopping Centre

Miramar

Copthorne
King's

Jalan Minyak

Thong Chai
Building

Thong
Kwang
Road

Tan Si Chong Su

Magazine Rd

Cumming

Fisher St

Tew Chew St

Riverside
Point

Read
Bridge

Merchant
Road

Cres

Swissotel
Merchant
Court

Thong Chai
Medical Instit

Cen
Tew Chew

Keng Chew St

New

Central
Mall

Upper

Ministry of
Manpower

Omar Kampung
Melaka Mosque

Apollo
Centre

Furama
City Centre

HO
PAM
Upp
Pickering

HO
PAM

**YORK
HILL ESTATE**

Furama
Riverfront
Singapore

Outram
Road

The Jubilee
Presby Church

York Hill
Road

Swee

Road

Manhattan
House

San
Centre

Pearl's

Hill Road

Cross

Subordinate
Courts

HAVELOCK
SQUARE

Havelock
Rd

Eu
Tong

Market St

4

Ho Lim
Kong Temple

Outram
Road

Outram Hill

Swee

PEARL'S HILL

*Pearl's Hill
Reservoir*

Police National
Service H.Q.

People's
Park Centre

OG Bldg

Majestic
Mall

Ywe Hwa
Emporium

Hotel 81

Upp. Hokki

Chinatown
Point

Hong Lim
Complex

Fook
Build

Qi Tian
Gong Temple

Chin

Outram Park

Park Crescent

Terrace

CITY PARK

Chinatown
Rd

People's Park
Complex

Lucky
Chinatown

CHINATOWN

Mosque St

Street

3

Central
Expressway

Chin

Outram Park

Outram
Flyover

Central
Police
Station

Pearl Bank

Pearl's
Bridge

Eu Tong

Kreta Ayer

New Bridge
Centre

Oriental
Plaza

The Inn
Yes
Chinatown

Chinatown
Complex

Smith St

Temple

Pagoda St

Trengganu

Chinatown
Heritage
Centre

Sago

**Jamae
Mosque**

Moh. Ali
Lane

**Sri
Mariamman**

Outram
Road

Avenue

College
Road

Hospital

Yangtze
Theatre

Pearl's
Centre

Layan Sithi
Vinayagar Temple

Hotel 1929

Kreta Ayer

Sago St

Banda St

Kreta Ayer
People's
Theatre

Buddha
Tooth Relic
Temple &
Museum

Sago
Lane

South

A Siang

Club St

Club St

Lai Chun Yuen

A Siang
Hill

Erskine Rd

Scarlet

Third Hospital Avenue

Singapore
National
Eye Centre

HSA

Outram Park

The Keong Saik

Royal
Peacock

New Bridge

Bukit

Keong

Neil

Tropical
Chinatown

New Hong Kong St

Ann Siang Rd

Kadayanallur St

A Siang
Hill

Maxwell
Food
Centre

Jinriksha
Station

Murray
St

Siang
Kec

2

Singapore
General
Hospital

Hospital Drive

Central Circus

Second Hospital Avenue

First Hospital

National
Dental
Centre

Outram Park

Sen

New
Majestic

Bukit

Ch. Ph Rd

Teck Lim Rd

Jiak

Duxton

DUXTON
PLAIN
PARK

Chinatown
Plaza

Tanjong Pagar
Conservation
Area

Cantonment

Hill

Berjaya
Duxton

Duxton Rd

Cook
St

Maxwell
Hse

Maxwell

Tanjong
Pagar

Peck Seah

Street

Singapore
City Gallery

URA Ctr.

MND Cp

red dot
design
museum

TEL
AY
PA

Bus
Terminal

Eu Tong Sen

New Bridge

St Matthew's
Church

Neil
Road

Craig
Road

Wallich St

Tras

Wallich St

Neil

Baba
House

Everton

Road

Everton Rd

Park

Phoo Thor Jee

VANDA MS
JOAQUIM PK

Plaza

1

Kampong Bahru Rd

Blair Road

Everton Road

Maritime
House

SPOTTISWOODE
PARK

Spottiswoode

Spottiswoode Park Road

Raeburn Park

**Singapore
Railway
Station**

**former Tanjong Pagar
Railway Station**

Cantonment Link

Keppel   Road

Yan
Kit

Tanjong Pagar

Road

Kee Seng St

Keppel
Towers

Hoe Chiang Rd

Lim Teck Kim Rd

South
Point

Singapore
Technologies
Building

Jit Poh
Building

Tanjong Pagar
Complex

Keppel Road

Tanjong
Pagar Plaza

Gopeng
St

Tanjong

Tras

GE Tower

Enggor St

Bernam St

Seng
Wong Beo

Lim Huat
Building

Amara

Choon Guan Street

International
Plaza

Anson

Peck

M Hotel

Pen
Rd

Mar
Ho

Shenton Way
Bus Terminal

Ayer   Rajah   Expressway

A · **B**

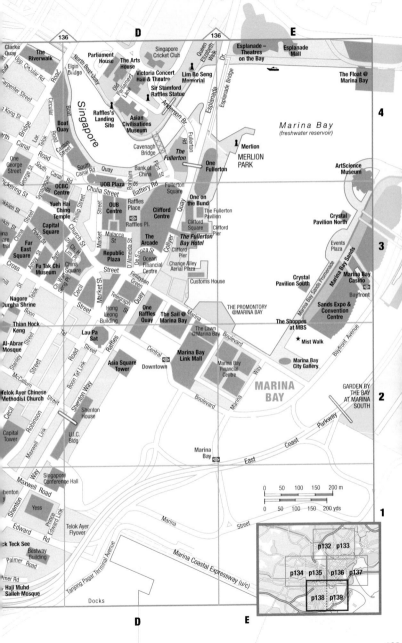

D
136
E

4

3

2

1

Clarke Quay
The Riverwalk
Upp. Circular Rd
Carpenter Street
Kong St
Boat Quay
Canal
North Bridge
One George Street
Pickering St
kkien St
Capital Square
China
are tral
Cross
mill
Nagore Durgha Shrine
Thian Hock Keng
Al-Abrar Mosque
Telok Ayer Chinese Methodist Church
Capital Tower
ck Teck See

Singapore

Parliament House
The Arts House
Elgin Bridge
North Boat Quay
North Bridge Road
Old Parliament Lane
Victoria Concert Hall & Theatre
Sir Stamford Raffles Statue
Raffles's Landing Site
Asian Civilisations Museum
Cavenagh Bridge

Singapore Cricket Club
Queen Elizabeth Walk
Lim Bo Seng Memorial
Anderson Br.

Esplanade Bridge
Esplanade Dr.

Esplanade – Theatres on the Bay
Esplanade Mall
The Float @ Marina Bay

Marina Bay
(freshwater reservoir)

Fullerton Rd
The Fullerton
Bank of China
Fullerton St
Flint St
One Fullerton
Merlion
MERLION PARK

Kong St
George Street
Canal
South Canal Rd
Chulia Street
Boat Quay
Carton Street
South Canal Rd
Bonham St
Battery Rd
Fullerton Square
ArtScience Museum

OCBC Centre
UOB Plaza
OUB Centre
Raffles Place
Raffles Pl.
One on the Bund
The Fullerton Pavilion
Clifford Pier
Crystal Pavilion North

Yueh Hai Ching Temple
Capital Square
Phillip Street
Church St
Ch Ch St
Malacca St
Lim St
De Souza St
Clifford Centre
Clifford Square
Events Plaza

Far East Square
Fu Tak Chi Museum
Amoy St
China St
Ch Kang St
China Square
Republic Plaza
The Arcade
Ocean Financial Centre
The Fullerton Bay Hotel
Change Alley Aerial Plaza
Crystal Pavilion South
Marina Bay Sands
Marina Bay Casino

Cecil Street
Market Street
Telegraph St
Finlayson Green
Customs House
Bayfront

Boon Tat St
Hong Leong Building
One Raffles Quay
The Sail @ Marina Bay
THE PROMONTORY @MARINA BAY
Marina Bay Sands Promenade
Sands Expo & Convention Centre

Lau Pa Sat
Raffles Quay
Central Boulevard
The Lawn @ Marina Bay
The Shoppes at MBS
★ Mist Walk

Stanley Street
McCallum
Asia Square Tower
Downtown
Marina Bay Link Mall
Marina Bay Financial Centre
Marina Bay City Gallery

Cecil
Robinson
Boon Tat Link
Shenton Way
Shenton House
MARINA BAY
GARDEN BY THE BAY AT MARINA SOUTH

Maxwell Link
U.I.C. Bldg
Marina Bay
Boulevard
Bayfront Avenue

Way
Shenton
benton
Singapore Conference Hall
Maxwell Road
Coast
East
Marina
Parkway

Yess
Prince Edward Link
Telok Ayer Flyover
Marina
Street

Edward Rd
Bestway Building
Palmer Road
Marina Coastal Expressway (u/c)

mer Rd
Haji Muhd Salleh Mosque
Tanjung Pagar Terminal Avenue
Docks

0   50   100   150   200 m
0   50   100   150   200 yds

p132   p133
p134   p135   p136   p137
p138   p139

D
E

Selective Index for Street Atlas

Index

Insight Smart Guide: Singapore
Compiled by: Annette Tan
Updated by: Amy Van
Commissioning Editor: Rebecca Lovell

Photography by: Jonathan Koh/Apa and
Vincent Ng/APA, except: Alain Compost
128b; Alamy 19t, 76/77t, 122b, 122/
123t; Amara Sanctuary Sentosa Resort
75; Apa Archives 40b; Aramsa Spa
98/99t; Archipalego 94; Asian Civilisations Museum 82b; Au Jardin 102/103t,
107b; Bigstock 58b; Chijmes 78b; Civil
Aviation Authority of Singapore 123b;
David Henley/Apa 19b; Denise
Tackett/Apa 33; Dreamstime 36b, 52b,
90/91t, 91b, 126b; Front Row 54t; The
Fullerton Hotel 28, 93b; The Gallery
Hotel 70b; Halia 108; Hotel 1929 73l,
106; iStockphoto 126t; Jack
Hollingsworth/Apa 2/3t; 7t, 10, 11b, 12,
15b, 17l&r, 21b, 42, 43t, 44, 45b, 48/49t,
49b, 51b, 58t, 76b, 79b, 80, 81b, 100b,
129b, 130t; James Tye/Apa 22; Kazbar
94; Kevin Jones/Apa 5TR, 69, 100/101t;
Lifebrandz 97b; Leonardo 92l; Low Jat
Leng 110; Luke Duggleby/onasia 127;
Marina Bay Sands 92/93a, 95; Marina
Mandarin 102b; Mary Evans Picture
Library 68bl; National Arts Council 57b;
National Museum of Singapore 5cl, 86;
National Orchid Garden 101b; National
Parks Board 128/129t; New Majestic
Hotel 70/71t, 105; Hansel 52/53t, 53b;
Night Safari 5cr, 37b; NUS Museums

87b; Photobank Singapore 68tl; Raffles
Hotel 72, 81t; Rang Mahal 103b, 112;
red dot design museum 87t, 117b;
Roslan Rahman/afp/Getty Images 66/
67t; Royal Plaza on Scotts 74; Sentosa
18, 32/33t, 35b,85, 118/119t; The Sentosa Resort & Spa 98b, 99b; The
Shangri-La 107t; Singapore Art Museum
82/83t, 88; The Pond Photography/Sin-
gapore Dance Theatre 46/47t, 46b; Singapore Flyer Pte Ltd 131b; Singapore
Repertory Theatre 120/121t; Singapore
Tourism Board 113, 117t; Singapore
Tourism Board/Ryan Tan 54b; Swissôtel
The Stamford 104; T'ang Quartet 90b;
Tan Kok Yong 5c, 26, 29, 30, 31b, 38b,
116; Timbre 97t; Toy Factory Productions 120b; Thumper 92/93t; Tony Ying
40/41t, 56b, 59t&b; Zhaowei Films
60/61t, 61b
Maps: James Macdonald
Art Editor: Tom Smyth
Series Editor: Sarah Sweeney

Third Edition 2013
© 2013 Apa Publications (UK) Limited
Printed by CTPS-China
Worldwide distribution enquiries:
APA Publications GmbH & Co Verlag KG
(Singapore branch); 7030 Ang Mo Kio Ave 5,
08-65 Northstar @ AMK, Singapore
569880; email: apasin@singnet.com.sg
Distributed in the UK and Ireland by:
Dorling Kindersley Ltd (a Penguin Company);
80 Strand, London, WC2R 0RL, UK; email:

customerservice@uk.dk.com
Distributed in the United States by:
Ingram Publisher Services
One Ingram Blvd, PO Box 3006, La Vergne,
TN 37086-1986; email: customer.
service@ingrampublisherservices.com
Distributed in Australia by:
Universal Publishers; PO Box 307,
St. Leonards, NSW 1590; email: sales@uni-
versalpublishers.com.au
Distributed in New Zealand by:
Brown Knows Publications; 11 Artesia Close,
Shamrock Park, Auckland, New Zealand
2016; email: sales@brownknows.co.nz
Contacting the Editors
We would appreciate it if readers would alert us
to errors or outdated information by writing to:
Apa Publications, PO Box 7910, London SE1
1WE, UK; fax: (44 20) 7403 0290;
email: insight@apaguide.co.uk
No part of this book may be reproduced,
stored in a retrieval system or transmitted in
any form or by any means (electronic,
mechanical, photocopying, recording or
otherwise), without prior written permission of
Apa Publications. Brief text quotations with
use of photographs are exempted for book
review purposes only. Information has been
obtained from sources believed to be reliable,
but its accuracy and completeness, and the
opinions based thereon, are not guaranteed.

MRT & LRT System r

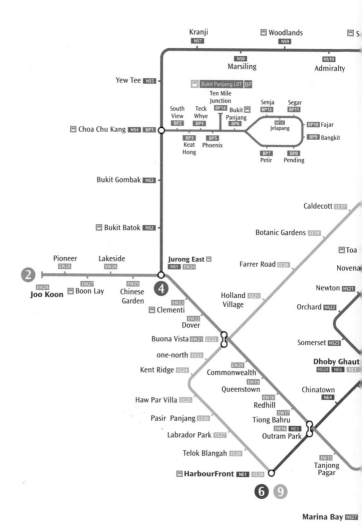

Kranji NS7
Woodlands NS9
S...

NS8
Marsling
NS10
Admiralty

Yew Tee NS5

Bukit Panjang LRT BP
Ten Mile Junction
BP14 Bukit Panjang BP6
South View BP2
Teck Whye BP4
Senja BP13
Segar BP11
BP12 Jelapang
BP10 Fajar

Choa Chu Kang NS4 BP1
BP3 Keat Hong
BP5 Phoenix
BP9 Bangkit

BP7 Petir
BP8 Pending

Bukit Gombak NS3

Bukit Batok NS2

Caldecott CC17

Botanic Gardens CC19

Toa

Pioneer EW28
Lakeside EW26
Jurong East NS1 EW24
Farrer Road CC20
Novena

EW29 Joo Koon
Boon Lay EW27
Chinese Garden EW25
Holland Village CC21
Newton NS21

Clementi EW23
Orchard NS22

Dover EW22
Buona Vista EW21 CC22
Somerset NS23

one-north CC23
Dhoby Ghaut NS24 NE6 CC1

Kent Ridge CC24
Commonwealth EW20
Queenstown EW19
Chinatown NE4

Haw Par Villa CC25
Redhill EW18

Pasir Panjang CC26
Tiong Bahru EW17

Labrador Park CC27
Outram Park EW16 NE3

Telok Blangah CC28
Tanjong Pagar EW15

HarbourFront NE1 CC29

Marina Bay NS27

2 4 6 9